Losing Political Office

'This is a great read and an important and wide-ranging book. Jane Roberts' interviews with former MPs, ministers and local council leaders bring out brilliantly what it is like to go through the loss of office and what happens next for the politicians concerned. It should be essential reading both for those in public office who will one day have to face their own political mortality and for academics and students working on political leadership and thinking about the phenomenon of the 'political class.'

— Professor Kevin Theakston,
University of Leeds, UK

'Losing their office hits politicians hard. They lose whatever power they have, their social status, and part of their identity. One of them, quoted in this book, describes the experience as a 'massive psychological and emotional and public hit all at the same time'. Their stories of loss and coping are in this wonderful, empathic, analytical and captivating book. Read it and get a deeper understanding of politicians as humans.'

— Professor Paul 't Hart,
Utrecht University, the Netherlands

'A thoughtful, sensitive - and long overdue - exploration of what it really feels like to leave political office and why it matters. Letting go of a cherished role and a deeply valued purpose that have been fundamental to one's sense of identity is a transition of enormous significance - and here it is laid bare.'

— Baroness Tessa Jowell,
DBE, MP for Dulwich and
West Norwood 1992–2015, UK

'Elected politicians get little public sympathy when they lose office or their seats. But the adjustment can be very difficult. Jane Roberts identifies a genuine problem in a sympathetic and perceptive way and offers responses which should not only help those who have lost office but also encourage those taking the risk of standing in the first place.'

— Peter Riddell,
Director, Institute for Government and former chair of the Hansard Society, UK

'Understanding more about the dynamics of losing political office tells us important things about how democracy works or falters. Politicians like us are people and their reactions to losing are varied but very human. Politics is a business the needs to be designed around the realities of flawed human nature and this book provides new insights into the democratic process.'

— Professor Gerry Stoker,
University of Southampton, UK

Jane Roberts

Losing Political Office

Jane Roberts
The Open University
United Kingdom

ISBN 978-3-319-81945-7   ISBN 978-3-319-39702-3   (eBook)
DOI 10.1007/978-3-319-39702-3

Cover illustration: © Karolina Larusdottir – 'Setting Off'

Printed on acid-free paper

This Palgrave Macmillan imprint is published by Springer Nature
The registered company is Springer International Publishing AG
The registered company address is: Gewerbestrasse 11, 6330 Cham, Switzerland

ACKNOWLEDGEMENTS

What started simply as curiosity about what happens to politicians when they leave office has to my surprise, some years later, ended up as a neatly bound tome considering psychological, sociological and political perspectives on political exit.

The research has drawn me into fascinating conversations with those whom I name below and with many from the research itself that I cannot identify. But you know who you are, and I am deeply indebted to all my interviewees who gave so generously of their time and thoughtfulness. I am enormously grateful to Lord David Blunkett, Rt. Hon. Paul Burstow, Sir Vince Cable, Sir Jim Paice and Jo Swinson, former MPs who left Parliament in 2015 who later agreed to talk with me on an attributable basis.

The research began while I was an Associate Fellow at Warwick Business School, and the remaining fieldwork, the analysis and the writing were undertaken while I was a Visiting Fellow at The Open University Business School. The Open University, a deeply admirable institution, provided support to the work including the publication of a summary report on losing political office launched at the House of Commons in February 2015.

In addition to my interviewees, there are many to whom I owe heartfelt thanks for going out of their way to advise and help: the Local Government Association (LGA) who kindly provided some funding for the fieldwork; Dennis Skinner and Morgan McSweeney at the LGA for invaluable factual help; Raj Chada, former leader of the London Borough of Camden, Phil Hope and Dr Doug Naysmith, both former MPs, for their comments on the interview protocol; Charles Walker, MP, for his continuing enthusiasm and help with this work; Pamela Chesters, Dame Moira Gibb, Steve Hitchins and Baroness Alison Suttie for their introductions; Bethan Garwood and John Chick at the Welsh Assembly and Baroness Dianne Hayter for assistance with specific questions; Anna Simpson at the Independent Parliamentary Standards Authority and Lady Sally Grocott of the Association of Former MPs for information on both organisations respectively; Dr Sebastian Kraemer for cheerfully volunteering to read through iterations of my manuscript; and the members of the Advisory Group for the research for their wise counsel: Professor Kevin Theakston, Annette Stansfeld, Joe Simpson, Rt. Hon. Peter Riddell, Sir Michael Lyons, Professor Tina Keifer, Karen Izod, Phil Hope, Professor Paul t' Hart, Lucy de Groot and Christina Dykes.

Professor Jean Hartley at The Open University Business School artfully chaired the Advisory Group, but she has done so much more to encourage, guide and support me through the vicissitudes of the work. Life tends to get in the way of writing, but she kept me on track and I am enormously grateful.

I have immensely enjoyed conversations with Dr Peter Allen, Dr David Bell, Professor Ken Coghill, Paul Goodman, Professor Robert Hazell, Professor David Howarth, Professor Paul Hoggett, Professor Mike Kenny, Dr Jane Milton, Professor Nick Pearce, Peter Oborne, Professor Gerry Stoker (who helpfully commented on one chapter), Dr Henry Tam and Professor Tony Wright. Each got me thinking more. None, of course, bears any responsibility for what finally emerged.

I thank the artist Karolina Larusdottir, for her permission (delightedly given) to use one of her wonderful etchings on the cover of this book, and lastly my husband, Professor David Dunger, who cast his rigorous analytic eye over the methodology. He will be thankful to regain a room.

CONTENTS

CHAPTER 1

Introduction

On resigning the crown, Shakespeare's Richard II makes plaintively clear,

> But still my griefs are mine:
> You may my glories and my state depose,
> But not my griefs; still am I king of those.

We may flock to see Shakespearean drama; television cameras may linger voyeuristically a little too long at the point of a dramatic defeat of a politician—any fall from grace momentarily grabs the attention. But behind the scene, what really happens when politicians leave office, either at the electorate's choosing or their own?

For those other than heads of state, we know little. Nor is the loss of political office much talked about except at the point of defeat. It is almost as if we do not really want to know what happens to the human beings behind the salacious flash of cameras. Norman Rockwell's compelling portrait of Casey *"The Losing Candidate"*—instantly a diminished and ignored figure—in 1958 powerfully conveys the human drama. For those unfamiliar with this painting for the cover of the magazine, The Saturday Evening Post in the USA, it shows the beaming smile of Casey in his election poster under which sits a very different Casey, dejected and slumped in a chair, having just learned of his electoral defeat as his erstwhile supporters are already streaming away from him.

The relative silence about what happens following the loss of political office—in academic literature, within political circles and in common

© The Author(s) 2017
J. Roberts, *Losing Political Office*,
DOI 10.1007/978-3-319-39702-3_1

1

parlance—is curious. Politicians are, after all, a very necessary part of our representative democracy; they affect all our lives, like it or not. But it is part of the democratic "deal," it may be argued: politicians stand for election with their eyes open: democracy depends on politicians exiting office, often involuntarily. So it does. But what might be the effects on individual politicians and on their families? Should we care? Does it matter? Does it matter to them? Does it matter to us as citizens and for society?

David Runciman (2013 p. XVII) maintains that,

"Successful democratic politicians are constantly reminded of their own mortality. They can hardly get away from it: ... no one in a democracy should ever be taken unawares by failure. If democratic politicians become complacent, it is because they have become inured to the whispers of mortality, not because they have been shielded from them."

"Inured to the whispers of mortality" is a powerfully resonant phrase. Have politicians become so inured? Might there be forces inuring them from the quiet, susurrating sounds of political mortality? I wondered if this might be so.

Rockwell's powerful image of Casey lay dormant in my mind for many years. It surfaced every now and then, for example, during my time in elected political office as a council leader of a London borough (Camden) with my puzzlement at learning how few of my peers had made succession plans. Surely, this was an essential task of leadership? I chose to step down in 2005 from my position as council leader, a role I had unashamedly loved and deeply valued. It was far from an easy decision and I had long wrestled with it, but in the end, I felt that I owed it to my then 14-year-old son, Jack, to be reliably at home in the evenings and available for him on his terms rather than on mine. I am a child psychiatrist after all. I know about loss and change professionally, and I was expecting my experience of walking away from leadership to be difficult. And so it was. It was nevertheless, I think, the right decision. But my experience fed my curiosity.

I discovered subsequently how relatively little there was in the academic literature on leaving political office (Roberts 2011). On a practical level, many Westminster Members of Parliament would inevitably lose their seats at the next General Election—might there be any political party interest in thinking about how best this could be handled? To my enquiry of one political party at the time, it appeared not. What did council leaders do when they left office? Few people had any idea. It was difficult even to find out who had been the leader of a council, even very recently, let alone what they were doing. This fed my curiosity still further. Why was there such relative silence?

I decided to explore the experience of leaving political office in more depth and, with the encouragement of Professor Jean Hartley, I embarked on a research project to interview former Westminster MPs and local government leaders to hear directly their experiences. I had not intended to write a book: I was simply curious and wanted to find out more about political exit. But I found such a rich seam of powerful experience—a veritable maelstrom of emotions and reflections—that a book emerged.

In this book, I start by reviewing relevant literature on what happens when politicians step down or are ejected from office. I draw on the much more extensive literature on job loss—redundancy, retirement and unemployment—later. I briefly sketch the context in which my research was conducted: meaning, we know from systemic thinking, depends on context. A brief description of the research and study design that lies behind this report follows. The methodology is included more fully as an appendix at the end of the book.

Given that the experience of leaving political office can only be understood in the context of what holding that office meant in the first place, I deal initially with the experience *of* office. I go on to explore the thinking of current politicians about how they might seek to shape their time in political office. Only then do I come on to the main findings from the research, the experience of leaving office in or around 2010 of former MPs and former council leaders, and their partners, considering separately those who chose to stand down and those who were electorally defeated. The findings are thematically presented rather than as case histories. Some of the material is emotionally very raw, and the interview material remains scrupulously unattributable. To this end, I have used the inelegant device of "her/his" for the possessive pronoun.

In seeking to explain the findings, I begin from an individual psychological perspective, but I bring in a family systemic perspective in a section considering the position of partners and families. Drawing on factors that may help or hinder the transition from political office, I suggest a series of practical steps that might make a difference. I go on to suggest possible implications of the findings for our system of representative democracy.

I have sought to explain my findings drawing on frameworks from psychology and sociology. I subsequently arc over into wider considerations, drawing on research from political science—ambitious, perhaps, not least from one who is not a political scientist, but a practitioner in psychological medicine and, formerly, in politics. In mitigation, from the opposite direction, I draw on Blondel et al.'s (2013) study of political leadership where it is argued that political scientists could usefully expand their range of analytic tools and become more accustomed to dealing with psychological concepts.

Since the initial research was completed, there has been a General Election in the UK in 2015, the first since Fixed Term Parliaments were introduced in the UK. Five MPs who left Parliament in that year reflect on the findings of the research, summarised in a report published in February 2015 (Roberts 2015), in the light of their own experience. Bravely, they agreed that our conversations would be attributable.

A brief word about the use in this book of the term "politician": I have used the term as a pragmatic short hand for one who is holding political office, that is, not one who has left office. I am aware that many former political office holders would still regard themselves as "politicians" whether they remain elected or not. Questions of identity and its relationship to role are at the heart of this and are explored in this work.

It should be borne in mind that the research was conducted with only one cohort of politicians, all of whom left political office relatively recently, in or around 2010, and they were interviewed on one occasion only. It therefore portrays a snapshot of the experiences of the participants rather than a more longitudinal view. The data and the conclusions drawn reflect a picture of contemporary political office loss and cannot necessarily compare with previous (or future) cohorts of politicians. While there may be principles that hold true over time, the context of holding and losing political office at any particular time must be considered in order better to understand the experience of current and former politicians. The context in 2010, quite aside from the electoral cycle—the Labour Government had been in power for 13 years—was dominated by the 2009 "expenses scandal."[1] The cohort of MPs leaving parliament in 2010 had all been embroiled in the effects of the "scandal," whether they had been directly involved or not. The issue had a profound effect on individual politicians, their families and UK political culture more widely (Byrne and Theakston 2015), and this is evident from my interviews.

NOTE

1. Following a long tussle over publication of MPs' expenses, the newspaper, The Daily Telegraph, in 2009 published leaked details of MPs' expenses in instalments that dominated the headlines in the UK for a number of months with information on alleged over-claiming of expenses and manipulation of the rules on property by some MPs and peers. There was widespread public outrage, further detailed on page XX.

REFERENCES

Blondel, J. and Thiébault, J.L. with Czernicka, K., Inoguchi, T., Pathmanand, U. and Venturino, F. (2013). *Political Leadership, Parties and Citizens. The Personalisation of Leadership*. Abingdon: Routledge.

Roberts, J. (2011). Losing political power. What happens next? Why care? *Public Money and Management* September, 1–3.

Roberts, J. (2015). *Losing Political Office*. Milton Keynes: The Open University Business School.

Runciman, D. (2013). *The Confidence Trap*. New Jersey: Princeton University Press.

CHAPTER 2

Why Focus on Losing Political Office?

First, why bother about the leaving of political office?

Let me take head on the charge that politicians leaving office do not merit any particular consideration. Politicians know, after all, the score on standing for elected office before entering the fray. Furthermore, it might be argued that leaving political office is a transition much as any other and can be informed by the wealth of literature that already exists on redundancy, retirement and life transitions in general.

While politicians do indeed share elements of their role with other occupations—many occupations are just as intensely and relentlessly demanding, for example—it is the *combination* of a number of elements associated with the political role and the leaving of it that is distinctive:

- Political office as an MP or a council leader is immensely hard work that intrudes upon family life, unconfined to any normal hours of work, requires working in more than one locality and more than one arena. MPs face weekly travel from Westminster to possibly far distant constituencies, disruptive to family life;
- The attraction of politics for many is all consuming, not only of time but of identity: personal and occupational boundaries are often deeply intertwined;
- Public expectations of accessibility to their elected representative are higher now than they ever have been. No longer, quite rightly, does an annual visit to the constituency as in yesteryear suffice.

© The Author(s) 2017
J. Roberts, *Losing Political Office*,
DOI 10.1007/978-3-319-39702-3_2

Social media and digital communication have transformed the ease with which constituents can contact their MP. There is therefore often little time to develop or maintain interests, other than political. Any precious spare time may be understandably pocketed away for spending time with partners or other family members;

- Media scrutiny and public exposure are now part of the package, often edged with cynicism at best, through to distrust and sometimes contempt given current public attitudes towards politicians;
- Yet seeking positive perceptions of what they do on the part of their constituents is a legitimate and intrinsic element of a politician's role. On these perceptions rest votes and thus both the individual and their political party gaining office. Few other roles are quite as explicit in this regard;
- When the time in office comes to an end, involuntarily or not, the cliff edge is very steep: loss of office may be sudden, unexpected and entirely unrelated to individual poor performance. It is supremely difficult even for the ablest politician in a marginal seat to withstand a strong national tide against her/his political party. Council leaders experience ice-cold turkey: they are out immediately with no redundancy pay, not even the statutory minimum;
- Whereas a senior or chief executive officer may move to another organisation without loss of status, even if they are departing because of performance concerns, there is usually no political equivalent. Politicians mostly have to build up local support to be elected, and they therefore cannot move on so quickly, even if they wish to;
- In common with others made redundant, politicians may lose office at a young age, well under retirement age. But in contrast to others made redundant or retiring, there is little in the way of anticipation of a significant transition let alone a package of support (such as coaching or advice with writing a curriculum vitae) on exit for politicians, now almost standard in the other areas. Quite the reverse: a politician's demise may be greeted with glee.

It may be instructive to look at an historical perspective of attitudes towards redundancy. Until the 1980s or so, redundancy was widely seen as a deeply shameful occurrence and certainly not one for affected individuals to talk about. But there have been profound changes over the last 20 years now that redundancy has become more commonplace with at least two recessions in the UK and major changes in the labour market. It is still an enormously significant event, but over the last 30 years, the implications of redundancy—financial, personal and social—have become widely acknowledged. It is now expected that more care will be taken to prepare a workforce threatened with redundancy, that a proper process will be followed, and that a package of support is offered to those individuals who are subsequently made redundant. The world of politics seems to lag far behind.

- Finally, politicians are private individuals, but they are in public office as elected representatives and they explicitly carry wider obligations. Their leaving of office is not just a private affair; not only are they subject to the expectations of their constituents but also to their own expectations of a wider responsibility to serve. Politicians cannot help but be the recipients of a wide range of emotions projected on to them by others. Anger, guilt, anxiety and disappointment are just some of the powerful emotions that the public may commonly bring to the encounter. But such emotions may be troubling and unsettling for the bearer and hence need to be dealt with, sometimes by repudiating and projecting them on to another. Elected representatives are then in pole position to absorb, and ideally to diffuse and to contain such emotions. In such circumstances, it is especially easy for the boundaries between the personal and the political to become blurred.

    Gabriel (2011) bring psychoanalytic insights into the study of leadership generally and view leadership as the management of meaning and the management of emotions. Astute political leadership has a deep understanding of the importance of managing meaning and emotions. That a political role in any case demands a strong value base further compounds the closeness of the personal and the political.

It is the combination of all of the factors above that provides the justification for the focus of this book on the loss specifically of political office.

A useful parallel to the challenges of leaving political office may be with top athletes. Athletes may have set their hearts on their sport at a young age; they face gruelling training demands precluding other interests; their identity may well be wholly invested in their sport; they face highly competitive challenges against their peers and yet they spend much of their time with fellow athletes away from family and friends. They may achieve high status, often at a young age, and be subject to considerable media interest.

But they may find themselves losing unexpectedly, being de-selected and facing retirement, through injury or age, although they are likely to be still at a relatively young age. They may have no continuing source of income, be very uncertain about the future, not least their own identity outside sport. There are many journalistic articles documenting the retirement of specific athlete personalities and, over the past few decades, a burgeoning academic literature on athlete retirement (e.g. Taylor and Ogilvie 1994; Wylleman et al. 2004; Cecić Erpič et al. 2004; Lally 2007).

That retirement from high-level sport is a transition not a one-off event is now widely accepted. It is recognised that adjustment to retirement is dependent on a number of factors, both athletic and non-athletic related, including the degree of voluntariness of the termination, the degree of athletic identity, subjective perception of sporting achievement and educational status. Many athletes adjust with relatively little distress, but some struggle. The Professional Cricketers Association, in response to concerns about the wellbeing of retired professional cricketers, researched their needs in 2013 and came up with "Top Ten Tips"[1] to help retiring cricketers make the transition from professional sport. While athletes may well find adjusting to the end of their sporting career problematic, there are opportunities for them to go into coaching or broadcast commentating, an avenue less available to most former political office holders.

The blurring of the personal and the occupational is seen in some other groups too. Leaving the army or the clergy may offer some insights into the exit from political office. The armed services and ecclesiastical office exist to serve, albeit different masters; there are heavy work demands at unsocial hours; and very close working relationships within an institution. Politicians in comparison are however far more in the public eye, and they have a very distinctive role as elected representatives that no other occupational group has. Nevertheless, it is surely no coincidence that politics, the army and the clergy may all be seen as having a vocational element?

Nearly one hundred years ago, in Berlin, Weber (1919) gave probably the most influential lecture of modern times on political theory, Politics As Vocation. His observations have stood the test of time despite the very different and turbulent political, social and economic context of post First World War Europe compared with the early twenty-first century.

While we are all *"occasional"* politicians, Weber said, even if actions are simply limited to casting a vote, politics may be a vocation for some: such men (as they mostly were) might either live *"for"* or *"off"* politics, although the two were not seen by Weber as necessarily mutually exclusive, *"He who lives 'for' politics makes politics his life, in an internal sense. Either he enjoys the naked possession of the power he exerts, or he nourishes his inner balance and self-feeling by the consciousness that his life has <u>meaning</u> in the service of a cause."* On the other hand, *"He who strives to make politics a permanent <u>source of income</u> lives 'off' politics as a vocation, whereas he who does not do this lives 'for' politics."*

Understandably, in those revolutionary times, Weber was pre-occupied by the struggle for and the experience of power—the essence of politics. He said, *"The career of politics grants a feeling of power. The knowledge of influencing men, in participating In power over them, and above all, the feeling of holding in one's hands a nerve fibre of historically important events can elevate the professional politician above everyday routine even when he is placed in formally modest positions."*

He went on to discuss the qualities necessary for a man to have the calling for politics: a combination of passion, conviction and a more pragmatic sense of proportion and political realism. He cautions against excessive vanity in a politician and, *"The vain self-reflection in the feeling of power … the serving of a cause must not be absent if action is to have inner strength. Exactly what the cause, in the service of which the politician strives for power and uses power, looks like a matter of faith."*

Nearly one hundred years on, leading politicians at all but the most local level are more generously remunerated for their activities and in a Weberian sense, live *'off'* politics. But most, whatever their political allegiance, would profess to a cause, a strong sense of what is right, a faith—albeit perhaps a secular one—that drives them on. Certainly, the politicians whom I interviewed for this study all had a strong sense of values and were highly motivated by public service. Notably, a very few had contemplated a religious calling. While the public image of politicians may be very different in our cynical, distrustful times, my research demonstrated politicians at their best—thoughtful, reflective and mostly, brutally honest.

NOTE

1. http://www.thepca.co.uk/top-ten-tips.html

REFERENCES

Cecić Erpič, S., Wylleman, P. and Zupančič, M. (2004). The Effect of Athletic and Non-athletic Factors on the Sports Career Termination Process. *Psychology of Sport and Exercise* 5 pp. 45–59.

Gabriel, Y. (2011). *Psychoanalytic approaches to leadership.* In A. Bryman, D. Collinson, K. Grint, B. Jackson, and M. Uhl-Bien (Eds.), In *The SAGE Handbook of Leadership.* Sage: London. http://www.yiannisgabriel.com/2013/05/psychoanalytic-appraoches-to-leadership.html

Lally, P. (2007). Identity and Athletic Retirement: A Prospective Study. *Psychology of Sport and Exercise* 8 pp. 85–99.

Taylor, J. and Ogilvie, B.C. (1994). A Conceptual Model of Adaptation to Retirement Among Athletes. *Journal of Applied Sport Psychology* 6 pp. 1–20.

Professional Cricketers' Association. http://www.thepca.co.uk/top-ten-tips.html. Accessed 23/11/15.

Weber, M. (1919). http://anthropos-lab.net/wp/wp-content/uploads/2011/12/Weber-Politics-as-a-Vocation.pdf. Accessed 17/10/11.

Wylleman, P., Alfermann, D. and Laverlee, D. (2004). Career Transitions in Sport: European Perspectives. *Psychology of Sport and Exercise* 5 pp. 7–20.

CHAPTER 3

What Is Known About Losing Political Office?

John Keane, the widely respected writer and academic, qualifies Enoch Powell's much quoted observation that,

> All political lives, unless they are cut off in midstream at a happy juncture, end in failure, because that is the nature of politics and of human affairs. (Powell 1977, p. 151)

At least for those who have held the highest political office, Keane (2011) contends that political lives no longer necessarily end in failure. Taking a long view, he makes a compelling case that those who have held the highest offices of state in democratic governments now are no longer sent into exile, nor subjected formally to ostracism as in ancient Greek democracies and nor are they consigned to the *"ranks of nobodies"* (Keane 2011, p. 282).

Indeed, in more recent times, with increased longevity, better health and the relative youth of some, many former heads of state enjoy rising public prominence, often on an international stage. Keane (2011, p. 294) talks of this as *"a new form of sinecure system."* Bill Clinton spoke of losing *"your power but not your influence"* (Skidmore 2004, p. 3), happily for him, still, of course, addressed as "Mr. President" for the rest of his days.

But what of political office holders lower down the food chain: parliamentarians who may or may not have achieved ministerial office;

© The Author(s) 2017
J. Roberts, *Losing Political Office*,
DOI 10.1007/978-3-319-39702-3_3

13

leaders of devolved administrations; or local government leaders who may have wielded considerably more authority than a parliamentarian, albeit within a smaller domain? The fate of those who have occupied prominent but less exalted political positions is the subject of this study. There has been much less written about such former political office holders. And the issue of ex-office holders as a whole, even now, has been described as *"under-theorized, under-researched, under-appreciated, and – in many cases – under-regulated"* (Keane 2011, pp. 282–3).

US Presidents

The earliest attempts to pay attention to the study of former office holders were in the USA, with a focus, unsurprisingly, on US presidents. The dominance of studies of former US presidents continues even now in the literature, although it has been broadened by studies from elsewhere in recent years, as described below. The focus in the academic literature is on what former leaders do in their post-leadership life, and there are a number of attempts to suggest typologies according to their activities in this period.

The first survey was published in 1925 in Sheldon's The Ex-Presidents of the United States: How Each Played a Role (cited in Theakston 2010), but it was many decades later before Martin (1951) picked the subject up again in his study of ex-presidents up to and including Herbert Hoover. He relayed the story of the earlier life of each man, and his family, before considering in more detail the succession and their life after the White House, when they had been, as written in the preface, *"at liberty for the first time in their lives to act and speak freely."* While full of fascinating biographical detail, Martin did not attempt to pull together his findings, nor come to any conclusions.

In that same year, the Twenty-second Amendment, the 1951 constitutional change that set a two-term limitation on the presidency, perhaps concentrated the minds of incumbents of the White House on what was to come. The Former Presidents Act, enacted by Congress in 1958 that granted an office, pension (the term *"lifetime salary"* (Hecht 1976, p. 188) was preferred) and staff to former presidents, reinforced the significance of the post-presidential period.

Twenty years or so elapsed before Marie Hecht's study of former presidents' *"twilight years"* (Hecht 1976, p. xiii). As a historian, she sought to explore their residues of power and how they were used or misused by their political parties of the administration currently in power. She considered a number of areas of possible activity, such as war or peace making, partisan politics or, in a couple of cases, a second career. Although ex-presidents varied widely in what they did after leaving office, and how, if at all, they sought to exert influence, many put pen to paper. And this was long before the monumental edifices of presidential libraries of the later twentieth century. Hecht quoted Eisenhower's son, *"Writing is almost the only dignified occupation a President can follow after leaving office"* (p. 289). Indeed, Richard Nixon was in the process of writing his memoirs at the time that Hecht's book was published. How else could a former president have conducted his defence? In the end, Hecht contended that the proper use of ex-presidents' twilight years should be determined by those individuals' own preferences and abilities.

Schenker (1982) had a different view. He examined the lives of 30 former presidents, seeking to stimulate interest and discussion about their *"penultimate career experience."* They had remained physically and mentally vigorous for most of this time with four former presidents having been in their early 50s when they left office. He observed, *"We, the people elevate a politician to the most prestigious and highest office in the land and then more often than not dump him on the trash heap of politics."* Schenker suggested a pattern of post-presidential activity that might inform a more constructive use of such nationally significant figures. He proposed a broad threefold classification of their activity based on: their personalities and orientation to the private or the public sphere; their formal involvement in government and the degree to which they were active or passive in shaping their post-presidential life. He recommended that increased attention be paid to these *"far from twilight years"* and that ex-presidents' experience was a national resource that could be drawn on more systematically.

There has since been a steady increase in attention given to former presidents: a comprehensive overview of research until the presidency of Ronald Reagen is provided by Norton-Smith and Walch (1990). But it was not until President Jimmy Carter left office and went on to carve out a distinctive, international and high profile role in humanitarian causes and conflict resolution, that the role of the Office of the Former President was redefined (Chambers 1998). Carter transformed his previously battered reputation as president as a result, a lesson likely to be heeded by his successors.

Carter's post-presidential role as an elder statesman was included as one of six typologies proposed by Belenky's (1999) study of the activity of ex-presidents: the Still Ambitious; Exhausted Volcanoes; Political Dabblers; First Citizens (the elder statesman model); Embracers of a Cause and the Seekers of Vindication. She suggested that future ex-presidents are most likely to seek to emulate Carter post-presidential life. They may aspire to greatness in their role as an ex-president, just as they are likely to have done while in the White House, but they *"will continue to find their destinies shaped by prevailing circumstances and by the largeness or the limitations of their individual character."*

The focus of Skidmore's (2004) study of former occupants of the White House was their influence on public affairs once they had left office. He suggested four main ways in which influence could be brought to bear: running again for the presidency (unlikely now given the 22nd Amendment); securing other public office (Taft, for example, the 27th president, later becoming Chief Justice); contributing to education and public understanding and becoming active in humanitarian causes. They are not, of course, mutually exclusive. The pace of activity in office does not predict activity in post-presidential years, nor even does age, despite its probable impact on former President Reagan. Skidmore referred to suggestions that have been made to make use of former presidents' expertise, for example, a non-voting seat in Senate or former President Clinton's proposal of some sort of council for active ex-presidents, a group said to have no vested interests. Such a group, Clinton suggested, might be able to make a valuable contribution *"to really constructive debates about our honest disagreements"* (p. 168).

Runciman (2013) observes the hurt rather than surprise manifest in politicians' experience of defeat. Of George Bush Senior's defeat in 1992, for example, he suggests it was as if he had thought, *"I heard the abuse you have been directing my ways. How could I not? I read the newspapers. But that's democracy. I didn't realise you really meant it"* (p. XVII).

The last three US Presidents, Bill Clinton, George W. Bush and Barack Obama, have been relatively young men—age 55, 62 and 55, respectively—at the end of their presidencies. All three had won two terms and therefore knew four years in advance when they would be stepping down. But Clinton and Bush have taken different paths after leaving the White House. As is now the norm, both men have written autobiographies and established presidential libraries, but Clinton has remained on the global stage, making many high profile speeches to promote education, public understanding and humanitarian causes (two of Skidmore's ways of maintaining influence, as we have seen above). Bush, in contrast, has adopted a low profile, settling quietly in his home state of Texas and making clear that he has no desire anymore to influence public affairs or for fame and power. He has described such a presidential afterlife as "*awesome*"[1] in a CNN interview in 2012. Clinton, uniquely, faces the possibility that he will be the first ex-president and first man to return to the White House as the spouse of a sitting US president if his wife Hillary is inaugurated in 2017. Speculation in 2016 is rife with regard to how Obama will use his time after office but, especially with his popularity riding high internationally, he is likely to be in high demand and hardly consigned to the "ranks of the nobodies."

UK PRIME MINISTERS

The interest in US commanders-in-chief sparked a similar interest across the Atlantic and elsewhere. Just (2004) was one of the first to study "*the largely neglected*" subject of the role of former British Prime Ministers, from Churchill in 1955 to his latest recruit, John Major, in 2001. What did these former prime ministers do when out of office? How much did they intervene in political debate? Just (2004) put forward a typology for "*premiers emeritus*," either statesman or politician, having examined the number of their parliamentary interventions and the degree of their ideological drive. He concluded that former prime ministers have had a continuing role in the political life of the nation, albeit a different kind of leadership role to that which they had previously played.

Theakston (2010, p. 2) took up the baton with a comprehensive historical account of former UK prime ministers from Walpole to Blair. He commented, "*The 'club' of ex-prime ministers is rarely one that they really want to join. Few left Number 10 as happy, contented or fulfilled people, or at a time and in a manner of their own choosing.*" Many former prime ministers would echo Lord Aberdeen's sentiments in 1855, "*I do not know how I shall bear being out of office. I have many resources and objects of interest; but after being occupied with great affairs, it is not easy to subside to the level of common occupation*" (pp. 80–81). Others adapted better, Lord Grey, for example, from the nineteenth century or James Callaghan from more recent times who "*seems psychologically to have been more able to accept, and more reconciled to, the loss of office and power than some other prime ministers*" (p. 191). Looking into the longer term and at the broader landscape now of former leaders in the USA and Europe, Theakston suggested that with the growth in the number of international organisations in modern times and the relative youth of many former leaders, there are many more opportunities on a global stage potentially available to such leaders than once was the case.

The literature relating to high office has been informed by other works that have sought insights into who politicians are and what motivates them. With regard to the British prime ministers, Lucille Iremonger was unusual in her study: It investigated the childhood, family and subsequent life of a series of nineteenth and twentieth century Prime Ministers (Iremonger 1970). She suggested that for many, it had been the loss of a parent at a young age that drove her subjects' ambition to gain the highest political position in the land, desperate as they were to be loved and admired. How much more difficult then might have been the fall from grace. Of Neville Chamberlain, she wrote (p. 303), "*Yet he never gave up. Like all these men – except Rosebery – he fought on, during those final few months, despite it all, clinging to his place, kicking against his bitter fate, that driving ambition which had taken him so far, so late, riding him still.*"

Not necessarily academic works, but biographies, autobiographies and diaries of UK prime ministers inform our understanding of them as people (for example, Jenkins 2002a, b; Major 2000; Blair 2010; Powell 2010; Hattersley 2012).

Autobiographical accounts inevitably concentrate most on the time in office with any attention to the exit from office focusing on the events leading up to it and perhaps just a little on the immediate aftermath. Biographical accounts may take a longer-term view, able both to marry both what happens subsequent to leaving office and a view of how the transition was experienced, and thus can richly inform the analysis and discussion.

There are some hints of the impact of the transition from high office from the formidable political figures of the nineteenth and early twentieth century. Gladstone, for example, was said by one biographer (Jenkins 2002a, p. 379) to have minded greatly "*the sense of rejection*" by the electorate the loss of office of his first premiership in 1874. But he had the pressing issue of the loss of £5000 income to distract him, at least until he was drawn back into politics and public life, temperamentally disinclined to stay away for long. By the time Gladstone resigned as prime minister for the last time in 1894, he was "*un-tormented by the loss of office*" (p. 619), but he was in his mid-eighties and certainly not in the best of health. Observing that politicians rarely choose the right time to say goodbye, Hattersley described Lloyd George as *"temperamentally incapable of accepting that after 1922, his day was done"* (Hattersley 2012, p. 617).

Despite having wanted to avoid Wellington and Palmerston's fate of clinging to office for too long, arguably Churchill, over fifty years later, did just that. He was described by one biographer as having *"a limpet-like attitude to the surrender of office"* (Jenkins 2002b, p. 897).

Even Harold Wilson, one of the very few to have departed as British Prime Minister entirely on his own terms in 1976, was said to have found retirement a great shock (Riddell 1996, p. 251) despite initially having remained as a very active backbencher, standing again for election in his Huyton constituency in the 1979 General Election.

The most dramatic and memorable departure from prime ministerial office in recent times was that of Margaret Thatcher. Its brutal suddenness divided the nation politically, but even Mrs. Thatcher's most hostile foes do not forget the poignancy at a human level of her leaving Number 10 Downing Street. Her visible distress was scrutinised by television cameras and in newspaper columns in unsparing detail. She herself never hid her bitterness towards those whom she considered had betrayed her. Over the years, as one obituary made clear, *"in private, she could not come to terms with her dismissal, or with what she saw as John Major's betrayal of her legacy"* (McSmith 2013). Timing, of course, is all. As Moore (2010) wrote, if Mrs. Thatcher had picked her 10th anniversary in 1989, to go, *"she would have retired with the most unassailable political reputation in our history. Wanting to go 'on and on and on' was not such a brilliant idea."* Theakston (2010) stated that Thatcher *"hated the whole idea of retirement, feeing a sort of existential angst about the loss of office, power and activity"* (p. 198). He vividly described her as having *"burned, raved and raged"* (p. 201) in the years after office.

With more equanimity and insight, John Major wrote in his autobiography, *"even as my political profile rose ... I knew it would not last for ever. Senior politicians spend only a limited time in the sun, and I did not want to leave the front line of politics as a husk, bereft of everything but a backward glance to memories of my political noontide"* (p. xviii). When the time came for Major to leave Number 10, he acknowledged that *"leaving was very painful"* (p. 725), but he soon felt relieved at the lifting of pressures and the weekend after the election, *"went to bed thinking not what had been, but what was yet to come"* (p. 729).

John Major reflected subsequently that while he had been buoyed up by an ocean of supportive letters from people far and wide, *"I should have immediately set about writing to those many Conservative MPs who had lost seats. I did not. This was unforgivable … I was exhausted."* He later—with some difficulty no longer having the same level of administrative support—did get letters out, but by his own admission, it took too long (p. 728).

Jonathan Powell, Tony Bair's former Chief of Staff, advises, *"To hold on to power successfully, a leader must not mind losing it. Some politicians have what Denis Healey called a hinterland. Others don't. Tony started talking about what he might do after leaving office as early as 2001. He had other things that he wanted to do with his life"* (Powell 2010, p. 304). Blair choreographed an elegant exit and *"his last weeks were the longest goodbye in British political history"* (Rawnsley 2010, p. 454) after having, unusually, initially announced his departure in September 2006. He did not however specify a date at that time, thereby provoking the festering fury of his eventual successor, Gordon Brown. Theakston (2010) refers to a radio interview in 2006 in which Blair stressed the importance of finding a meaningful role and doing something after leaving the premiership that had *"a real purpose to it … a real life purpose"* (p. 217). Some years on, Theakston reflected that *"hyper-activism, restlessness and a continued craving for the limelight"* (p. 224) marks Blair's post-premiership, *"…. a huge political personality trying to fill the void, and find something as challenging and satisfying as being prime minister"* (p. 225). Unlike Major, Blair has retained a high profile on the global stage, but increasingly he has attracted criticism for the nature of some of his international consultancy work.

In contrast to his recent predecessors, Gordon Brown has not written a personal post-prime ministerial memoir, although his account of the global financial crash of 2008, the measures taken to stabilise world economies and Brown's recommendations for the future, was written very quickly after he left office. His wife, Sarah Brown, has however given her account of their time at Number 10 with the briefest mention of the experience for her of Brown's last few days as prime minister (Brown 2012, p. 430), that she *"can't quite cope with the level of emotion … recognising that this is his big departure more than mine at the moment."* Of Brown's immediate adjustment to post-prime ministerial life, we know little other than Seldon and Lodge's (2010) picture of a vulnerable and introspective period. He remained as an MP for the next Parliament but kept a relatively low profile apart from intervening in the Scottish independence referendum debate of 2014. Brown stood down as an MP in 2015 and has since focused his energy on charitable work involving global education.

David Cameron's resignation as Prime Minister in 2016 was sudden and unexpected following his defeat in the European Union referendum debate. It brought about his exit from high office far sooner than he had previously announced. The research presented in this book may have resonances for him.

HEADS OF GOVERNMENTS IN OTHER DEMOCRACIES

Theakston followed up his study on British prime ministers with an in-depth look at former leaders in democratic governments from wider afield through an edited collection of accounts from authors in Europe, North America, Israel and Australia (Theakston and de Vries 2012). Booker's Masters thesis examined former New Zealand premiers (Booker 2013) while Abjorensen (2015) made a detailed study of the exit from office of Australian prime ministers.

Theakston and de Vries's collection of case studies from countries with very different systems and political cultures illustrates that success or failure in office does not predict the success or otherwise of what comes later, "*the afterlife.*" And there are very different paths commonly available to former leaders in different countries: the degree to which, for example, they may serve again in government, or seek positions in local and powerful fiefdoms (as in France). The editors pointed to the growing number of leaders who have taken advantage of increasing opportunities to get involved with international or sub-regional organisations, but they were clear that the activities and roles of former leaders have to be analysed on a number of different levels: personal ambition and choices as well as a range of contextual factors—the immediate political situation, institutional structural factors and broader environment of modern politics with the international meshing together of business and government.

In his contribution from Australia, Strangio (2012) quoted former prime minister, John Howard, musing that his country needed "*a more mature approach*" to its ex-leaders. While recent former Australian prime ministers are younger, healthier and noisier than their predecessors, there is little patience in Australia for any notion of venerating their position as a former leader, in contrast to the USA. Nor is there recognised space for any public service that they may wish to undertake.

Abjorensen (2015) has made a comprehensive study of the circumstances in which Australian heads of government have left office from the time of the first prime minister who took office in 1901 to Tony Abbott's exit in 2015. He noted how all had shared a marked reluctance to leave with the possible exception of Robert Menzies in 1966 after his second period in office. The study dealt less however with the personal experience of the transition from office, although the book makes clear the bruising effects of internecine conflicts most recently between Kevin Rudd and Julia Gillard. Abjorensen (2015, p. 3) astutely observes how,

"To look at how power is lost or relinquished is to be reminded of all that is transient; it is the story of Ozymandias."[2]

Booker (2013) examined former premiers and prime ministers of New Zealand from 1856 to 2008. Drawing on both individual and situational variables, she suggested three distinct groups, although the key distinction between them seems to be chronological. First, Booker describes Colonial Premiers from the nineteenth century, who had undertaken a range of post-leadership activities, in part in order to stabilise their financial situation that had deteriorated in office. Second, Kiwi prime ministers who stretched from 1856 to 1960, a time when New Zealand came to establish its identity, confidence and maturity. Many of these Kiwi prime ministers suffered significant physical or psychological decline while in office. Third, Modern New Zealand prime ministers (1960–2008) who set a new trend in high profile post-leadership activity, often however, outside New Zealand, or *"behind the closed doors of the business world."* Booker concluded that New Zealand misses out on the benefits that its former leaders' skills and experiences otherwise might bring.

Former President of the Czech Republic, Václav Havel, is unusual in having written a play, entitled "Leaving," about transition from political office (Havel 2008): a Chancellor who had given his whole life to politics, with his family and staff dealing with practicalities of leaving office, musing on his time in office and his legacy.

More recently, former Australian Prime Minister Julia Gillard (2013) described her immediate experience of electoral defeat, characteristically not mincing her words, *"I know too that you can feel you are fine but then suddenly someone's words of comfort, or finding a memento at the back of the cupboard as you pack up, or even cracking jokes about old times, can bring forth a pain that hits you like a fist, pain so strong you feel it in your guts, your nerve endings."*

Gillard was a relatively young age (51) when she exited high office, in common increasingly with other former heads of government. Former leaders now often enter and then leave politics at a younger age than their predecessors and with increasing longevity, they now face many more active years ahead of them (Theakston and de Vries 2012). This is perhaps a welcome but different predicament compared with only relatively.

Given their very different political contexts, personalities and fortunes, politicians' and their biographers' reflections about the adjustment to loss of office vary substantially. That life following high office changes abruptly, and to a life for which there is often little preparation, however, is not in question.

Democracy demands that some politicians win and some lose. The inevitable exit from office is therefore an integral and vital part of the democratic process. But this creates dilemmas. As Anderson (2010), in her overview of not just US ex-presidents but of many former leaders across the world, starkly wrote, *"Democracy imposes some difficult demands. Among others, it asks its leaders to risk defeat in elections or (perhaps even more boldly) to retire from office at the end of a limited term."*

OTHER COUNTRIES

This review does not look in any detail at leaders in countries outside western style democracies. However, it may be instructive to highlight a few leaders from the African continent where entry to the political club may be relatively more closed (Lane 2015). Senegal's former democratically elected president Abdoulaye Wade created a storm of protest in 2012 when, despite having introduced constitutional amendments in 2011 bringing in a two-term rule, he reneged on his previous commitment and announced an (ultimately unsuccessful) bid for a third term. Similarly, but more successfully, and very controversially, Pierre Nkurunziza, president of Burundi, stood for a third term in 2015, despite a two-term limit. It divided the country bringing violence in its wake and brought pleas from the African Union to Nkurunziza not to pursue a third term. In the same vein in 2015, President Denis Sassou Nguesso in Congo-Brazzaville sought a mandate to change the two-term limit in office, established in the 2002 constitution, to a third term. Wade, Nkurunziza and Sassou Nguesso join a number of leaders from the African continent—for example, Museveni (in Uganda), Mugabe (in Zimbabwe), Kagame (in Rwanda) and Mbasago (in Equitorial Guinea)—who have been reluctant to relinquish office. Giving up is so very hard to do, even despite the best of intentions.

In order to recognise good governance including a willingness to leave office and to take on other public roles within the continent, the Mo Ibrahim Foundation instituted a $5 million Prize for Achievement in African Leadership in 2007. The first recipient was Joaquim Chissano from Mozambique. He had announced in plentiful time that he would not seek a third mandate to allow the county to prepare itself for peaceful transition. The Mo Ibrahim Foundation has since chosen not to award the prize in some years.

Term limits have been introduced in different parts of the world in an attempt to prevent heads of government from outstaying their welcome. The USA introduced two-term presidential rule, six years after Franklin Delano Roosevelt won his fourth term in office.

In countries other than democracies, the transfer of political power is thornier still and requires far greater examination than is possible here. China however may be worth highlighting because of generational changes that have occurred only relatively recently. China has a very long tradition in which political power *"has not passed from one person to another until the death of the leader, a tradition that the Leninist political organisation has not helped"* (Fewsmith 2002). Attempts have been made gradually to bring in the notion of retirement from leadership, and the systematic training of a younger generation of political leaders has been introduced. But institutionalising the transfer of supreme political power is a major challenge.

So much for high profile leaders of nations. What do we know of how those who did not gain the dizzy heights of president or prime minister, either their experience or how they fare? Much less. What about those politicians who ascended to the leadership of their parties but never won executive power?

Party Leaders

While there are studies of party leaders, their survival and the pitfalls of even a managed succession (for example, Bynander and `t Hart 2008; Laing and `t Hart 2011; Ennser-Jedenastik and Muller 2013), there is little on the fate of those who have lost a party leadership rather than a head of government position, in the published literature. Anecdotally, Moore (2010) quotes *"an angry backbencher famously warned Ted Heath, in 1974, that the party leadership is a 'leasehold, not a freehold',"* a warning that went unheeded by Heath who appeared unable to come to terms with losing the Conservative Party leadership to Margaret Thatcher for many years.

There are some personal and biographical accounts. Despite the suggestion that Neil Kinnock, Leader of the British Labour Party, *"would find it difficult to accept that he could not, or adjust to it"* if he did not win the 1992 General Election (Leapman 1987, p. 199), Paxman (2002, p. 281) quoted Kinnock wisely saying after the Labour Party was defeated, *"you've got to go on. It didn't come as a total surprise after all. And anyway, it's not like losing a child. God knows how people cope with that."* Of course, this does not at all preclude a more private sense of political failure, not least on behalf of a party to which Kinnock had been passionately committed to lead into government: *"Nothing will have replaced for Neil the sense of loss he has about losing the 1992 election. He is the kind of man who will carry it with him always"* (Gould 1998, p. 148).

One of the richest and insightful accounts is from Michael Ignatieff, Liberal Party leader in Canada from 2008 to 2011, who ultimately failed in his bid to become prime minister. As both an academic and a former politician, he has since written analytically and ruefully of the experience of his and his party's overwhelming defeat in the 2011 federal election (Ignatieff 2013). Ignatieff (2013, p. 178) recognised that *"embracing a political life means shedding your innocence. It means being willing to pay the costs before you even know what they are going to be."* He is still nevertheless a staunch admirer of those who enter the political fray; politics, he has no doubt, is indeed a vocation, as Weber suggested in 1919. Ignatieff was fortunate to be able to return to a senior academic position, his understanding of politics and government immeasurably enhanced by his experience of frontline politics and of the bitter taste of defeat.

There is increasingly less tolerance in the UK for party leaders to remain in office after they have lost an election. Their key task is to win power. If they do not, they have failed and they go. Nonetheless, two recent former Conservative Party leaders—William Hague and Iain Duncan Smith—returned to influential frontbench Cabinet positions while Michael Howard entered the House of Lords in 2010. Ed Miliband, Labour Party leader from 2010 until 2015, and Nick Clegg, Liberal Democrat leader (and Deputy Prime Minister in the coalition government of 2010–15) from 2007 until 2015, currently remain parliamentarians but with relatively low profiles. Miliband wryly related his six-year-old son's passing comment on how his father *"used to be famous"*[3] only days after Labour's defeat under Miliband in the 2015 General Election.

PARLIAMENTARIANS

There are memoirs, increasing in number, and some biographies and auto-biographical accounts of those who did not quite make it to the leadership of their party but nevertheless attained senior positions in government, the so-called "big beasts" of British politics (for example, Healey 1989; Crick 1997 (of Michael Heseltine); Cook 2003; Waldegrave 2015). But mostly such politicians return first to the backbenches, thus gradually letting go. Denis Healey chose to return to the backbenches after the 1987 General Election when Labour was defeated. He famously talked of having "*far too much hinterland. My wife and family have always meant more to me than the House of Commons … Nothing is more dangerous than the politician who uses politics as a surrogate for an unsatisfactory personal life*" (Healey 1989, p. 564). Waldegrave (2015) had a similar view and described "*the simplest lesson of all: if you wake up one day and think, 'There is no significant life beyond politics,' then that is the time to quit. You are an addict, in the grip of an addiction that threatens both yourself and others*" (p. 277).

Some Cabinet members resign over a specific issue: Michael Heseltine, for example, from a senior Cabinet position in 1986 over the Westland helicopter affair; and Robin Cook as Leader of the House of Commons in 2003 over the decision to invade in Iraq. It is highly plausible that such individuals adjust better to their change of status than those who are reshuffled out, although there is only anecdotal evidence. Cook regarded his life following resignation as "*personally more fulfilling*," and he was relieved to have got back a life of his own (Cook 2003, p. 359). Unsurprising sentiments, of course, from any politician leaving the frontbench, but Cook's account did not touch on his adjustment then to being more distant from the centre of government. Nor, more surprisingly, did Crick's (1997) biography of Heseltine, a man who had spent nearly 17 years in ministerial office and who had reputedly longed to be prime minister.

Proceeding further down the political hierarchy, through the world of front- and backbench parliamentarians and of politicians at a provincial, state or municipal level, there is progressively little literature on either the experience of leaving office or of what happens subsequently.

Blondel's (1991) longitudinal study of ministers from 14 Western democracies was one of the first of a very small number to investigate life after being in the Cabinet. He examined occupation post-ministerial office from 1945 to 1984. Among those not returning to the Cabinet, 32 per cent moved to the national parliament, 30 per cent went back to their previous career and 33 per cent started a new career. In the UK, Cabinet ministers must all in any case be parliamentarians.

More recent work in Germany that has studied the post-Cabinet careers of regional ministers in German Lander from 1990 to 2011 (Stoltz and Fischer 2014) focuses on political career "*pathways*." This study did not look at what ministers went on to do other than in elected political office.

A study by Claveria and Verge (2015) examines the immediate occupation of former ministers in a cross-sectional study across 23 advanced industrialised democracies. From 430 departing ministers, they found that the commonest post-Cabinet position is public or party office (47 per cent), followed by ministers returning to the Cabinet (28 per cent). Some are employed in private business (10 per cent), others in international positions (7 per cent) and a few returned to their previous job (8 per cent). They found no significant gender differences in this respect.

A study examining post-ministerial careers in the USA and Britain (Stolz and Kintz 2014) found that British former Cabinet ministers from John Major's Conservative government of 1992 to 1997 almost all stayed within the realm of professional politics, showing "*an extreme fixation with Westminster*" in contrast to the USA. They comment that in the quest to understand political careers as part of the study of political elites, "*the question of what comes after position x is at least as interesting as the question what has preceded this position*." They suggest that part of the explanation for the relative lack of academic attention to post-ministerial careers may be because the subject has been seen as part of elite studies and hence what ministers go on to do becomes irrelevant in this context. But they comment also on the methodological difficulties of tracking individuals who may be dispersed across a wide area.

There has been extensive work on areas such as the career paths of politicians in various legislatures, on recruitment of candidates, the determinants of turnover in the US Congress, in state legislatures, on the broad motivations of politicians, ministerial resignations and some of the factors leading to a decision to quit (for example, Blair and Henry 1981; Hibbing 1982; Francis and Baker 1986; Dowding and Kang 1998; Matland and Studlar 2004; Mattozzi and Merlo 2007; Cristofoli and Crugnola 2012; Keane and Merlo 2010; Kerby and Blidook 2011; Karol 2012; Hix et al. 2012). Even death in the US Congress has been the focus of study (Maltzman et al. 1996).

While works such as these have some relevance to this study, this review focuses specifically on the experience of transition from office and what happens subsequently to former office holders. And in this latter area, there is considerably less work.

North America and Britain have provided the most fertile ground for considering what happens to former political office holders at a parliamentary level. Given that my study focused on parliamentarians (and local authority leaders), I shall include go into more detail about these studies.

NORTH AMERICA

In Canada, Doherty (2001) sought to determine the types of experiences that MPs faced both in office and after leaving public life. The Canadian Association of Former Parliamentarians (CAFP) sent surveys to over 850 former members of both the Senate and House of Commons. Questions probed former members' experience of their time in office, the costs to their quality of life of being in office and life after office. "*Over 200 completed surveys*" were returned—the precise number is not stated— but the author wrote that the response rate was "*just over*" 25 per cent. Doherty distinguished between those who had left office voluntarily (69) and those who had been defeated at the ballot box (98). It is not clear from his paper, however, what had happened to the 33 or so who are not accounted for in these figures.

The results demonstrated that this was a group of former members who had been very dedicated to public service but for whom the personal and family costs had been high. Most former members in the survey were relatively satisfied with their transition from elected life to post-elected life: 83 per cent responded that transition had been "*somewhat*" or "*very*" successful. This high overall figure masked a cohort, albeit a small minority, who had experienced considerable problems. The most vulnerable group was those who had been electorally defeated, especially if they had served only one term and therefore had no parliamentary pension. This tends generally to be a numerically significant group given Canada's exceptionally high parliamentary turnover rates. While even a majority of those who had been defeated had experienced a relatively smooth passage from office, there was a significant difference between "*retirees*" and defeated members: the defeated members were twice as likely as those who had stood down to experience "*a rocky switch.*" Doherty maintained that, "*Those who leave office by choice, who retire, have the luxury of planning their exit. For these former office holders, the transition takes place on their terms.*" There was a similar difference between those who returned to their previous careers and those who had begun afresh, with the former finding the transition less problematic.

The survey revealed a mixed picture from a financial point of view, with some former members earning higher salaries and others lower, than they had in office. This, Doherty stated, is in contrast to former senators and representatives in the USA, the majority of whom do substantially better after serving in office. There was some indication from the survey respondents that specific experiences in office played a part in the softness or otherwise of the subsequent landing, "*there are some Cabinet ministers who spent all their time in social policy. They helped a lot of people, but no companies were knocking on their doors after they left [elected life]. But if you were in something with lots of contacts in the business community,*" more possibilities opened up. Most respondents nevertheless appeared relatively sanguine about their transition to life after political office. It should be borne in mind, however, that the quarter of CAFP members that had chosen to respond to the survey might well have had a different perspective from the much larger percentage of non-respondents. In conclusion, the author hoped that his survey would enhance public understanding of the issues facing Canadian parliamentarians both in office and once they leave office.

From the perspective of a journalist in Canada, Paikin (2003) wrote more of "*the dark side*" of political life. He offered a fascinating account of the highs and the lows, and the price to be paid for entering the political arena. He profiled a number of provincial premiers, but he had long observed Canadian politicians of all hues and ranks. He painted an intensely vivid picture of their experiences of gaining political office, of being in office, and of losing it. His interviews and conversations with politicians convey a powerful sense of the exhilaration of office, of what can be achieved and of the relationships forged in battle—and of the deep bitterness from any betrayal. One interviewee even likened politics to his military experience, "*Politics is like a substitute ... in civilian life it's the only comparable experience you have. It's the intensity of the battle. It's the friendships you form*" (p. 100).

From his interviews, Paikin suggested a more negative experience of transition from office than that from Doherty's survey. He observed, "*I've met hundreds of politicians over the years, and I'm constantly surprised at how ill-prepared many of them are for life after politics, particularly if they're starting that life after an election loss*" (p. 64). Even with extensive preparation, however, departure from the intoxication of political office is not easy. Paikin quoted the former premier of New Brunswick, Frank McKenna, who had planned his chosen departure and succession in the 1990s with the utmost care, and went on to enjoy an impressive post-political career. Nevertheless six years after leaving political office, " '*I miss it terribly*,' Frank McKenna sighs. '*I miss it every day*'" (p. 236).

An exploratory study of how ex-politicians come to terms with electoral defeat was carried out in Canada by Shaffir and Kleinknecht (2005). The work is based on the transcribed interviews of 45 former federal and provincial parliamentarians from the three main political parties who had been electorally defeated, looking at their experience of defeat in the immediate term. These 45 were drawn from a larger group of about 70 interviews, but it is not clear how they were selected. They included not only defeated former politicians but also parliamentary clerks and administrative officials employed by the political parties. Interviewees had from 3 to 30 years of legislative (mostly backbench) experience between them, and the majority was male. The interviews were carried out within five years of defeat. Their results powerfully convey the intensity of the trauma of defeat and its impact "*Defeat represents rejection at its extreme: 'You didn't get fired by one person; you got fired by 6,000'.*" Imagery of death, sometimes striking, was volunteered by about a third and acknowledged by about two thirds of the total sample. One interviewee, for example, compared the experience of loss to a miscarriage, "*It's a different death. It's a death that no one grieves with you.*" The authors went on to consider the means by which the defeated politicians had come to terms with their loss, referring to that they called "*deflection rhetoric.*" In order to avoid blame and cope with defeat, perhaps associated with guilt and shame, interviewees attributed their defeat to a range of external factors over which they could have had little control: the party leader; policies that had been adopted; the timing of the election; negative portrayal in the media and poor personal health. The authors went on to observe that while the rhetoric absolves the individual of responsibility, "*it fails to totally alleviate the sense of failure and disappointment associated with the loss.*" The vast majority of their group would stand again, given the opportunity. They went on to comment from other data that they have (not in the paper), that the stigma of defeat impedes an ex-politician's efforts to secure gainful employment.

Williams (2011) later study of post-Cabinet life in the Ontario legislature explored the attitudes and behaviours of ex-ministers, that is, those who had lost their frontbench position but who remained in the legislature, rather than having lost their constituencies. She conducted a qualitative study with 11 ex-ministers who had either resigned or left the Cabinet as a result of a reshuffle, over a four-month period in 2011. Williams argued that while Cabinet membership is often regarded as the pinnacle of political achievement in the legislature, her research undermined any notion that ex-ministers disappear into obscurity on the backbenches and/or experience disenchantment and tension. While there may be an initial shock and a period of disappointment at being dropped from the Cabinet, *"they are not disillusioned, frustrated or embittered by not having this opportunity anymore."* It should be borne in mind, however, that the interviews were relatively short (half an hour or under). Williams suggested three personality types—the Maverick, the Valedictorian and the Good Soldier—that encapsulated the ex-ministers' approach to having sought office, to serving in Cabinet and to the trajectory of their future careers, but it is hard to gauge how robust this classification is from the paper. She suggested that ex-ministers should be nurtured as mentors, *"Their skills must be cultivated in order to maximize their potential to lead outside of Cabinet."*

From the USA, Thomas Volgy offered a persuasive perspective as both a political scientist and a former mayor of Tucson. He set out to shine a light on to the reality of democratic governance, rather than its coarsely characterised image. He was clear from the start that his book was to challenge public cynicism in government. It was based on the premise that modern American democracy *"requires citizens to have a sense of empathy toward politicians"* (Volgy 2001, p. xiii). Despite its flaws, the worth of the American democratic system and its political actors should be recognised; he highlighted what the public did to its politicians, drawing attention to *"the many good people retiring from public office"* (p. xiii). He illustrated colourfully the life of an elected politician, the demands, the joys and the exhaustion; but he divulged little about the transition from office or on his experience of having failed to be elected to Congress. Volgy ran twice for Congress, losing by very narrow margins, and was being urged to run again at the time of writing.

In a similar vein, but from the perspective solely of a political scientist in the USA, Reeher (2006) garnered the personal stories of state legislators to portray what it is really like to be a politician, against a background of the general public's increasing distrust, low regard for and cynicism about politicians. Reeher set out to hear the narratives of how legislators had come to enter politics; their experience of serving in office and of their decision to stay or leave the political arena. Despite the plethora of work on legislators in academic political science, he too found it strange that there had been so little work on them as *people*, what motivated them to run, what they risk and what may drive them away. He was clear that, "*any valid theory about representation or legislative behaviour must ultimately play itself through a process involving people, and thus understanding the people involved is essential to a full understanding of the explanatory work that the theories purport to do*" (Reeher 2006, p. 2).

Reeher interviewed 77 legislators serving in the lower houses of Connecticut, New York and Vermont during the 1990s, and conducted 23 follow-up interviews four to five years later. In addition, he drew on survey responses from 233 legislators in the same three states, together with data from official records of individual legislators' characteristics and activities. Although his focus was on state legislators, Reeher, drawing on both his own work and Volgy (2001), maintained that his arguments apply both upwards (to Congress) and downwards (to the municipal level). Through their stories, the politicians in Reeher's work are portrayed very differently from the public's caricature of them. They were an ambitious lot—no bad thing in itself—but they shared a commitment to serving the public good and had deep roots in their communities. Their job satisfaction was fuelled by a sense of personal efficacy, that what they did really mattered, "*the joy of mattering*" (p. 71). But it was at some cost: of overwork, overwhelming demands and often, a strained family life. Decisions to stay or to go were complicated affairs, a product of many different factors, both personal and political. But regardless of any particular set of factors or outcome, many legislators "*agonised*" over the decision. Reeher's study did not interview legislators after they had left office except for the few who had previously lost office but had subsequently been re-elected. With issues of governance becoming more complicated but public political discourse more coarse, Reeher makes a plea for the understanding of politics, not least of its practitioners, to be more nuanced and discerning.

UNITED KINGDOM

On the other side of the Atlantic, Kevin Theakston has led systematic attempts to understand what happens to MPs once they have left the House of Commons (Theakston et al. 2007; Byrne and Theakston 2015). In the 2007 study of MPs leaving the Westminster Parliament in 2007, Theakston and colleagues sent a 43-item questionnaire in October 2006, to all of the then 343 members of the Association of Former Members of Parliament (AFMP), to which 184 (54 per cent) responded. Of these, 72 (39 per cent) had been electorally defeated and 112 (60 per cent) had "retired," that is, they had not stood in the election. Membership of the AFMP is open to all former MPs and hence respondents had left Parliament at different elections, from 1970 to 2005.

The survey covered a range of areas including reasons for standing down, reasons for defeat, the reactions of the former parliamentarians themselves as well as others, the practicalities involved with leaving the Commons, as well as next steps, not least looking for work. Their sample of former MPs contained broadly three groups: those who were around the age of 65 and had decided that their parliamentary career should come to an end; those, mostly younger, who had lost their seat in the election or, fewer, as a result of boundary changes; and a smaller group who chose to leave to pursue other career possibilities. Note that nearly 25 per cent of the respondents had been appointed to the House of Lords, a figure that seems significantly higher than for MPs generally. It is difficult to make exact comparisons as the percentage of MPs who are appointed to the Lords varies from time to time. But, for example, 4.96 per cent of MPs who left during or after the 2001–05 Parliament were appointed to the Lords, and 4.4 per cent of those who sat in the 2005–10 Parliament (House of Lords Library).

The research highlighted common issues. Emotional reactions to leaving the Commons varied widely but were most problematic for those who had experienced electoral defeat (or had been de-selected), that had been unexpected in a third of cases. In the immediate period of defeat, a significant minority acknowledged having felt shocked, angry and upset. A number mentioned how much constant campaigning had been needed to nurse their marginal constituency, only then to be swept away in the tide of a national swing.

The effect of defeat was acknowledged to last a considerable time for about a quarter (24 per cent), for a couple, "*still continuing*" or "*for six years.*" Nearly half, however, responded that leaving the Commons had not led to any decline in self-perception.

Family and friends, unsurprisingly, were cited as the main source of support and some respondents felt that the parties or Parliament itself could offer more help to defeated MPs to adjust and to find employment. Many missed the buzz of the Commons and being at the centre of things, but this had to be weighed against the long hours and the strain on family life.

Almost all the respondents in this survey had continued to be active in public life in some guise, whether in their political party, local organisations or on public bodies. They felt that they had skills honed as parliamentarians that could have been drawn on, yet over half felt that not enough use was being made of what they could offer. Theakston et al. commented that their respondents appeared "*overwhelmingly as a group of public-minded individuals*" and they question whether the skills and experience that they have are used by civil society to the extent that they could be.

Theakston's Leeds group returned to a similar theme in their survey of former MPs who left Parliament in 2010 (Byrne and Theakston 2015). They sent a postal survey to all 225 of those who had left: 149 had stood down while 76 had been defeated. In addition, they conducted a number (unspecified) of personal interviews, although there are no details about the nature of these interviews or how interviewees were selected. They received 67 responses, a rate of 34 per cent, which is not unreasonable but it was significantly lower than in their previous survey. The authors attributed this in part to the fact that their survey from 2010 contacted all departing MPs, whereas their earlier study contacted only members of the Association of Former Members of Parliament who, for a variety of reasons, may have been more likely to reply.

Byrne and Theakston highlighted the profound effects of the MPs's expenses scandal of 2009 on both the former MPs themselves and their families that in part accounted for the almost record number of MPs who left the House of Commons in 2010. The most common reason in this study for standing down given was age, cited by 60 per cent of respondents, followed by 25 per cent who cited a desire to spend more time with their family. In contrast to the findings of Shaffir and Kleinknecht's (2005) study, most of the former MPs who had been defeated in Byrne and Theakston's survey, replied that they had not been surprised to lose their seat. The authors speculate that one of the reasons for their contradictory findings might have been that former MPs claimed retrospectively to have been less shocked than they had been as a way of coping with their loss. Former MPs missed much the same aspects of being in the House of Commons as in the earlier study: being able to make a difference; being in the political centre of things and the social aspects of being an MP. The incessant demands, long working hours and the incursions into family life were however not missed. That the rules around MPs' housing arrangements had changed so significantly, thus further compromising family life was described as a bone of contention for Bryne and Theakston's departing MPs. Of note, former female MPs were likely to leave at a younger age, and they tended to have had a shorter time in Parliament than their male counterparts.

Byrne and Theakston pointed to the significant differences in the way that former MPs reacted to their exit from Parliament in their research. Although *"overwhelmingly"* their respondents were relieved to have left, there were notable differences between those who had chosen to stand down and those who had been defeated. Fourteen per cent of the former group reported feeling depressed after the election compared with half of the latter. Of those who had been defeated, 11 per cent reported feeling angry, whereas none of those standing down had. Many commented that they had experienced a sense of grief or a loss of identity after leaving political office. Fifty-seven per cent of respondents had taken up paid work after leaving Parliament, but a higher figure, 70 per cent, of those under the age of 65 had done so. Half the sample was paid more than they had been as an MP, 39.5 per cent less and 10.5 per cent about the same. A clear majority reported that their post-parliamentary career was more satisfying than their parliamentary one with women significantly more likely to report higher satisfaction with their subsequent careers. On the other hand, it took some time for many to find employment: 42 per cent of those seeking paid employment in Byrne and Theakston's study were out of work three months after leaving Parliament and 11 per cent of the total were out of work a year after leaving. A large number felt that their status as a former MP had hampered their efforts to find employment in addition to their having taken a substantial period out of a career prior to entering Parliament. The more senior the former MP had been, unsurprisingly, the less difficult it had been to find work. As in the 2007 study, many respondents believed that their skills and experience were being wasted in the labour market and in public life more generally, although many were involved in charitable work. Byrne and Theakston concluded that,

> *"The transition out of political office needs to be made less problematic, perhaps through the efforts of parliamentary authorities and political parties to help departing MPs navigate the labour market: and, in light of the frenzied reporting of the MPs' expenses scandal and the spread of a broader anti-political populism, more needs to be done – even if this is perhaps wishful thinking – to recognise that most MPs are hardworking people motivated by a genuine desire to serve the public interest, and who pursue that interest in uniquely challenging circumstances."*

Weinberg has investigated quite how challenging the circumstances of MPs can be. He conducted a study on the psychological impact of "*surviving*," losing or leaving the role of an MP in the Westminster Parliament following a General Election (Weinberg 2007). Questionnaires were sent to 132 MPs six months after the election and again about two years later. They found that there had been small decreases in levels of physical symptoms of stress reported by former MPs compared with two years previously, but both psychological and physical symptom levels were still higher than those of surviving MPs. Increased psychological symptoms of stress were reported by those losing their jobs compared with those who had taken the decision themselves to leave. Weinberg (2012) called later for more longitudinal research into the differential impact of either losing or deliberately leaving a political job. He wrote:

"Continuing debate about the 'career' politician who is ill-prepared for any other kind of occupation suggests that the type of support offered by many modern organisations to employees who are being made redundant is also needed by ex-MPs" (p. 137).

Having explored the culture of the House of Commons through interviews with MPs over 20 years, Kwiatkowski (2015) wrote a reflective piece about how psychologically difficult it may be to leave the Commons. Parliament is replete with traditional and powerful symbols; MPs are rapidly socialised into the institution and strong friendships formed. No wonder then that,

"There will be an inevitable period of mourning for what they have lost, and can never have again."

Otherwise, there is little else in the academic literature on the fate of British parliamentarians, but both Peter Riddell and Jeremy Paxman have written well-researched, thoughtful and convincing accounts about the politicians who govern us, who they are and what drives them (Riddell 1996, 2011; Paxman 2002). Their books each devote a chapter, appropriately enough at the end, to "*Failure*" and "*Being history*," respectively.

While Riddell (1996) acknowledged that many ministers do not leave office voluntarily, there are notable examples of those who have and a larger number who have gone on to successful post-ministerial lives. Very few now return to ministerial office, and if they do, they seldom attain their previous position of influence. Riddell (p. 239) quoted William Waldegrave opining that, *"in politics, everyone has fifteen years ... but for*

the whole of that fifteen years, you may be in opposition or the wrong section of your party may be in power … you have to recognise that you are taking a gamble and you may just miss."
Paxman (2002) was curious about the magnetic, spellbinding draw of political office. He talked with MPs, past and present, in order to try and get the measure of this strange beast, the political animal. Among much else, he was puzzled by how unprepared many politicians are for their political end. Governments outstay their welcome, *"the longer governments stay in office, the more dangerous the arrogance of power"* (Paxman 2002, p. 267). Ministers oddly *"do not seem to realise that, just as one day they were elevated, so another day they will be jettisoned"*; and *"further down the dramatis personae, once they are on the stage, the proportion willing to leave it voluntarily is tiny"* (Paxman 2002, p. 265). With Paxman's description of how quickly and completely the political waters close over even a former prime minister, and of how restless, invisible (and sometimes unemployed) many former MPs are, it is less surprising that political oblivion is so resistible. Perhaps unusually, former backbench MP, David Watkins (1996), whose seat disappeared courtesy of his constituency's abolition, immediately in 1983 found employment to which he was eminently well-suited. He was invited to accept the vacant directorship of the Council for the Advancement of Arab-British Understanding, a cause he had long championed as an MP. Watkins wrote (p. 227) that this had brought *"both job satisfaction and international renown and arguably enabled me to exert more influence in important places than as an MP"*; but how common is this now? Despite the widespread perception that former MPs easily pick up positions in the corporate sector, only a tiny number at the very top of the political tree do so (Gonzàlez-Bailon et al. 2013; Byrne and Theakston 2015). It is simply not the case in the UK that there is a lucrative revolving door into business for the vast majority of former politicians, a point I return to in Chap. 13.

Memoirs again provide an insight although Paxman (2002) commented on how few reflect on *"what it is like to put politics behind you"* (p. 270). He dourly described the genre as a whole as *"largely dismal"* (p. 269).

Far from dismal are the diaries from *"the foothills"* penned by former MP, Chris Mullin (2010). He was *"unceremoniously dismissed"* (p. 1) as a minister in 2005, an act he wrote that was *"a hammer blow to my fragile self-esteem"* (p. 4). Four months later, Mullin found, *"To my surprise and slightly to my disgust, I still find myself moping over the loss of office.*" But he qualified this by writing that it was, "*Not office per se but the particular job I had.*" Yet, he went on to wonder what it might be like for others who had lost positions, "*What must it be like after ten years – and at the top? Presumably, it all depends on the manner of your exit. If your tenure comes to a natural conclusion – courtesy of the electorate or by your own hand – you feel you've done your best and move on. But when it comes out of the blue and with the inevitable implication that you weren't up to it, that's what hurts*" (Mullin 2010, pp. 36–37). Mullin both insightfully and wittily went on to describe the following five years in Parliament on the backbenches and his growing realisation that his useful life in politics was over. In 2008, after considerable private agonising, he told a few close colleagues that he had decided to stand down at the next election in 2010, whereupon he "*went home feeling sick … a hollow feeling. Like bereavement*" (p. 243). Readers are left in suspense to know how Mr. Mullin fares in his post-parliamentary life other than, "*If all else fails, I shall grow vegetables*" (p. 449).

Austin Mitchell's valedictory reflections from his 38 years as an MP until 2015 cast a somewhat sad and diminished light on the working of the House of Commons in recent years (Mitchell 2015). While he has no doubt that, "*You're forgotten once you're gone, and written out once you announce your departure,*" he writes little of his own experience of the transition from office. However, he acknowledges frankly that despite the tiresome evidence of his advancing years, there were still attractions of remaining in office,

"*Me? I'd like to stay on. There's trouble to be had, constituents to be served and issues to be taken up, but my conscience and Ed Miliband tell me it's time to go.*"

There are, of course, many newspaper, other journalistic articles and now blogs written about (or by) former and soon to be former MPs (for example, Brown 2010; Macrory 2011; Porter 2011; Rustin 2012; Helm 2013; Bland 2015). They are, unsurprisingly, mostly written in the wake of an election or following the announcement that an MP is standing down. While they give some insight into what happens after a parliamentarian has left office, it is likely that these pen portraits focus on those former MPs who feel more confident in post-parliamentary life than others. At the other end of the spectrum, the expenses scandal of 2009 led to the criminal conviction of a number of MPs and peers in whom there has been both a legitimate but sometimes salacious interest by the media.

Graffin and his colleagues (2013) took the opportunity of the expenses scandal to examine the potential hazards of high status associated with political office, and their work does have some bearing on the reasons for MPs leaving Parliament in 2010. They found that while *"high status"* MPs (those who had received an honour and/or who had sat on the front bench) were not more likely to have abused the expenses system than *"low status"* MPs, they were more likely to have been targeted by the press for any inappropriate expenses claims. They were therefore more likely to exit Parliament as a result.

LOCAL AND DEVOLVED GOVERNMENT

As sparse as the literature on leaving office may be at a national level, there is virtually nothing about the experience of local government politicians leaving office. Given that local authority leaders have considerably more responsibility and authority than most parliamentarians, albeit within a smaller geographical domain, this should be surprising. Somehow it is not, in the context of the lack of recognition accorded to local government generally in comparison with national government, and to local politicians compared with MPs. Yet, arguably, local politicians and the decisions that they make have far greater influence on the day-to-day experience of citizens, although this is often not recognised.

There is however a considerable body of work on the recruitment of councillors, their turnover, their demographic representativeness of the communities that they are elected to serve and the factors leading to their exit (for example, Councillors Commission 2007; Allen 2012; Hjelmar et al. 2010; Rallings and Thrasher 2014). I have not been able to find anything, however, that has been written on council leaders' transition from office. With new democratic structures in place— the devolved governments of Scotland and Wales, and directly elected mayors—it is possible that there will be more attention to this area in the future.

The former Mayor of London (and former backbench MP), Ken Livingstone, in his memoirs after his first defeat in 2008 but before his second candidature in 2012, acknowledged how in the weekend after his defeat, he had felt *"overwhelmed with a sense of loss ... without warning every now and then I found myself quietly weeping"* (Livingstone 2011, p. 633). He had been a self confessed workaholic for 46 years and very quickly came to focus his considerable energies on a re-run four years later, perhaps in order to deal with the sudden vacuum from the loss of office. Of his second defeat, in 2012, we know even less.

OVERVIEW OF THE LITERATURE

In essence, there is a reasonably well-established literature with regard to the lives and activities of US presidents once they leave office although little that probes their lived experience of transition from office and their adjustment to post-presidential life. US presidents, of course, if they are re-elected for a second term, not only know when they will be leaving office four years before but the transition itself is two months or so, before the inauguration of their successor. This is very different from most leaders' experience. There is an emerging literature on what happens to other government leaders once they leave office, mostly from western style democracies. This literature has focused on what such leaders have gone on to do, and the political roles and influence that they may or may not have.

There is little however examining the experience of transition from office of politicians who have not achieved the highest office, although the literature from Canada is richer than elsewhere. There are reflections, mostly of a self-justifying nature from autobiographies, but little about the emotional and psychological consequences of leaving office; and barely anything about impact on partners and wider family impact. There is relatively little systematic in the UK except that spearheaded by Kevin Theakston and his colleagues from Leeds and that from Ashley Weinberg. There appears to be a vacuum with regard to local government leadership: I have not been able to find anything about the transition from local government leadership. Given these gaps, there is nothing that considers what, if any, the impact may be on our democratic system of the experience of transition from political office.

OFFICE DEPENDENCY

Going back to Keane (2011), he took a longer-term and more analytic perspective. Representative democracy came to be understood from the eighteenth century on as a new, different and inherently better model of government in which people had a genuine choice about who governed them; representatives were elected to act in defence of the interests of those who had put them into office; those very same people could eject them from office too; and the notion of "*office holding*" came into being. But Keane was struck by the odd silence about the fate of leaders once they have been efficiently but peacefully dispensed with. That they should be so dispensed of was, of course, part of the democratic advance. Keane quoted approvingly Thomas Jefferson's advice in 1811 that there is *"a fullness of time when men should go, and not occupy too long the ground to which others have a right to advance"* (p. 280).

Keane's starting point was that, Jefferson's advice notwithstanding, the experience of holding high office is a habit that can be hard to kick and *"often synonymous with the collapse of a personal world"* (p. 283). *"Office dependency,"* a malady in his terms, is partly fostered by the perks of office but more saliently, by the deep personal satisfaction both from advancing cherished policy goals and the narcissistic fulfilment gained. Keane quoted Gareth Evans, a former Australian foreign minister's term, *"relevance deprivation syndrome"* (p. 284), to describe the pain of leaving office. A range of checks to office dependency may be in place in different democratic systems (such a limiting the number of terms that can be served, recall by the electorate), but Keane argues that the key test of democratic strength is the degree to which a distinction is made between those who hold office and those who have left office. He points to the growing intolerance in the last 100 years or so of the British parliamentary system to prime ministers hanging on to high office. Few now even remain in Parliament. This is in contrast to nine former premiers of the eighteenth and nineteenth centuries who held very senior positions under subsequent prime ministers, the so-called *"Balfour syndrome."* Keane here concentrated on the holders of very high office, but he acknowledges that *"the malady may affect office holding at all levels"* (p. 283).

Of relevance but from a different perspective, from the UK Lord David Owen, himself a medical doctor as well as a politician, has written of the risks for some heads of government of holding office for too long, and what the consequences might be on decision-making (Owen 2006). From his investigation into illness in heads of governments, Owen identified a *"hubris syndrome"* that includes behaviours such as excessive self-confidence, messianic zeal and the conflation of self with nation or organisation. Owen warned that *"The intoxication of power, not just illness in Heads of Government, can be as great a menace to the quality of their leadership as are conventional illnesses."*

There has been some debate in the psychiatric literature about the diagnostic validity of such a syndrome with a suggestion that it may instead be better understood, for example, as a sub-type of narcissistic personality disorder (Russell 2011; Owen 2011; Freedman 2011). Rather than a separately defined category of hubris syndrome, the features seen may simply be a *"widespread psychological tendency, observed in many and, due to normal variation (of character and personal life history), extremely developed in a few"* (Loch 2016, p. 105). In other words, we may be seeing exaggerated personality traits that may have facilitated the seeking of power in the first place: It is known that many individuals with a narcissistic personality organisation will search out leadership roles (Volkan 2014). On leadership, Kets de Vries (2003b) writes more from a psychoanalytic perspective and he observes that, *"One of the dangers of narcissism is the difficulty leaders have in letting go"* *(p.xvi)*.

In Mulgan's (2007) masterly overview of power, good and bad, in government, he writes (p. 114) of *"The drive for permanence"* that *"shapes how rulers use their power. Often they appear to hoard it, and therefore tend to cling on, resisting challengers, real or imagined."* Mulgan suggests that this is in part because of rulers' fear that they will lose everything that they value once they have lost office. While rulers in democratic countries do not lose their lives—as they may do in some parts of the world—they do lose control over their legacy and their reputation. Although Mulgan regards trying to hold on to power as natural, it brings problems, *"Storing it up guarantees atrophy"* (p. 115).

In a similar vein, Horiuchi, Laing and `t Hart (2015) observe of party leader succession that, *"Very long-serving leaders may stifle innovation within parties and governments and generate internal conflicts and stalemates."* But even when attempts are made to manage a party leader's succession, the process may be far from smooth (Bynander and `t Hart 2008).

Structural mechanisms such as term limits have been introduced, predominantly in the state legislature of the USA since the late 1980s in response to grassroots popular pressure (Caress and Kunioka 2012). Of course, as noted earlier, the USA ratified a two-term limit for its president long before, in 1951. Although there was little hard evidence either in support of against term limits when they were introduced, it has become more evident that term limits have had profound effects on how state governments operate depending on the term restriction imposed, and some consequences have been unexpected. Term limits, for example, have changed career paths as incumbents seek election in other chambers, but they have not changed the type of people who were elected as legislators. They have reduced the experience of legislative leaders and potentially therefore legislators' powers. But in any case, Riddell (1995) argues that formal term limits would not be appropriate in the UK, not least because there is no separation of powers between the executive and the legislative as in the USA.

While there may be checks to office dependency in any democratic system, there have been some changes in the composition of politicians in the UK and the wider context that might tack in the opposite direction and instead foster office dependency.

Changing Trends in Who UK Politicians Are

Prior to the latter half of the twentieth century, MPs were often not full-time politicians. With Conservative and Liberal MPs either from the aristocracy and landed classes, or later as the Labour Party grew, from a trade union background, politics was not necessarily a full-time occupation. As the century went on, there was an increasing convergence towards MPs coming from an urban, middle class and professional background (Rush and Cromwell 2004; Cairney 2007). Changes put in place towards the end of the century—the modern allowance system introduced in 1969 and successive increases in salaries, pensions and expenses most notably since the end of the 1990s—facilitated the increasing professionalisation of politics with MPs able to make a living *off* politics, from being a politician alone. This has given rise to the "career politician" (King 1981), a term that King applies to one who is wholly committed to politics,

"He regards politics as his vocation, he seeks fulfillment in politics, he sees his future in politics, he would be deeply upset if circumstances forced him to retire from politics. In short, he is hooked."

For King, a career politician would not necessarily have to work full time in politics, although s/he might like to, in contrast to a "professional politician." He goes on to write of a career politician,

"Being psychologically committed to politics does not preclude someone's having other interests, and these interests, although secondary, may be genuine and absorbing."

Cowley (2012), on the other hand, in his examination of UK party leadership, uses the term "career politician" to describe a pathway in which individuals have worked in politics professionally—as advisers, researchers and similar roles—prior to gaining elected office in the Westminster Parliament.

Many have decried the ascent of career politician. Indeed, Neil Kinnock's biographer (Westlake 2001, p. 711) relates how one of Kinnock's pet hates was,

"The young person who asks, "How do I have a career in politics? I always say, "You don't. You go away and you do something useful, and then if you're lucky you might be selected for some sort of public office, but you can't see it as a career in that way."

Kinnock's advice has mostly not been heeded as the career politician became much more commonplace over the latter half of the twentieth century. Riddell (1995) describes how the proportion of newly elected MPs who had had what he termed "proper" jobs, that is, jobs that were wholly independent of politics, fell between 1951 and 1992 elections from 80 per cent to 41 per cent. In contrast, the number of newly elected MPs who had been fully involved in politics prior to this election rose from 11 per cent to 31 per cent in the same period. Riddell acknowledges that this trend has reflected a greater specialisation in all occupations, and it has continued apace. Now, as Cowley (2012) makes clear, if an ambitious politician wants to reach the top,

"Being a career politician is the only game in town."

Becoming a career politician is made more straightforward if parliamentary candidates come from certain occupational backgrounds. MPs have increasingly been drawn from so-called "politics-facilitating" occupations (Cairney 2007) in which useful skills and contacts for a political life can be developed such as law, journalism and education. Within this category of politics-facilitating occupations, there has been a further recent change with more MPs coming from occupations with direct links to politics such as researchers, journalists and advisers—"instrumental" occupations—rather than the traditional "brokerage" professions such as law and teaching. There are some party differences, however: Labour MPs in the early twenty-first century are increasingly likely to come from instrumental politics-facilitating backgrounds compared with their Conservative colleagues whose backgrounds have been more stable albeit with some rise in those with a business background.

Figures from the most recent UK General Election in 2015 bear out this trend in the narrowing of the occupational background of MPs (Lamprinakou et al. 2015). Lamprinakou and colleagues also point to the rise in the numbers of MPs from a business background, especially from the Conservative party, possibly suggesting wider experience.

Howarth's closer scrutiny of the nature of the business experience of MPs in the two parliaments from 2005 to 2015 however suggests that the increase during that time was nearly all accounted for by the number coming from a background in public relations, marketing and advertising

(Howarth 2013). A wider experience to some extent perhaps, but these arguably could be considered "instrumental" occupations, since skills in public relations and marketing are increasingly useful to the modern British politician. Mitchell (2015) more pithily comments,

"Public relations has replaced policy, electoral calculus has driven economic management, and we've ended up with fewer skills but more political obsessives, all of them with little experience of the real world of work, living or business building and hinterlands restricted to pop music and telly."

Even if MPs do enter the Westminster Parliament having forged a successful career outside of politics, more stringent rules introduced in 2009 on MPs' registers of interests and any additional work they undertook make it more difficult than once it was for MPs to maintain their professional skills. Howarth (2013) observes how difficult it can be for barristers, previously more numerous in the Commons, now to maintain their professional skills while practising politics, unlike PR and marketing practitioners and long-term political professionals. He notes how few of the 20 lawyers who left the Commons in 2010 returned to the law—and some took up jobs that were significantly less well paid than the law. Of those lawyers, Howarth comments (p. 57) that,

"Political experience seems not to be prized at all."

His concern is echoed with regard to a different profession, medicine, by the decision of former MP, Dr Howard Stoate, to stand down at the 2010 General Election because he felt otherwise he would have been unable to continue to practise as a GP, albeit very part time (BBC News, 28 July 2009).

A lowering of the age at which MPs first enter Parliament confirms the shift to professionalised politics (King 1981; Riddell 1995; Lamprinakou et al. 2015). With an increase in the number of MPs first elected from their 20s to early 40s, more are likely to have been set upon a political career from an early age, to have less experience of the wider world and therefore to have less to fall back upon should they lose their seat.

In such circumstance, with more invested in holding on to political office once it has been gained, the risks of office dependency may increase. I consider this possibility more fully in Chap. 13. Riddell called for an end to *"the closed shop"* by allowing people of wider experience to become parliamentary candidates in mid-career so that they might spend a decade or so as MPs and involving more outsiders as members of governments or advisers outside Parliament.

The picture is emerging in the devolved governments of Scotland and Wales. Scottish Members of the Scottish Parliament (MSPs) are very similar in demographic character to their Westminster counterparts, except that there are relatively more female MSPs (35 per cent in the 2016 MSP intake, lower than in the peak year of 2003 when there were 39.5 per cent women).[4] Since the 2015 UK General Election, however, the gap between the two has diminished, with 29 per cent female Westminster MPs currently. Notably, MSPs are just as likely to come from a politics-facilitating occupation prior to their election (Cairney and McGarvey 2013, p. 108).

In Wales, there is a relatively high proportion of female Assembly Members (AMs): It was 50 per cent in 1999 when the Assembly was first established and it has since dipped slightly to 42 per cent in the fifth Assembly from 2016, the same figure as in the preceding Assembly from 2011 (Garwood 2016, personal communication). The average age of an AM starting in 1999 was 47, whereas in 2011, it was 51 (Garwood 2015, personal communication). The 23 new members of the Welsh Assembly after the 2011 election came from a variety of backgrounds, although the most common were ex-councillors, lawyers and teachers/academics. Of the 24 AMs since 1999 (until 2015) who have been defeated, a number have remained directly in politics (as councillors, or candidates for the Westminster Parliament or for election as a Police and Crime Commissioner), others have gone into consultancy and lobbying or working for the voluntary sector (Garwood 2015, personal communication). Of the 22 new members of the fifth Assembly in 2016, over half came from a political background (previously having been an MP, Member of the European Parliament (MEP), AM, councillor or having worked for an MP). Of the remaining eight, two were lawyers, two had worked for a trade union and the rest were from a mixed background (Garwood 2016, personal communication). AMs are expected to work full time in their role.

There is a similar trend towards full-time council leaders in local government, although there is much less information available regarding council leaders than there is about MPs or about councillors as a whole.

The last census of councillors was done in 2013 (Kettlewell and Phillips 2014). This showed that the proportion of councillors in full-time employment had decreased steadily from 27.2 per cent in 2001 to 19.2 per cent in 2013 while the proportion of retired councillors had increased from 36.8 % in 2001 to 46.6 per cent in 2013, suggesting that councillors may be spending relatively more time on council duties than they had been previously.

Council leaders have often continued in their previous employment or some might have been retired. Increasingly, however, the trend has been for council leaders and now even Cabinet members to carry out their roles full time (Simpson 2014, personal communication), encouraged by the change in political management structures in the Local Government Act 2000. There is little hard evidence of this trend, but it is widely reported anecdotally. With the advent of directly elected mayors, albeit still relatively few in number (17 in 2016), who are expected to work full time in the role, the trend towards full-time local leadership is reinforced. This is a profound change over a relatively short time.

In contrast to MPs, the age of councillors generally and council leaders specifically has changed relatively little over time. The age of councillors has been increasingly very slightly over time (from 57.8 in 2004 to 60.2 in 2013) with only 12 per cent aged below 45. The age of leaders of party groups (rather than necessarily of a council leader) was 58 in 2013 (Skinner 2015, personal communication).

In summary, over the last few decades, Westminster MPs have become more single-mindedly focused on a political career at an early age, younger when they are first elected to parliament, still far more likely to be male, and less likely to have worked in a job unrelated to politics prior to their election. They are now coming from a narrower occupational background, and they are less likely to continue working in any other role during their time as an MP, concentrating instead exclusively on their work as an MP and thus not able to keep up their professional skills. These trends are seen in many other western-type democracies (Riddell 1995). The evidence regarding council leaders is less clear, but it is likely that they are increasingly working full time in their role as leader. These changes may enhance the likelihood of office dependency, an issue I return to in Chap. 13 in the light of the findings from the research presented in this book.

All the more necessary, therefore, is a *"politics of retreat,"* proposed by Keane (2011), that is, the capacity to concede power gracefully to others. But, *"stepping down is a capacity learned reluctantly, and with the greatest difficulty, usually in trying circumstances; it is a talent that has few supporting role models and virtually no philosophical mentors or political guidebooks"* (pp. 283–4).

OTHER INSIGHTS

There is a wealth of literature studying other transitions that has considerable relevance. Most relevant are redundancy, retirement, bereavement, loss and change more generally. Literature from these areas will be considered in subsequent chapters. There is also some interest in what happens to specific post-holders, for example, chief executive officers or people in specific occupations, such as top athletes or members of the armed forces, once they move on, as discussed earlier.

ROLE EXIT

Sociological insights into the possible impact of the loss of political office may be gained from wider sources. Studies carried out by Ebaugh (1988), for example, provide some of the richest insights into the experience of "exes." A former nun turned academic, Ebaugh became interested in what she terms, role exit, that is, *"the process of disengagement from a role that is central to one's self-identity and the reestablishment of an identity in a new role that takes into account one's ex-role"* (p. 1). She was curious that so little scholarly attention had been paid to the area, in contrast to the interest that there had been to role entrance and the process of socialisation into a role. Some years later on, Ashworth (2012) observes still the lopsidedness of research between role entry and exit.

Ebaugh's book drew on data from four separate samples of interviewees: a group of 57 ex-nuns in 1971; a follow-up of 12 ex-nuns in 1985; 106 exes of different types, for example retirees, widows and former doctors; and 10 transsexuals in 1985. Interviews were semi-structured in style and lasted about two hours with reflections encouraged. All interviewees had chosen to leave although, as Ebaugh argued, their decisions to go had not always been entirely voluntary. From her data, she drew 11 properties of the role exit process that emerged as central variables influencing the nature and consequences of the process:

- The degree of voluntariness—having more choice in whether to go or not favours a better adjustment;
- The centrality of the role—we all have different roles and they differ in the extent of their centrality to self-identity. Leaving a role that is core to an individual's identity is potentially more problematic;
- The reversibility of the process—some exits may be irreversible, a surgical change of gender, for example, but others may be more

reversible. The more irreversible, unsurprisingly, the more extended is the decision-making process;

- The duration of the role exit process—a longer time for deliberation is often helpful, but there seems no advantage for a very extended period when no new insights can be gained;
- The degree of control over the process and the degree to which role exit is dependent on other individuals or institutions;
- Individual versus group exit—individuals may leave a role on their own or as part of a cohort of people leaving around the same time, new graduates, for example. The cohort effect may encourage others to exit that same role in their wake and it can provide support to all those exiting;
- Single versus multiple exits—some exits inevitably involve exits from related roles, for example, a nun leaving a teaching role as well as her vocation, whereas leaving a job can be just a single exit. The greater the awareness and anticipation of other role exits, the better the adjustment;
- Social desirability—the process of establishing a new ex-identity is influenced by the perceived desirability of exit, for example, an alcoholic who has given up drinking may be seen more benignly than someone leaving a highly socially desirable profession;
- The degree of institutionalisation—some exits are marked by known and expected rite of passage (giving gold watches or graduation ceremonies, for example) and may even involve the acquisition of a name, such as alumnus. Others transit without any ritual;
- Degree of awareness—the degree to which an individual makes the decision to exit with deliberation and awareness;
- Sequentiality—the more an exit disrupts social expectations regarding role sequences, the more pressure is placed on an individual if they exit, for example, breaking off an engagement close to the wedding.

Ebaugh made clear that disengagement from an old role is a complex process that *"involves shifts in reference groups, friendship networks, relationships with former group members, and most important, shifts in a person's sense of self-identity"* (p. 181). She distinguished an ex-member of a group from a non-member: the new identity of the ex incorporates the vestiges of the previous role, and to a much greater extent where there had been very high intensity of attachment to that role. She wrote that *"the process of role exiting involves tension between an individual's past, present and future"* (p. 149), and she pointed to the adjustment and adaptation required not just by the individual making the transition but on the part of significant others associated with them. Ebaugh's central contention was that role exit is a process that can be generalised to all types of exits. Most, but not all, of her interviewees had exited roles with varying degrees of voluntariness. She advocated further studies that compared voluntary and involuntary exits.

While Ebaugh argued that people historically were much less mobile in terms of role change, thus accounting the lack of attention to role exit prior to her work, the mobility associated with leaving political office has long been an essential prerequisite of a representative democracy. The relative lack of attention to this specific role exit may therefore be all the more surprising. Ebaugh did not include former politicians in her study. In the next chapter, I describe my research that focused on this group alone.

NOTES

1. http://politicalticker.blogs.cnn.com/2012/07/18/george-w-bush-presidential-afterlife-is-awesome/
2. Ozymandias, a Greek name for the Egyptian pharaoh Rameses ll, is the title of a sonnet written by both Percy Bysshe Shelley and Horace Smith in 1818 exploring the impermanence of leaders and their empires and the decline into oblivion to which that their legacies are inevitably consigned.
3. http://www.independent.co.uk/news/uk/politics/watch-ed-miliband-reveal-how-his-son-brought-him-crushing-down-to-earth-by-telling-him-you-used-to-10297411.html
4. http://www.heraldscotland.com/news/14477630.Election_2016__Number_of_female_MSPs_unchanged

REFERENCES

Abjorensen, N. (2015). *The Manner of Their Going: Prime Ministerial Exits from Lyne to Abbott.* North Melbourne, Victoria: Australian Scholarly.

Allen, P. (2012). Last In, First Out: Gendered Patterns of Local Government Dropout. *British Politics* pp. 1–18.

Anderson, L. (2010). The Ex-Presidents. *Journal of Democracy* 21 (2) 64–78 doi: 10.1353/jod.0.0166.

Ashforth, B.E. (2012). *Role Transitions in Organizational Life: An Identity-Based Perspective.* East Sussex and New York: Routledge.

Belenky, I. (1999). The Making of the Ex-Presidents, 1797–1993: Six Recurrent Models. *Presidential Studies Quarterly* 29 (1) pp. 150–165.

Blair, D.K. and Henry, A.R. (1981). The Family Factor in State Legislative Turnover. *Legislative Studies Quarterly* 6 (1) pp. 55–68.

Bland, A. (2015). You get sacked by thousands of people. *The Guardian* 12 May 2015.

Blair, T. (2010). A Journey. London: Hutchinson.

Blondel, J. (1991). *The post-ministerial careers*. In J. Blondel and J.L. Thiébault (Eds.), *The Profession of Government Ministers in Western Europe*. London: Macmillan.

Booker, J. (2013). Life After Politics? The Post-Leadership Activities of New Zealand Premiers and Prime Ministers, 1856–2008, *A thesis submitted to the Victoria University of Wellington in fulfillment of the requirement for the degree of Master of Arts in Political Science*. Victoria: University of Wellington.

Brown, M. (2010). To those MPs who lost their seats, I know how you feel. *The Independent* 7 May.

Brown, S. (2012). *Behind the Black Door*. London: Random House.

Bynander, F. and `t Hart, P. (2008). The Art of Handing Over: (Mis)Managing Party Leadership Successions. *Government and Opposition* 43 (3) pp. 385–404.

Byrne, C. and Theakston, K. (2015). Leaving the House: The Experience of Former Members of Parliament Who Left the House of Commons in 2010. *Parliamentary Affairs* doi: 10.1093/pa/gsv053.

Cairney, P. (2007). The Professionalisation of MPs: Refining the 'Politics-Facilitating' Explanation. *Parliamentary Affairs* 60 (2) pp. 212–233.

Cairney, P. and McGarvey, N. (2013). *Scottish Politics*. Basingstoke: Palgrave Macmillan.

Caress, S.M. and Kunioka, T.T. (2012). *Term Limits and Their Consequences*. Albany: State University of New York.

Chambers, J.W. (1998). Jimmy Carter's Public Policy Ex-Presidency. *Political Science Quarterly* 113 (3) pp. 405–425.

Cristofoli, D. and Crugnola, P. (2012). To run or not to run (again) for political office … at the crossroads between public values and self-interested benefits. Yearbook of Swiss Administrative Sciences pp. 91–105.

Claveria, S. and Verge, T. (2015). Post-ministerial Occupation in Advanced Democracies: Ambition, Individual Resources and Institutional Opportunity Structures. *European Journal of Political Research* 1 doi: 10.1111/1475-6765.12107.

Cook, R. (2003). *The Point of Departure*. London: Simon and Schuster.

Cowley, P. (2012). Arise, Novice Leader! The Continuing Rise of the Career Politician in Britain. *Politics* 32 pp. 31–38.

Crick, M. (1997). *Michael Heseltine: A Biography*. London: Penguin Books.
Department of Communities and Local Government. (2007). *Representing the Future: Report of the Councillors Commission*. London: Communities and Local Government Publications.
Doherty, D.C. (2001). To Run or Not to Run? *Canadian Parliamentary Review* 24 pp. 16–23.
Dowding, K. and Kang, W-T. (1998). Ministerial Resignations 1945–97. *Public Administration* 76 pp. 411–429.
Ebaugh, H.R.F. (1988). *Becoming an Ex*. Chicago: The University of Chicago Press.
Ennser-Jedenastik, L. and Muller, W.C. (2013). Intra-party Democracy, Political Performance, and the Survival of Party Leaders: Austria, 1945–2011. *Party Politics* doi: 10.1177/1354068813509517.
Fewsmith, J. (2002). Generational Transition in China. *The Washington Quarterly* 25 pp. 23–35.
Francis, W.L. and Baker, J.R. (1986). Why Do US State Legislators Vacate Their Seats? *Legislative Studies Quarterly* 11 pp. 119–126.
Freedman, L. (2011). Mental States and Political Decisions. Commentary on... Psychiatry and Politicians. *The Psychiatrist* 35 pp. 148–150.
Garwood, B. (2015). Personal communication.
Garwood, B. (2016). Personal communication.
Gillard, J. (2013). Julia Gillard writes on power, purpose and Labor's future. *The Guardian* 14 September.
Gonzàlez-Bailon, S., Jennings, W. and Lodge, M. (2013). Politics in the Boardroom: Corporate Pay, Networks and Recruitment of Former Parliamentarians, Ministers and Civil Servants in Britain. *Political Studies* 61(4) pp. 850–873.
Gould, P. (1998). *The Unfinished Revolution: How the Modernisers Saved the Labour Party*. London: Little, Brown and Company.
Graffin, S.D., Bundy, J., Porac, J.F., Wade, J.B. and Quinn, D.P. (2013). Falls from Grace and the Hazards of High Status: The 2009 British MP Expense Scandal and Its Impact on Parliamentary Elites. *Administrative Science Quarterly* 58 (3) pp. 313–345.
Hattersley, R. (2012). *The Great Outsider: David Lloyd George*. London: Abacus.
Hável, V. (2008). *Leaving*. London: Faber and Faber Ltd.
Healey, D. (1989). *The Time of My Life*. London: Penguin Group.
Hecht, M.B. (1976). *Beyond the Presidency: The Residues of Power*. New York: Macmillan Publishing Co., Inc.
Helm, T. (2013). It's Time to End this Chapter. *The Observer* 7 September.
Hjelmar, U., Olsen, A.L. and Pedersen, L.H. (2010). Should I Stay or Should I Go Now? Voluntary Retirement from Danish Local Government. *Scandinavian Political Studies* 33 (4) pp. 402–416.

Hibbing, J.R. (1982). Voluntary Retirement from the US House of Representatives: Who Quits? *American Journal of Political Science* 26 (3) pp. 467–484.

Hix, S., Hobolt, S.B. and Høyland, B. (2012). Career Paths and Legislative Activities of Members of the European Parliament. *Paper prepared for presentation at the Annual Conference of the American Political Science Association* August 30-September 2, New Orleans.

Horiuchi, Y., Laing, M. and `t Hart, P. (2015). Hard acts to follow: Predecessor effects on party leader survival. *Party Politics* 21(3) pp. 357–366.

Howarth, D. (2013). *Lawyers in the House of Commons.* In David Feldman (Ed.), *Law in Politics, Politics in Law.* Oxford: Hart pp. 41–63.

Ignatieff, M. (2013). *Fire and Ashes.* Canada: Random House Canada.

Iremonger, L. (1970). *The Fiery Chariot.* London: Martin Secker & Warburg.

Jenkins, R. (2002a). *Gladstone.* London: Pan Books.

Jenkins, R. (2002b). *Churchill.* London: Pan Books.

Just, P.D. (2004). United Kingdom: Life After Number 10 – Premiers Emeritus and Parliament. *The Journal of Legislative Studies* 10 (2–3) pp. 66–78.

Karol, D. (2012). Forcing Their Hands? Explaining Trends in Retirement Announcement Timing in the U.S. Congress. *Paper Prepared for Presentation at the 2012 Annual Conference on Congress and History, University of Georgia, Athens, Georgia.*

Keane, J. (2011). *Life after political death.* In J. Kane, H. Patapan, and P. `t Hart (Eds.), *Dispersed Democratic Leadership.* Oxford: Oxford University Press.

Keane, M.P. and Merlo, A. (2010). Money, Political Ambition, and the Career Decisions of Politicians. *American Economic Journal: Microeconomics* 2 pp. 186–215.

Kerby, M. and Blidook, K. (2011). It's Not You, It's Me: Determinants of Voluntary Legislative Turnover in Canada. *Legislative Studies Quarterly* 36 pp. 621–643.

Kettlewell, K. and Phillips, L. (2014). *Census of Local Authority Councillors 2013* (LGA Research Report). Slough: NFER.

Kets de Vries, M.F.R. (2003b). *Leaders, Fools and Imposters: Essays on the Psychology of Leadership.* Lincoln: iUniverse, Inc.

King, A. (1981). The Rise of the Career Politician in Britain – And Its Consequences. *British Journal of Political Science* 11 pp. 249–285.

Kwiatkowski, R. (2015). Our House. *The House* 37 no.1513 27 March 2015.

Laing, M. and `t Hart, P. (2011). *Seeking and keeping the hot seat: A comparative analysis of party leader successions.* In P `t Hart and J. Uhr (Eds.), *How Power Changes Hands: Transition and Succession in Government.* Basingstoke: Palgrave.

Lamprinakou, C., Morucci, M., Campbell, R. and van Heerde-Hudson, J. (2015). Shuffling the House of Cards? The Profile of Candidates and MPs in the 2015

British General Election. *Paper prepared for the 2015 British General Election: Transition or Crisis?' 2 September 2015, University of California.*

Lane, J-E. (2015). Entry and Exit in Politics. *International Journal of Political Science and Development* 3(2) pp. 79–84.

Leapman, M. (1987). *Kinnock.* London: Unwin Hyman.

Livingstone, K. (2011). *You Can't Say That.* London: Faber and Faber.

Loch, C.H. (2016). *It's not just others: Conquering the hubris in Yourself.* In P. Garrard and G. Robinson (Eds.), *The Intoxication of Power. Interdisciplinary Insights.* Basingstoke: Palgrave Macmillan.

McSmith, A. (2013). Obituary of Margaret Thatcher. *The Independent* 8 April.

Macrory, S. (2011). Been There, Done That. *The House Magazine. 7 March.*

Major, J. (2000). *John Major: The Autobiography.* London: Harper Collins.

Maltzman, F., Sigelman, L and Binder, S. (1996). Leaving Office Feet First: Death in Congress. *Political Science and Politics* 29 (4) pp. 665–671.

Martin, A.E. (1951). *After the White House.* Pennsylvania: Penns Valley Publishers, Inc.

Matland, R.E. and Studlar, D.T. (2004). Determinants of Legislative Turnover: A Cross National Analysis. *British Journal of Political Science* 34 pp. 87–108.

Mattozzi, A. and Merlo, A. (2007). Political Careers or Career Politicians? *Discussion Paper* No. 6164 Centre for Economic Policy Research.

Mitchell, A. (2015). Goodbye to All That. *The Political Quarterly* 86 (2) pp. 307–313.

Moore, C. (2010). Margaret Thatcher's resignation: A career that did not die in vain. *Daily Telegraph* 22 November.

Mulgan, G. (2007). *Good and Bad Power: The Ideals and Betrayals of Government.* London: Penguin Books.

Mullin, C. (2010). *Decline and Fall.* London: Profile Books.

Norton Smith, R. and Walch, T. (1990). Eds. *Farewell to the Chief.* Wyoming: Herbert Hoover Presidential Library Association, Inc.

Owen, D. (2006). Hubris and Nemesis in Heads of Government. *Journal of the Royal Society of Medicine* 99 pp. 548–551.

Owen, D. (2011). Psychiatry and Politicians – Afterword. Commentary on … Psychiatry and Politicians. *The Psychiatrist* 35 pp. 145–148.

Paikin, S. (2003). *The Dark Side.* Canada: Viking.

Paxman, J. (2002). *The Political Animal.* London: Penguin Books.

Porter, D. (2011). Ex-MPs: Life After (Parliamentary) Death. http://www.davidporter.co.uk/2011/06/ex-mps-life-after-parliamentary-death/

Powell, E. (1977). *Joseph Chamberlain.* London: Thames and Hudson.

Powell, J. (2010). *The New Machiavelli.* London: The Bodley Head.

Rallings, C. and Thrasher, M. (2014). Stand Down or Run Again? *First Magazine Local Government Association* 20 May.

Rawnsley, A. (2010). *The End of the Party: The Rise and Fall of New Labour.* London: Viking.

Reeher, G. (2006). *First Person Political.* New York: New York University Press.

Riddell, P. (1995). The Impact of the Rise of the Career Politician. *The Journal of Legislative Studies* 1 (2) pp. 186–191.

Riddell, P. (1996). *Honest Opportunism: How We Get the Politicians We Deserve.* London: Indigo.

Riddell, P. (2011). *In Defence of Politicians: In Spite of Themselves.* London: Biteback Publishing.

Runciman, D. (2013). *The Confidence Trap.* New Jersey: Princeton University Press.

Rush, M. and Cromwell, V. (2004). Continuity and change: Legislative recruitment in the United Kingdom 1868–1999. In H. Best and M. Cotta (Eds.), *Parliamentary Representatives in Europe 1848–2000. Legislative Recruitment and Careers in Eleven European Countries.* New York: Oxford University Press.

Russell, G. (2011). Psychiatry and Politicians: The 'Hubris Syndrome'. *The Psychiatrist* 35 pp. 140–145.

Rustin, S. (2012). Is there life after politics? *The Guardian* 15 September.

Schenker, A. (1982). Former Presidents: Suggestions for the Study of an Often Neglected Resource. *Presidential Studies Quarterly* 12 (4) pp. 545–551.

Seldon, A. and Lodge, G. (2010). *Brown at 10.* London: Biteback.

Shaffir, W. and Kleinknecht, S. (2005). Death at the Polls. Experiencing and Coping with Political Defeat. *Journal of Contemporary Ethnography* 34 (6) pp. 707–738.

Simpson, J. (2014). Personal communication.

Skidmore, M.J (2004). *After the White House.* New York and Hampshire: Palgrave Macmillan.

Skinner, D. (2015). Personal communication.

Strangio, P. (2012). *The evolution of prime ministerial afterlives in Australia.* In Theakston and De Vries (Eds.), *Former Leaders in Modern Democracies. Political Sunsets.* Basingstoke: Palgrave Macmillan.

Stolz, K. and Fischer, J. (2014). Post-Cabinet Careers of Regional Ministers in Germany, 1990–2011. *German Politics* 1–17. Accessed 2/9/14.

Stolz, K. and Kintz. M. (2014). Post-Cabinet Careers in Britain and the US: Theory, Concepts and Empirical Illustrations. *Paper prepared for the ECPR General Conference 2014.* Accessed 9/10/15.

Theakston, K., Gouge, E. M. and Honeyman, V. (2007). *Life after Losing or Leaving: The Experience of Former Members of Parliament.* A report for the Association of Former Members of Parliament by the University of Leeds.

Theakston, K. (2010). *After Number 10.* Basingstoke: Palgrave Macmillan.

Theakston, K. and De Vries, J. (2012). *Former Leaders in Modern Democracies: Political Sunsets.* Basingstoke: Palgrave Macmillan.

Volgy, T.J. (2001). *Politics in the Trenches: Citizens, Politicians, and the Fate of Democracy.* Tucson: University of Arizona Press.

Volkan, V.D. (2014). *Psychoanalysis, International Relations, and Diplomacy: A Sourcebook on Large-Group Psychology.* London: Karnac Books.

Waldegrave, W. (2015). *A Different Kind of Weather. A Memoir.* London: Constable.

Watkins, D. (1996). *Seventeen Years in Obscurity: Memoirs from the Back Benches.* Lewes: The Book Guild.

Williams, L.-M. (2011). The Queen's Park After-party: Post-Cabinet Life in the Legislature. *Paper prepared for the Canadian Political Science Association Conference, Waterloo, Ontario.*

Weinberg, A. (2007). Your destiny in their hands: Job loss and success in Members of Parliament. BPS Annual Conference, York. *Proceedings of the BPS,* 15 (2).

Weinberg, A. (2012). *Should the job of national politicians carry a government health warning? The impact of psychological strain on politicians.* In A. Weinberg (Ed.), *The Psychology of Politicians.* Cambridge: Cambridge University Press.

Westlake, M. (2001). *Kinnock: The Biography.* London: Little, Brown and Company.

CHAPTER 4

The Research

This book is drawn from an exploratory study to understand more about the experience of losing political office, the consequences of the loss of such office on individuals and their families and what, if anything, could be done to mitigate the consequences. It was a small qualitative study, and it did not aim to be able to produce statistically significant figures, but instead to hear directly the lived experiences of a number of different former politicians.

The study went on to explore the views of current politicians about their role and how they think, if at all, about shaping the duration of their time in office. It sought to address whether there are any wider implications from the findings for our democratic system.

The issues examined in this book concern the experience of losing political office whatever the level of governance: any elected representative whether at national parliamentary level, in a local council, a devolved administration or at European level. Given the gaps in the literature demonstrated in the preceding chapter, this study chose to focus on former MPs in the Westminster Parliament and former leaders of unitary (single tier) local authorities.

UNDERSTANDING THE ROLE OF MPS, COUNCIL LEADERS AND DIRECTLY ELECTED MAYORS

Any MP, whether on the green frontbenches or backbenches, has at least two distinct roles: as member of the House of Commons, playing a part in parliamentary debates and questions, and participating in committee

© The Author(s) 2017 57
J. Roberts, *Losing Political Office*,
DOI 10.1007/978-3-319-39702-3_4

work; and as a constituency member, a parliamentary representative of the local area, active and visible there. Ministers, as part of the executive, have added departmental roles, a third, and highly time consuming element of their role.

The role of a council leader and directly elected mayor is arguably more varied, responsible and challenging than that of a backbench MP. The office of a directly elected mayor is relatively recent introduction into the political arrangements of local government in England and Wales, brought in first in London by the Greater London Authority Act 1999 and then by the Local Government Act 2000. Directly elected mayors have a similar role to that of a council leader, but owing to their election by the population of a local authority as a whole rather than leaders who are elected by members of their party grouping, they have a more direct accountability to the wider electorate. Their only constituency is the local authority area. Council leaders represent their ward or division, hold constituency advice surgeries, just as MPs do, and they lead the council executive, with its different portfolios, as well as being the key public face of the authority as a whole.

The council leader or directly elected mayor is ultimately responsible for whatever challenges are thrown at them, some totally unexpected, from one day to the next. An MP's role, of course, may change significantly depending on a change of government and any rise (or fall) through the ministerial ranks in government or in a shadow position. Even then, unless at the most senior level, ministerial portfolios are relatively narrow, albeit over a national rather than local terrain.

As we have seen, MPs now are generally expected to work full time in the role. Unless they represent a constituency either in or very close to Westminster, MPs and their families must make very significant accommodation to the demands of the role. They might move to a previously unfamiliar part of the country, and/or there will be significant periods of the week when the MP is absent from the family.

Council leaders and directly elected mayors do not have to move, nor do leaders have to stop working in their previous employment, although it appears that increasing numbers of them are choosing to do so. A directly elected mayoralty is a full-time role and is paid accordingly. "Allowances," not salaries, for council leaders vary from authority to authority and may be sufficient for an individual not to seek income from elsewhere, but not in all authorities.

Despite the numbers of hours worked each week by both council leaders and directly elected mayors, they are no longer eligible to be part of the Local Government Pension Scheme (LGPS). Councillors were only first able to access the scheme in 2003, but this provision was removed by the Secretary of State for Communities and Local Government to take effect from 1 April 2014. MPs' pensions, however, introduced by the Ministerial Salaries and Members' Pensions Act in 1965, remain generous.

While MPs can be challenged for re-selection, in practice this is rare (two MPs were de-selected before the 2015 General Election), especially for assiduous constituency MPs. The majority of MPs sit in seats that mostly do not change their party political representation in elections. Political tsunamis aside, many MPs, therefore, unless they fall foul of scandal, a boundary change or represent marginal constituencies, can be relatively assured of remaining in office should they wish. There was of course one such recent tsunami, in Scotland, in the 2015 General Election.

The position for council leaders varies far more depending on the electoral cycle and the political culture of the authority. There are no figures available on the length of tenure of council leaders: The census of councillors carried out under the auspices of the Local Government Association does not distinguish leaders from other council members and evidence is therefore hard to come by. Some local authorities have a tradition of long-standing leaders, others less so. While some leaders may remain unchallenged for many years, for others, often in metropolitan areas and especially in London, the tenure of council leadership may be shorter. Until recently, leaders were normally subject to an annual election of their party group and many still are.

The position for directly elected mayors is emerging. So far, in most authorities, it appears that those who are widely judged to be doing a competent job, whatever their party affiliation, remain in office, having been re-elected by constituents after four years. It may, however, not have been experienced in this way by present incumbents, many of whom were elected in the very early days of the elected mayoral system. At that time especially, it may have felt very high stakes: Mayors are required to work full time, and successful candidates may well have left their previous employment and pension. London is perhaps an exception to likely re-election: It is a much more high profile mayoral election nationally, and it has been a tightly contested election both in terms of individual personalities and party politics. And in Bristol in 2016, the incumbent directly elected mayor was defeated after only four years in office, underlining the risks that candidates for such a position face.

THE RESEARCH QUESTIONS

This study focused on MPs who had left office and on leaders of unitary local authorities who had lost both their leadership position and their seat. The study asked five research questions:

- What is the experience of losing elected political office for the office-holder?
- What are the consequences of the loss of political office on individual and their families?
- What, if anything, could be done to mitigate the consequences?
- What can current politicians tell us about the period prior to exit and how the matter is (or is not) approached while in office?
- Are there any wider implications from the information gathered for our democratic system?

STUDY DESIGN

Semi-structured interviews were conducted with three groups: a group of ten former MPs and council leaders who had chosen to stand down from political office; a group of ten former MPs and council leaders who had been defeated electorally and a group of ten current MPs, council leaders and directly elected mayors.

Former council leaders had to have lost both their leadership position and their seat in order to fulfil the criteria for the study. Those former politicians who had the same partner as the time of their exit from office were asked for permission for me to contact their partner. The study was designed to ensure that former and current politicians came from all three main political parties; they had represented geographically diverse constituencies within the British Isles; and that as a group, they had been in different positions, some in government, some on an opposition frontbench and other on the backbenches. By design, all the MPs interviewed had to have lost office at the 2010 General Election. Very few council leaders had lost their position and seat in 2010 and therefore the span of years was widened, from 2008 to 2012.

Only one former (defeated) MP, one former (defeated) council leader and three current MPs of those contacted either declined to participate or did not reply to my initial approach.

THE FORMER POLITICIANS

The former politicians had been in office, either as a council leader or as an MP for widely varying lengths of time: from under 1 year to 27 years.

All the former MPs were interviewed about both their experiences of holding office and of the experience of the transition from office about two years after they had left office following the May 2010 General Election. Some had been Cabinet ministers, some in either more junior or shadow positions and others had remained on the backbenches.

The former council leaders had left office from 2008 to 2012, with half having left in 2011. The time that had elapsed between their leaving office and my interview ranged from 12 months to just under four years with most interviewed between 12 and 18 months after they had left office. All but one of the council leaders interviewed had undertaken the role on a full-time basis with no other paid employment, although this was not a requirement of the post.

THE PARTNERS

Not all of the former politicians were currently with the partner that they had had at the time of leaving political office: 17 of the 20 did have the same partner. Of those 17, 6 partners did not respond to my invitation. Ten partners and one adult child of a divorced interviewee (suggested by them) were interviewed, 11 in total. Seven of the 11 were partners of politicians who had been defeated, and four were partners of politicians who had stood down.

THE CURRENT POLITICIANS

The ten current politicians interviewed had been elected to their current position for widely varying times, from 2 to over 30 years. They were interviewed from the end of 2013 to May 2014. In addition to questions about their experience of holding office, interviewees were asked about how long they were thinking of seeking to remain in office, the factors that influenced their thinking and what they may have learnt from seeing colleagues move on from elected office.

Interview Participants

	Former politicians who stood down (Group 1)	Former politicians who were defeated (Group 2)	Current politicians (Group 3)
Number of interviewees	10	10	10
Number of partners interviewed/number still with the same partner at the time of loss of office	4/8	7/9	N/A
Number who declined to be interviewed or did not reply	1	1	3

Further details about the study design and methodology are in the Appendix.

The influence of the "expenses scandal" of 2009.

The intention had been to exclude those MPs who had been caught in the centre of the expenses maelstrom of 2009 from the study on the grounds that the issue would significantly distort the findings. But it turned out that the expenses issue had affected virtually every MP, whether or not they were directly implicated. Although the expenses issue did not directly involve councillors, there was no escaping the issue for some council leaders either, tarred by association with a similar brush by their constituents on the doorstep.

The "expenses scandal" has been much publicised within the UK, but a brief explanation here may be helpful. The Freedom of Information Act 2000 came into force in the UK in early 2005. A request for information on the expenses of certain MPs was then made as part of a campaign. The parliamentary authorities were reluctant to disclose the information, and the request was passed to the Information Commissioner. At the end of considerable legal wrangling, the High Court ruled in 2008 in favour of releasing the information. In 2009, attempts were made to exempt MPs from the Freedom of Information Act, but the proposal was subsequently dropped and it was announced that there would be full disclosure of all MPs' expenses on 1 July 2009. Two months before this scheduled date however, the newspaper, The Daily Telegraph, published in instalments leaked details of MPs' expenses. This had an explosive effect on public debate with outrage at the alleged abuses of expenses—such as over-claiming of expenses and manipulation of the rules on property—by some MPs and peers. The scandal resulted in a number of sackings and resignations from government and a very small number of prosecutions. Many MPs announced that they would stand down at the next election such was the fury directed towards them by the electorate. MPs who were thought to be culpable were hounded and even those who had been entirely blameless felt deeply affected by the public opprobrium towards them, and sometimes their families. It was a deeply scarring experience for many MPs, and its legacy continues to this day. The issue was widely seen as having heightened public distrust and cynicism in politicians.

The cohort of MPs standing down in 2010 was unusually large (149 in number) in part as a result of the expenses issue (Weinberg 2015). Seventy-six MPs were defeated, and for some, the expenses issue played a role in their defeat. The turnover rate in 2010 was 35 per cent (Byrne and Theakston 2015) compared with 15 per cent in 2001 and 21 per cent in 2005. A higher turnover rate was seen again in the 2015 election (28 per cent), all the more reason Byrne and Theakston maintain, to study parliamentary exits.

****

Although my interviewees in the first two groups had in common the loss of political office, they brought with them a very wide range of different backgrounds and experiences. They differed widely in terms of personality, motivation to stand for elected office in the first place, expectations of office and experiences once elected, quite aside from the circumstances around their loss of office. Inevitably, therefore, I report wide differences as well as some commonalities of experience of losing political office.

Whether thankful and relieved to be out of office, or still in the midst of dealing with the raw intensity of the loss, or somewhere in between, interviewees gave very generously of their time. Most interviews went on for longer, often considerably so, than the time we had agreed at the outset, and, for many, the subject matter was visibly emotionally stirring.

REFERENCES

Byrne, C. and Theakston, K. (2015). Leaving the House: The Experience of Former Members of Parliament Who Left the House of Commons in 2010. *Parliamentary Affairs* doi: 10.1093/pa/gsv053.

Weinberg, A. (2015). A Longitudinal Study on the Impact of Changes in the Job and the Expenses Scandal on UK National Politicians' Experiences of Work, Stress and the Home-Work Interface. *Parliamentary Affairs* 68 pp. 248–271.

CHAPTER 5

The Current Politicians: Views of Political Careers and Motivations

I begin with the perspective of current politicians—council leaders, directly elected mayors and MPs—about their motivations for seeking office, their experience of holding it and how long they might seek to remain in office. What factors might influence such their decision on their preferred duration in office? In order to maintain confidentiality, I shall include both directly elected mayors and council leaders under the rubric of 'council leaders'.

VIEWS ON PREFERRED DURATION OF OFFICE

Obviously Not in Their Hands

Few leaders or MPs had given any thought to how long they might remain in office when first elected, whether in a marginal seat or not. As time goes on, there may be stronger forces compelling a council leader (but perhaps not a directly elected mayor or an MP in a safer seat) to contemplate their length of time in office. In highly contested areas and in inner London authorities especially, few leaders remain in office for years measured in double figures. In other areas, however, there may rarely be challenges to a council leader. Even MPs in relatively safe seats may face significant uncertainty about the future if there are significant boundary changes to their constituency.

© The Author(s) 2017
J. Roberts, *Losing Political Office*,
DOI 10.1007/978-3-319-39702-3_5

All the current council leaders and MPs whom I interviewed conveyed a sense that to be elected to political office—*"to do something in politics"*—had been the goal; from there on, even the leaders were open-minded, intending to see how it went. Council leaders especially had welcomed the potential of office to make a significant and lasting difference to the physical and social fabric of their area, and that there was almost always a new challenge to face.

COUNCIL LEADERS

Even if, in the case of the leaders, they had continued to work in their previous job while a councillor, few had given more than a glancing thought to how long they might stay in office. One leader, thinking back, said that s/he would have been surprised then to know how long s/he turned out to have remained in post. Had s/he been asked the question then, s/he thought that s/he would have been likely to reply,

"Four years or so and then probably stand down."

My interview took place considerably more than four years on. Another had originally envisaged staying a similar length of time, but new challenges to the structure of the authority had led her/him to stay on too. Another had been enabled to stay on by successfully contesting the mayoralty that had come with a salary (and fresh challenges) that the previous role of leader had not.

Two leaders explicitly acknowledged that they had never planned anything much in life. One of these, who had come into local government "*by accident*" but who had nevertheless given up her/his previous career to devote more time to council work, acknowledged that s/he had never been one to plan and s/he was a bit of a risk taker. There is perhaps something in standing for political office that attracts the risk-taking element: putting yourself in front of an electorate is an exposing business, fraught with risk. Certainly, Paxman (2002, pp. 264–5) thought that there was something in this notion,

"There is no notice period, no right of appeal, no trades union representation, no industrial tribunal, no compensation. It is another reason for the trade attracting the sort of people who like to take risks."

Perhaps politicians are inherently less cautious than others and less likely to plan ahead? As my interviews progressed, I was struck by how many seemed not to have failed in anything much before. Perhaps an element of invulnerability had helped to carry them forward too?

Even among the leaders, only two, and possibly one other, had a probable plan for the (fairly distant) future in terms of a date by which s/he would step down. Most were continuing in post for the time being with some thoughts, of varying degrees of fleetingness, of what the future might hold. None (bar one) envisaged remaining on the council post-leadership. The idea for most of being a member of the council without leading it was anathema, for example,

"You can't go back. I don't believe I could ever stay in that council chamber not leading it ... You can't do it and I've made that decision very, very clearly that there's no going back once you're leader."

One of the two leaders with a definite (and private) plan about the date by which to go was clear that the post should be time limited,

"I think that there is a danger that you stop seeing things that you should see when you've been incumbent for a while. I think that's almost inevitable in any job."

The other had been considerably longer in post and was clear that there was no perfect time to go. But, at a specified year in the future, acknowledged to be pretty arbitrary, it was likely that it would,

"Be time to hand over to the next generation."

S/he had seen leaders stay too long and was determined not to fall into a similar trap, having witnessed the *"sentimentality"* of the Labour Party that allowed people to go on for too long. S/he was driven by achieving explicit outcomes for her/his area and felt confident that s/he would know when to bow out. How can you be so sure, I asked? S/he replied,

"On the balance of probabilities, I think that I am not deluding myself."

Another acknowledged that the duration in office of the leader of a council, as of any organisation, was something that should be thought about,

"Is it time for a different view, a different idea?"

Having also seen some leaders who had lasted too long and departed as sad figures, s/he too has determined that there was to be a definite end point—but one that had so far shifted forwards more than once.

Even for one leader with a definite plan to stand down, the options for the future after that were less clear: s/he was unconvinced at this stage that standing for Parliament was the right course and a return to her/his previous professional role was no longer possible, such were the scale of changes that there had been. So, s/he looked ahead and,

"I don't like what I see. I think you've got all these skills and passion for things and it's kind of what do you do with it? It's quite difficult to see where

you go with it actually ... I think about doing sort of non exec things but they're quite hard to get into."

S/he portrayed the dilemma: in any other field of endeavour,

"You don't leave a job without another one to go to. It wouldn't be a problem in any other walk of life but yet it is in politics."

It was too late now to return to her/his former highly regarded profession,

"That door closed."

There had been too many changes in recent years yet s/he was clear that s/he had always imagined doing something and working,

"I just don't quite see what it is yet and it is a bit scary."

S/he was aware that her/his predecessor had left the area. Although not seeking to emulate this, s/he only now had some understanding of why he had done so,

"I probably feel I'd go through a grieving process, I'm sure ... I wouldn't want to be Banquo's ghost or ... just be the critic on the side and things like that, so kind of disappearing is an attractive option in some ways, you know. I now understand why he did it."

S/he could acknowledge, even some years in advance, that stepping down would be a major life event,

"That's why I have to control when I go."

Yet, it is not always possible for a leader to control when to go, even those who are widely regarded as having done a good job, as one council leader commented,

"Of course, in local government, we all pay the price for our colleagues in Westminster. You know they do stupid things and we lose our seats."

"Some of the former leaders, I mean some of them are brutally treated, absolutely horribly treated. You wouldn't treat a dog like some of them ...."

Two leaders had toyed with the idea of standing down before, but one had deferred the idea at the behest of pleadings from the party group, and the other had put it off as the possible time approached. It sounded as though neither had really wanted to go.

One was acutely aware however that,

"Every leader has to think about what I call the Margaret Thatcher scenario. You know, I want to go at the top of this. I'm not going to be pushed ... many, many leaders in my time have had a sad departure and I don't want a sad departure."

How can the point—*"the top of this"*—be reliably recognised?

S/he reflected on the need to be self-critical,

"Are they still looking up to you? Are they still respecting you? Have I done everything I possibly can and is it time for a new face in the organisation?"
S/he did not think that s/he would fall into,
"The Thatcher trap ... I'll not go because I think I'm powerful and you know, nobody can touch me. I will have that insight."
S/he was alert to the need that,
"That's the time when you need friends and colleagues that will quietly tell you ... as far as knowing the truth, you do need some very close friends."
"I think the ones I've seen that have lasted too long, I think they've gone out as being sad figures and not gone out as being always successful leaders with a really good sort of ... you know, they haven't gone out at the top of their ... It's like a sportsman, isn't it?"
This leader attached great importance to regular communication with her/his group, both formally and informally, and appeared to have considerable emotional intelligence.

But s/he was explicit now that s/he was not going to dwell on the likely duration of office for at least another two or three years. The only certainties were that s/he was indeed going to stand down at a time of her/his choosing and not be pushed, and the manner of her/his going—in some raucous musical style! But what then? The prospect was,
"Horrible, absolutely horrible."
S/he recalled how her/his predecessor had not only lost the leadership role but also a national role in local government and had,
"Never been the same person since ... he lost that standing ... and to go from that to nothing ... in a way, it broke him."
This leader was not going to "*hang around*" locally, but a national role in local government did not appeal, nor much the House of Commons. The House of Lords was more attractive. This same leader on the one hand relayed how the duration of office was a subject that s/he and other leaders,
"Often talk about over a glass of wine at some conference or other ... 'Is it time? Should I go'. Yeah, they do talk about it. They also talk about their colleagues that have gone and why. We talk about our colleagues that have gone and why they've gone and does anybody see them, but it's really interesting you don't see them and that's a cautionary tale."
On the other hand, the only recourse was therefore not to think about going,
"Live in the moment, live in the day, live in the issues that I've got now ... and don't think about it."

When pressed harder, s/he wondered about chairing roles locally or nationally, or consultancy. But s/he was under no illusions about the latter,

"You think you can do that, but once you're out of the business, you're out of the business … but if you're away from the real sort of centre of it, you don't … it'd be sad, wouldn't it?"

On reflection during the interview, s/he ruefully thought that there was no point in planning to do anything post-leadership; opportunities might arise as and when,

"So, I think I'll just do it and wait and see what happens."

The other, past normal retirement age, who had postponed standing down was a long-established and highly respected leader; s/he still felt s/he had a contribution to make, particularly in the challenging times facing local government currently. S/he acknowledged however both this public motive and,

"A private motive probably. I think what the hell would I do if I didn't do it. You know, it's gripped my life for so long. I like gardening but not that much."

S/he, nevertheless, was toying with thoughts about stepping down at a future date. Perhaps partly because this was some way off, s/he maintained later that this was not something that s/he was worried about much and expressed the view that,

"The thing to do is to try and get away from your previous life as much as possible and build up something that's different and not sort of sit there privately saying, 'Oh god, the council's going to the dogs now that I'm not running it."

Age was the determining factor personally for one other long-standing leader. But s/he was very clear that all leaders throughout their period in office should question themselves relentlessly on their purpose: on what they were trying to achieve; what outcomes they were seeking and the extent to which they were making a difference. Echoing another who put great store on conversations with others, s/he too stressed the importance of simply talking to many people in order to get a rounded and reasonably objective view of how they were doing. Despite the length of time in office, but perhaps because of the age s/he would be on leaving it and that it was some years ahead, s/he was sanguine about how it would be. S/he was very clear that,

"When you stop, it stops."

Having kept up with a range of interests and activities outside politics, s/he felt confident that s/he would be fine.

Age featured for another: s/he acknowledged that s/he had over the last year started to think that s/he would need to take stock. During the course of her/his leadership, much that s/he had set out to achieve had been accomplished but, despite being younger than the normal retirement age,

"Well, age gets you in the end."

S/he had a tentative idea about how long more s/he would seek to remain in office, subject to her/his preferred successor being able to take on the leadership role together with other personal and professional responsibilities. S/he had had some thoughts about a year in transition as (civic) mayor but did not voice undue concern about leaving the leadership,

"I'll be able to cope with that, I mean it's like if you leave a job and you've done something, run a department or whatever, you have to let go and let somebody else do it."

This later became,

"Well, I'm hoping I'll be able to cope with it."

Notably, this was the only leader who envisaged staying on as a councillor, at least for a while, despite also having other, less specific, ideas for the future that would take her/him further afield. Directly elected mayors, of course, do not have the option of remaining as a councillor.

This leader went on to note the electoral impact on local government of policies pursued at Westminster but,

"There's no programme for decommissioning a leader and there should be especially for those who are suddenly ejected from office."

This compared unfavourably with the support packages that s/he had witnessed for senior executives in the private sector. For those in their 40s and 50s who,

"Have put their career on hold – and that is a euphemism for basically screwed their careers ... the longer they've been leader, the less employable they are anyway. Leaders are notoriously unemployable anywhere because they get used to just doing what they want."

The lack of any thinking about transition from council leadership was echoed by another who might have moved on had there been somewhere to move on to,

"I think there needs to be an exit strategy ... I gave up something that I can't go back to ... you want to make it easy for people to leave."

Many council leaders, and especially directly elected mayors, may well have given up their previous career, professional opportunity and a pension in order to run for office. A couple of current leaders volunteered how they had left a much better paid job (and pension) and how incensed they were by the decision of the Secretary of State at the time to deny access to the LGPS to council leaders and elected mayors. Financial considerations loomed large,

"So, you know, being able to pay your mortgage is quite a big consideration actually and certainly when it's an election and you're thinking, 'I could be out of a job on Friday because the election is a Thursday'. You know, no redundancy, nothing. Boomph, end. There's nothing else like it."

Given that most council leaders feel that they should have a clean break from the council once they have left so as not to be a spectre at the feast for their successor, and that directly elected mayors have no choice, the cliff edge that they then experience is very steep.

Succession planning may well not, therefore, be a priority. Yet, as Ghislieri and Gatti (2012) make clear,

"From the time the idea of transformational leadership was first introduced, turning followers into new leaders has been seen as the fundamental task of change."

Yet succession planning inevitably envisages a time when a politician will no longer be around—political mortality, often a deeply uncomfortable thought. Had these council leaders given much thought to their succession? Having thought about standing down over some time, they could after all have paved the way for others. Council leaders can encourage training and opportunities for their colleagues, and they will have worked closely with members of their political group, becoming familiar with their strengths and weaknesses. In contrast, the nature of MPs' work is more of an individual enterprise, at least at a local constituency level. In this small group of council leaders, however, most had not given much thought to succession planning.

Of those who had, a common theme was that they had wanted there to be a number of capable people who could acquire a range of experience and thus be part of a pool from whom the next leader could be drawn. They were aware that their job was to ensure a number of possible successors, not to make a choice between them. But they varied greatly in the extent to which they actively got involved to ensure that there was such a pool. One had had relatively little to do, commenting,

"I didn't really think much about a succession plan. I wanted to make sure that there were two or three people who were capable of being leaders of the group and who were different from each other and when I looked around

and discovered that there really were such people, I relaxed about the idea of succession."

But another, despite a lengthy leadership, thought that there was still no obvious person ready to take over the role,

"A bit more work was required."

It was only partially by intention that s/he had ensured that there were a number of younger, more able councillors now on the executive.

One very long-standing former leader was disarmingly honest, admitting that he did not have a succession plan until the last couple of years because,

"I didn't want a successor because I always wanted to carry on ... I'd never thought about who was going to succeed me. It hadn't crossed my mind really."

What do council leaders go on to do? We do not know, as the work has not been done, a deficit that this research in small part seeks to address.

Some may return to their previous career, an option that is likely to become more difficult as the pace of change in any job increases. Non-executive positions in the public sector have been seen as roles in which leaders' skills and knowledge might be well made use of, but opportunities are fewer than once they were. Quangos are thinner now on the ground. Consultancy within local government or to the private sector may be seen as an option for some at least in the short term. But as my interviewees observed, this may not be as promising as it sounds nor last much longer than networks remain current. And what about Parliament? While many MPs have served as councillors, fewer have been council leaders and relatively few council leaders go on to become MPs, although a number of MPs have been council leaders previously.

None of the leaders I interviewed showed much interest in being an MP (although at least one subsequently did stand, unsuccessfully, in 2015). One had been pressured to stand but,

"I don't know whether it's really me. I just feel I wouldn't want to just be backbench fodder."

S/he observed how one former leader whom s/he knew indirectly was now an MP, but

"You've just run xxxx ... and now you're just a backbench MP. You know, you've really made a difference to people's lives."

Another leader was ambivalent although s/he had stood unsuccessfully previously, again after persuasion from the party. Having been interested in politics from a young age, another had previously thought about becoming an MP but never did, soon coming to find local government totally absorbing. S/he mused,

"I can never understand these people who've chosen to take the route of being a council leader and then being an MP. I mean you see a lot of them and they're still very frustrated people."

But remaining as council leader in the long term may not be an option especially in more contested party groups. As tough as parliamentary selections can be, those leader-turned-MPs may have had little other way in which they could stay in the political fray.

The House of Lords appealed to at least a couple of my interviewees. Relatively few council leaders are appointed to the House of Lords, although this tends to vary by political party. The Liberal Democrat party has appointed a higher percentage of their council leaders to the Lords than any other political party. But as for MPs, this is a route that cannot be relied upon and is only for the very chosen few.

MPs

Perhaps because there may be less incentive for MPs to think about their preferred length of time in office, the MPs whom I interviewed, while extremely helpful in setting aside hard-pressed time to participate in this study, appeared less animated by the subject. Unsurprisingly, the one exception was an MP who had previously lost her/his seat by electoral defeat.

When first elected, the MPs had given little thought to how long they might remain in office. They had all hoped that this would be a job that would continue for the foreseeable future, that this was to be their future career, whether a first career or second. One (who had had a highly successful professional elsewhere first) viewed it *"as a career, a life-time career"* not least as her/his predecessor, and many other local MPs who had retired at the same time had been in Parliament for about 30 or 40 years. Another MP rejected the use of the word "career," having explicitly set out to develop business interests prior to entering politics, but s/he was clear nonetheless that,

"I'd chosen a political life and I didn't intend that it should be for a limited period."

As time had gone on, few had given the issue of duration in office any thought. This might be more expected of MPs than of leaders both for the reasons outlined earlier and because all the current, unlike some of the former, MPs whom I interviewed loved the role, wanting very much to continue for some time. Media intrusion was not an issue for them, one sanguinely quoting Enoch Powell that,

"Politicians who complain about the media are like sailors who complain about the sea."

Retirement or thinking about the possibility of losing, even in a marginal constituency, was simply not on the agenda for a number, whether of retirement age or not. An awareness of the financial strain that would ensue after a defeat did bother one, but s/he simply said,

"I want to keep going for as long as I can. If you love what you do then why stop? ... You have to commit."

This MP had experienced a setback previously and had come into Parliament later than many. S/he had come to the view that,

"One of the most important qualities, I believe, is your own self-resilience and self-awareness. As a whole, I don't think people are nearly self-aware enough ... so to know yourself and what you believe in, what you know are your strengths and weaknesses so that when bad things happen, as they will, you can, as I say, be quite rational about 'well, this is ...' and analyse things so that you can learn from it. Everything is a learning opportunity whether you lose, whether it's a job interview, or whether you win."

Another MP was adamant that retirement in general and standing down as an MP specifically were,

"Something I prefer not to think about. I just hope that when the moment ... my preferred life course is one where I wake up one morning dead."

Yet this particular MP had what sounded like a rich, productive and varied life outside politics. S/he had made a deliberate decision many years previously to pursue a life outside politics and outside London. S/he was all too aware of the volatility of politics,

"You don't need to know much about politics to know that it is a very up and down business and so I wanted a personal hinterland ...."

S/he had consciously planned a varied career, not just in politics,

"I'd never put all my eggs in that basket ... I would argue that it's a weakness of our modern political structure that there aren't many people who engage in it having an active commitment in a world outside."

Nevertheless, the proximity to major events that a parliamentary life involved was acknowledged to be an enormous pull. Nowhere other than Parliament could offer the same vista,

"The view that gives you the widest panorama is the view from a political stage."

Whatever the political context, standing down was out of the question at the time of the interview: ill health was the only conceivable trigger for going and that did not bear thinking about. There was just the possibility of standing down (emphatically not "retiring") to do something else, should the opportunity arise. But s/he had taken note from the experience of former colleagues that it would be best to leave any announcement as late as possible in order to avoid being seen as a "lame duck."

A demotion of ministerial or shadow ministerial position may trigger more sustained thoughts about the future, and a couple in my group had, as a result, briefly given some thought to alternative scenarios. One reflected that, for a while, s/he had thought,

"Maybe this is a moment where I need to think is this something that I want to do potentially into my sixties or is it perhaps something that having done it for a reasonable length of time, I might want to give up next time or the time after?"

Understandably, political contextual factors such as the relationship with the constituency party, whether or not their party was in government, who was party leader, and what, if any, ministerial position might be offered figured prominently.

Another had given some thought to her/his future but only after a number of parliamentary terms and precipitated by a sudden demotion. Her/his trajectory had at first been a smooth ascent up the ministerial ladder, but this was unexpectedly halted leading to the need to take stock and reassess the future: would a ministerial position be likely again; if not, would life on the backbenches suffice? Such scenarios are difficult to predict at the best of times, but the uncertainty at the time of the interview about the likely outcome of the General Election in 2015 heightened the political dilemma. The strong interest that this particular MP had developed in one policy area had, however, led to her/him pursuing other avenues for influencing its agenda, a source of considerable fulfilment. Despite having felt very angry initially about the undeserved demotion, s/he had come to accept the need to be,

"Philosophical about it if you want to move on … take advantage of the freedom."

S/he reflected that,

"Where else are you at the top of your game one minute and then your company says you're going back to the shop floor effectively and you're back on your starting salary and your expertise is no longer used but it's no longer used by a rival firm as well?"

In view of the many political imponderables, s/he had no clear view yet about the likely duration of her/his time as an MP but having seen former colleagues' difficulties following electoral defeat, s/he was determined not hang around. S/he recalled one former MP who had carried on holding surgeries after leaving office,

"Because they just couldn't let go and because there were so many people who, you know, had been around a long time they found the transition really hard. And so the rejection of the electorate is quite a biggie, I suspect ... What other job would half the population be dancing in the streets if you got made redundant?"

S/he quoted with approval a former MP who had stood down after eight years saying,

"Well, if I don't get out now, I never will."

This MP did not regard her/himself as a career politician not having come up through the special adviser/public relations/lobbying route but having had *"an ordinary job"* for some time before. S/he went on to reflect that,

"Where we go wrong in this country is the lack of interaction between the outside world and being in politics and where we don't use the expertise of the outside world as much."

Contrasting the UK with Switzerland where MPs are not full time but continue in their employment outside politics, s/he noted how,

"In this country, once you're on that political gravy train, the anticipation is that you will fight tooth and nail to remain on that political gravy train until you retire or are rejected through no fault of your own – and because of which we are viewed even more negatively ... the system does not permit a minister or even a backbencher to spend three months working away in a hospital, a school or whatever and yet it would be a hugely beneficial experience."

Another MP, on a similar tack, commented,

"I am in favour of a House of Commons that is in touch with real people, listens to people, expresses their views, is engaged in the life of the nation and I don't think that we're very good at that, but I don't think that means that you have to do two terms and that's enough."

One MP, scarred from a previous electoral defeat and all too aware of the precariousness of the role, was much more cautious about the future despite now representing a much safer seat. Boundary changes, for example, might thwart any long-term political career plan. The experience of defeat had influenced how s/he undertook her/his role as an MP now with much more emphasis on campaigning than previous incumbents of the seat.

Echoing many former MPs and council leaders whose experiences I shall shortly recount, s/he remembered the defeat as,

"A really, really horrible period ... a bit like a bereavement."

S/he had felt the defeat as a deeply personal wound even though it was clear to her/him (and others) that an antipathy against the government had been the overwhelming issue in the constituency. S/he just wanted to leave the constituency and not be around to hear—with some resentment—the sheepish apologies of her/his erstwhile voters,

"I just felt I didn't want to be there anymore."

It was only after having been selected for another seat over two years later that s/he had had some sense of release from the wounds of defeat. And even now, despite having regained a seat, s/he had not,

"Been able to have that sort of conversation properly with anyone really... it was very bottled up."

Given the experience of this interviewee—having been selected, elected, defeated and then selected and elected in a very different type of seat meant that s/he was able to give a particularly rich insight on the transition into and out of political office. S/he could give a perspective as both a current and a former MP, albeit from the safer ground of having regained political office. Unsurprisingly, s/he recounted experiences very similar to those expressed in the next chapter.

References

Ghislieri, C. and Gatti, P. (2012). Generativity and Balance in Leadership. *Leadership* 8 pp. 257–275.

Paxman, J. (2002). *The Political Animal.* London: Penguin Books.

CHAPTER 6

The Experience of Losing Political Office: Standing Down

WHAT WAS LOST?

The focus of this book is on the experience of loss of office, but in order to understand this better, it is important to know more about what had motivated the former politicians in the first place and what political office had meant to them. I will however deal more briefly with the experiences of holding office than that of the transition from office.

The experience of holding office was unequivocally positive for all the former council leaders whom I interviewed while it was more of a mixed picture for my group of former MPs. For a number of MPs, their experience of office was inextricably bound up with their decision to stand down. Most of my interviewees, whether leader or MP, were clear that the possibility of bringing about political change and making a difference was a key factor that had motivated and sustained them in political office.

FORMER COUNCIL LEADERS

Without exception, former leaders in my sample were wholly positive about their experience of council leadership. Of note, the one former MP in my study who had previously served as a council leader was clear that the latter was, by far, the better and more fulfilling experience.

All the former leaders talked about the role in similar terms: how demanding, fascinating and extraordinarily varied it was from one day to another. One said, for example,

J. Roberts, *Losing Political Office*,
DOI 10.1007/978-3-319-39702-3_6

"It was a bit like a roller coaster. It was unremitting, interesting, challenging. It was sort of utilising all of me."

Another, from a high profile borough, reflected in a similar vein,

"It's one of the most interesting jobs I have ever had and I've had a few ... It was one of the most demanding tasks and the variety was the most significant aspect of it. It was the gymnastics that you go through getting the flexibility of talking to a sabre-toothed developer, a nun, an older person and a policeman and a bunch of party activists and some journalists and the telly all in the same day. That's unusual and very exciting."

As council leaders, all my interviewees talked of how they had valued the ability to shape events locally. They had had the access to information and to the people that mattered in order to bring about significant changes in their area. For some, the degree of influence had exceeded their initial expectations.

One thoughtful former leader remarked how,

"Looking back I think it probably was a power rush and I think I felt good about that because all my life I'd been dancing to other people's tunes it seemed and all of a sudden I was playing the tune and that made a huge difference."

Many of the former leaders volunteered how important the camaraderie that they had experienced had been, mostly friendships within the party group but also for some, trusting working relationships with council officers. For one, it was likened explicitly to a family. This is not, of course, to deny that politics is all about a contest of views; attaining and maintaining a leadership role almost inevitably involves crossing metaphorical swords, often within a party group. One disliked *"the back-biting"* from some, and another experienced bitter betrayal from within the party. But both these former leaders kept in contact still with those former colleagues to whom they had been close.

That council leadership is such a positive experience is not widely acknowledged. It is presumably partly for this reason that relatively few council leaders choose to step down (Simpson 2014, personal communication). Again, there are no figures available on council leaders or their tenure. The picture for directly elected mayors will only emerge over the next few years, given their shorter history.

FORMER MPs

As might be expected, former parliamentarians enjoyed different aspects of the role—constituency work, parliamentary debates, work on select committees, party strategy or ministerial work in a department. One might be interested in the detail of legislation—constructing law—while another was dismissive of this aspect; some talked of *"falling in love"* with their constituency while others (many fewer) were less enthusiastic. Longer standing former MPs all agreed that constituency demands had gone up over time across the board quite aside from the advent of frenetic social media adding to those demands.

Former MPs all talked about the pull of the prospect of bringing about change. Those who had attained high government office most forcefully and persuasively conveyed how making major decisions and effecting change at a national level within their department was the key motivating factor. One was explicit that the power to make the changes that mattered could only come with political power, and this had been the lifelong driver for her/him. The attraction of office for this former MP and a number of others was to be in government rather than in the Commons per se. Opposition held much less appeal as opposition MPs,

"Don't have power but they can have influence."

Some MPs had revelled simply in the whole experience of being an MP, whether their party was in government or not. Terms such as *"exhilarating,"* *"fantastic"* and *"I loved every minute"* came from a number of former MPs who had attained varying ranks and none within government. Said one, speaking for others,

"It was fantastic. It was … every day was different. You'd wake up in the morning and, you know, you'd be desperate to get into work because you knew there was always going to be something interesting, something new and something different to do. So I did, I loved it."

Another in similar vein,

"It's not just spectator sport: you are part of it and you can influence it. I just enjoyed immensely the whole process of politics."

Echoing the vocational motivation, one partner described how,

"In some ways it was just a job, but it was also his life and that's what he wanted to be forever."

For these MPs, life in the Commons had been sufficient even if they might have longed to be in government: feeling close to power; being where things were happening; and mentioned by a few, the camaraderie. Achievements in the constituency brought a sense of satisfaction for many. One described,

"A massive buzz … the kind of political things that you could do in a patch and the levers that you could pull to make things happen. Yeah, it's power. It was power."

This was perhaps all the more heady an emotion given her/his non-political, modest family background: s/he felt that s/he had had to,

"Fight to get what I managed to get."

As much as the desire to make a difference was undoubtedly genuine and strong, a number acknowledged the attraction of the limelight, the attention and the boost to self-esteem that came with the status of having been elected to Parliament—an understandable narcissistic element. One referred to the initial:

"Glamour ... when people joke about MPs being failed rock stars and pop stars I can see what they mean."

Another pointed to the seductiveness of the role,

"The huge addiction to being where it's happening, particularly if you think you're part of it. So you're making it happen, you're not just an observer of it, and journalists are addicted to observing it and can't pull away."

One of the former MPs who had stood down volunteered,

"Shakespeare – what happens to all those guys in Shakespeare? Do any of them go voluntarily? And actually the only one that I can think of who goes voluntarily is the Duke in As You Like It. Very few people go willingly."

Other former MPs were much less enamoured of their experience in Parliament. They were, as might be expected, more likely to stand down after a limited number of terms, although one of them had only come to dislike the role after a considerably longer time. And, in my small sample, there was a suggestion that they had a quieter personality style, perhaps less extroverted, but no less passionate in their political views. Their experiences are detailed later as they explain why they chose to stand down. They paint a powerful and troubling picture.

Even those who came to dislike intensely the experience of being an MP had liked, or at least had been pleased to be in Parliament in the early days. But they had become increasingly aware of the downsides: escalating constituency demands; the costs to personal and family life especially from a marginal and/or distant constituency; the media scrutiny and intrusion that had been magnified many times over after the exposure of MPs' expenses and its repercussions. Given these considerations, one former MP postulated that there might be a higher turnover of MPs in the future. Others, however, mused about how a significant minority of their former colleagues felt trapped in Parliament, not at ease remaining in the Commons but anxious about being able to find an alternative career should they leave.

It must be stressed again that the Parliament of 2005 to 2010 had been particularly deeply scarred by the revelation of MPs' expenses in 2009.

Even those MPs in my sample who had thoroughly enjoyed the role had been greatly affected by the issue.

OVERVIEW

For some MPs, losing a Cabinet post or a more junior ministerial post was felt to be the more salient loss rather than the loss of the parliamentary seat itself. A Cabinet post is, after all, the apex of most political careers. For others, the failure to be promoted to Cabinet level was experienced as a more profound loss, a loss of opportunity possibly forever, and a more bitter pill. By design, the former council leaders interviewed had lost both their leadership role and their seat.

It might understandably be assumed that there would be a clear distinction in the experiences of loss between those office holders who chose to stand down and those who had been defeated at the ballot box (Weinberg 2007). Indeed, one interviewee quoted a former colleague who, having attended a gathering of former MPs, mostly of one political party, reported precisely this, and likened the experience of colleagues' losing a parliamentary seat to,

"A form of bereavement as though they'd been killed in battle."

Although this distinction is pertinent—and the next two chapters are separated in this way—it turned out to be not quite as simple. Choosing to leave a role that one may have relished brings its own dilemmas, not least that of being the architect of one's own political demise,

"It was the end of my political career basically and my government job and that was the end of my last big job because I was never going to go any higher, you know, whereas you all dream."

At least if defeated, a politician is not faced with the dilemma of whether or not to go, not cursed with "what if's," nor dealing with the knowledge, as former MP Tony Wright (2015, personal communication) puts it, *"you've done it to yourself."*

STANDING DOWN

The Decision: Why Go?

For those who had stood down, a few did so in a deliberate effort to shape the end of what had been a role much enjoyed over a number of years, mostly for personal and family reasons; a few in order to pre-empt a likely electoral loss or personal embarrassment; and a few, all MPs, no leaders, did so because the experience of being an MP was no longer one that they enjoyed, with its infringements of personal life and relentless media intrusion significant factors.

For one former MP, the role of parliamentarians was changing in such a way that s/he no longer wanted to be a participant. The expenses' issue figured significantly in the decision to stand down of the former MPs, and *not* just of those who were perceived to have claimed inappropriately.

Another former MP talked of how s/he could not bear having life dictated to all the time, despite having initially enjoyed the role, both in the constituency and in the Commons, acknowledging too that a certain amount of glamour had not been unattractive. Over time, however, the responsibilities of being an MP and a minister all took an increasingly damaging toll on personal life, with media intrusion a key factor. S/he observed:

"What had once seemed quite glamorous didn't feel quite so glamorous anymore."

Being a parliamentarian was to have been a long-term career, so to change radically a life plan by standing down required a considerable leap of the imagination for this former relatively young politician, not least as the future was very uncertain.

For a number of the former MPs, the degree of media scrutiny was the key factor in the decision to stand down. It was powerfully conveyed by one, but echoed by some others, as an experience akin to being stalked—followed, harried and threatened—and bringing in its wake, a wearying wariness. The expenses scandal spared no one even, and perhaps especially, those who were entirely blameless. That someone might have had the audacity to be on the side of the angels had acted almost a spur for the press to dig ever deeper into a politician's life for the relish of bringing them down. This has had such a powerful effect on the way in which MPs are perceived that, in this study, it had brought a sense of shame rather than pride into the wider family of one entirely blameless, immensely hard working former MP. This hardly bodes well for the state of our democracy. As if to underline this, one memorably stated,

"The powerlessness, which is really key to why I stopped, all came from the media. That's the great power in the land."

Even one former MP who had loved his job and who was defeated rather than who had stood down described how s/he had dreaded,

"Your phone ringing and you feel your heart surge a bit or you feel a tingling in your finger tips and you know that you're going to be on the back foot."

The level of media intrusion had not led her/him to stand down, but it had certainly considerably diminished her/his relish in the role and led her/him to wonder,

"Is it worth the aggro?"

The growth of social media, Twitter and cameras on mobile phones compounded the pressure. There was the ever present possibility that an MP, partner and family might be snapped on camera going about their ordinary lives, whatever they may be doing from day to day—even abroad, as happened to one luckless former MP—always at the mercy of a prying camera lens.

One former politician described the consequent corrosive effect on trust, never knowing quite whom one could trust, constant anxiety and hyper-vigilance. Even within the Commons, it was reported that there had been little sense of safety and confidentiality: gossip spread unfeasibly quickly. Surreptitious recording was not uncommon, with an array of opportunities to make mischief, for example, by extracting segments of a recorded audiotape that had then been taken out of context. There was no doubt for one that,

"The rate of increase of the price was much higher than the rate of increase of the job satisfaction."

One interviewee recalled the comment of a former colleague that in future, MPs were going to have to be *"Either psychopaths or billionaires ... or both."*

Another experienced former MP described the job of being an MP as, *"Immeasurably less attractive"* than it had been a couple of decades previously, in large part because of the abusive scrutiny directed towards them. In response, s/he thought that many MPs retreated into the Commons where they are treated better than often in the constituency,

"One of the reasons that they like this place is because this is one of the few places where they're treated well ... knocking on the door, you're more likely to have people proud of the fact that they don't vote. You're more likely to be regarded abusively than you were. So I think that there is a kind of retreating ... this place is definitely part of the comfort zone."

A former MP was less unhappy but increasingly uncomfortable with the changing role of an MP and came to stand down,

"If you go on the website of especially any MP elected in 2010, you find this transition from the elected representative to the professional politician is complete. You know, they'll put all the local campaigns there …"

S/he went on to say,

"People on the whole do want representatives who are like them, but what's happened without them taking too much interest in it is the system's changed in such a way as to produce people who are on the whole more unlike them."

For council leaders, media intrusion was much less of an issue. Relatively few have a national profile, and although the local press can be prying and highly distorting, there is nothing like the intensity of the scrutiny of national politicians. As one former politician who had been both an MP and a leading councillor put it,

"The media operates by threat … and in local politics, it doesn't."

But council leaders are now subject, as MPs, to the relentless pressures of social media feeding the demands and expectations of local constituents who are mostly very much closer at hand than is the case for parliamentarians.

Aside from the impact of media intrusion on MPs, the decision to stand down by both former MPs and council leaders was taken both for personal and family reasons and mostly in recognition that there was likely to be no further political advancement. One former leader was determined to choose the right time to go,

"There's something about bowing out at the top and I did."

But despite this, even s/he subsequently had some misgivings. And s/he had some years previously decided to stand down but changed her/his mind at the last minute. Another former leader talked dispassionately of wanting to leave the party before the end as it had been,

"Mission completed."

S/he expanded,

"You're in the middle of a party, you're talking to a lot of very interesting people and a few people have started to leave and you're getting a little bit drunk, you're beginning to get a little bit tired, you're becoming a bit loose with your tongue and so you decide perhaps it's time to go home."

S/he had been crystal clear from the start that this council leadership was going to be a time limited experience, a maximum of around five years,

"A reasonable innings."

Another had initially intended to remain in post for five or six years, having seen what had happened to the previous leader, widely thought to have stayed too long. In the event, however, s/he did not stand down for another few years, having been asked by group colleagues to remain in post. It was only later when there was a good successor in place that s/he had decided to go, by then wearying of the demands of office, some years past the normal retirement age. S/he pointed the culture of this particular authority of electing leaders for relatively long terms, in contrast, for example to many inner London councils.

A former MP was clear that s/he wanted to be in charge of deciding when to go,

"Stuff happens so it might not be completely under my control, but you could make a pretty good fist of deciding when you would go."

No misgivings either from this former politician who was one of the very few who had thought through her/his leaving with immense care. There was a poignant sense from a small number of older male former politicians that in deciding to stand down, they would have the opportunity to be better grandfathers than they had been fathers.

Another former MP who had finally decided to stand down from a very marginal constituency had recognised the potential difficulties,

"The main thing was my age and wish to do something else and if I'd left it much later to start to do something else, I'd have had difficulty in doing so."

In retrospect, s/he felt that the inexorable rise in constituency casework and correspondence had become oppressive with consequences that s/he regretted to the family,

"Looking back, I shouldn't have allowed it to so dominate my life. You know, I can see the damage it did now."

Representing a constituency that straddled such a large area took a huge toll and only compounded the pressures that had faced this former MP.

Being an MP for one youthful yet relatively long-standing former MP had no longer provided the challenge that this highly capable individual thrived upon.

Being an MP was, *"In the boring category"*: s/he could do casework *"standing on my head"* and s/he had repeatedly taken on portfolios to the point where they were no longer challenging enough. S/he decided that s/he did not want to spend all her/his life in the Commons having seen,

"A lot of old, alcoholic MPs who were doing European trips and you know, probably had once frankly been young, idealistic, wanted to make things happen and were so far past that and you just think that's not where you want to be."

Again, constituency issues—its distance from Westminster and boundary changes—and family factors played a key part in when to go and the elements had all come together so that the decision became *"Blindingly obvious."*

Her/his partner observed that it was,

"To do with not seeing it as ... entire life; seeing it as a patch ... and that at some time it would be time to move on."

Looking back, this former MP would find it hard to recommend to anyone that they get elected as an MP in their 20s: it is possible but *"There's more to life."* This was the decade, s/he thought, that people are better off sorting out *"Proper relationship stuff."* Maintaining intimate relationships as an MP at two ends of the country and especially now under increased scrutiny is very hard going. Another former MP who had stood down echoed similar sentiments,

"I would say to people, don't do it before you're 40 and they always ignore me. I mean, it's a drug for people ... it just swallows up your life ... and I think if I'd really felt that I'd enjoyed a normal life in my 30's, then I might have been able to put up with it for a bit longer in my 40's."

If s/he had her/his time over again, s/he would have sought a seat later in life, in a London constituency and not so far away and,

"I would have had a greater distance about it. I think I would have been stricter about maintaining sort of personal time and keeping up all those friendships and all that kind of stuff."

In a similar vein to the notion above of serving as an MP for a "patch" of life, s/he reflected on how it might now be possible to get into Parliament, get promoted, become a minister and get out in 10 or 15 years having had a perfectly good career. In the 1960s and 1970s, longer apprenticeships were expected,

"You know, there's not many Ken Clarkes around anymore."

This does, of course, depend on both the electoral cycle and a willingness to exit political office.

How Was the Decision Made?

There are different political considerations for council leaders and MPs, reflected among those whom I interviewed. Many of the former MPs may not have explicitly acknowledged their intentions while in office, but they thought that they had assumed that they would seek to remain in Parliament for the reminder of their career, however long that might have been. One in this study, having been elected in her/his twenties, had been clear that it would *not* be for a lifetime. Council leaders, in contrast, tend to be shorter-lived, although there is considerable variation between different areas and authorities. It might therefore be expected that council leaders will give more consideration to their desired time in office.

The time privately taken to make the decision to stand down was generally lengthy, and the time at which such thoughts began to emerge was hard to pin down in retrospect. Most came finally to their own private decision between from six to nine months before an election to as long as two to three years beforehand.

The length of time that elapsed between the private decision, perhaps only known to a spouse or very close confidantes, and the public announcement also varied considerably. For one or two, it was almost immediate (even if there was still well over a year to go before the election), while for others, there were many months before the decision had been made public.

Once the decision to go is made public, there is no going back. The political show moves on and quickly, at an almost unseemly pace. As one former MP relayed,

"You know what happens when an MP dies, everyone says 'what's his majority? What a shame' ... so I'm dead ... 'let's pick a new one' ... oh, well I'm discounted ... I knew that was going to happen."

One former leader, who had unusually little difficulty in making the decision, had a relatively short time—six months—after s/he had made up her/his mind before s/he told two confidantes, and then resigned one month later. Others generally knew for longer that they would later step down.

Obligations to constituents and a sense of responsibility to the local party featured, but at the end of the day, as might be expected, decisions were taken quietly and privately with partners and close family members. Mostly, the decision to stand down itself, even if it was under pressure and even if it had involved much agony and heartache, was straightforward in the end. As one former politician put it,

"It wasn't easy, but it was straightforward."

For one former MP, after months of agonising,

"It's a bit like when you flip a coin to find out ... and you suddenly realise that you don't want it to come back up heads. It was exactly like that."

Not so dissimilar for another former MP: s/he had chosen to stand down after a limited number of terms, and after considerable reflection, although the decision not to stand in the end came easily,

"A moment when everything seemed to cohere … and the knowledge that I wasn't going to stand came to me as something realised or complete in itself." No agonising, no drawing up lists of the relative merits and demerits of standing again, just a sudden realisation that the decision had at some level already been taken. It was,

"Like the alchemy of falling in love." And there was no mistaking it. But this had come after an assumption on first being elected as an MP, that this would be a role in which s/he would remain for most of the rest, if not all, of his/her working life,

"It was a vocational thing…. it's one of those things that's explicable only by being inexplicable." For other former politicians, even if the decision to stand down was in the end straightforward and they had come to have no doubt about its correctness, there had often been a time of considerable agonising. A former leader put it,

"Being in a position of such power and influence, if you like, locally, to willingly give that up is not something I was going to do on a whim or a drop of a hat or in an ill considered way, so I took my time." S/he, in fact, took a number of years finally to come to a decision. For another, a former MP,

"I always knew which way I had to make my mind up, but persuading yourself that you had to make your mind up the way you knew you had to make your mind up, was the difficult bit." And another was frank about how, despite the overwhelming rational reasons for going, the seesawing of emotions was difficult,

"I actually drew up a list at one point of 10 criteria and nine of them said go, but …" One former MP agonised long over the decision, vacillated several times feeling a nagging guilt, a sense of obligation to the constituency party and a fear of letting people down. But s/he too, once the decision was made, felt an overwhelming relief.

No agony for two. One announced her/his decision to stand down as an MP well in advance of the General Election to allow plentiful time for candidate succession, and although s/he was entirely confident that it was the right decision, s/he had not been sure if s/he might feel very differently after the announcement had been made,

"It's a bit like splitting up with a girl-friend – it seems like the right thing to do till the day after you've done it and then you miss them like heck."

It turned out that s/he remained immensely relieved to have stood down, with no regrets. By her/his own admission, s/he had never been clubbable in temperament and had felt no draw to this aspect of Commons life. S/he had however put enormous work and effort over many years, both in the constituency and at a more strategic level in the national political party. Yet s/he readily admitted that s/he had little personal political ambition. This may well have accounted for the ease of both the decision itself and making it public.

Only for two others, both former leaders, was the decision straightforward. One at the time found it "*very easy*": s/he had accomplished what s/he had set out to do and despite having found the role of council leader one of the most interesting jobs that s/he had ever had, it was simply time to go. This leader had had a highly accomplished, challenging and varied professional career aside from local government. At the time of the decision, s/he was,

"Relaxed about legacy. I was comfortable about what had happened. I thought my political career had been a reasonable success ... did I think I would miss it? Maybe. I was slightly worried about that but I only had the general anxiety that people have when they approach retirement. It wasn't anything specific to political office."

S/he later found however that the process of transition was not quite as simple as s/he had assumed.

The other leader who had found the decision very straightforward had been in post for many years and was feeling the strains of office, at the time well past retirement age. Stepping down as leader and councillor had been planned with care in collaboration both with her/his partner and likely successor so that the last year could be in a more ceremonial role.

THE EXPERIENCE OF STANDING DOWN

"Straightforward" in terms of the decision to stand down, however, does not necessarily mean that the actual experience—both the practical and the emotional experience—of the transition from office was not very keenly felt by many. It was recognised, certainly looking back, to have been an ending and a transition in life of enormous significance for most. Few had appreciated beforehand quite how significant it was to be.

There are different phases to the experience of standing down from political office: from initial private musings; to a definite but still unannounced decision possibly shared with intimates; to a public announcement when the die is cast; the approach to the election that is not being contested and the time after the election when the loss of office is formalised.

I was interested to learn about what had been experienced in the period between the public announcement of the decision to stand down and the election that would not be contested. At one end of the spectrum of experience, *"relief"* was the term used by a number of former MPs (but only one leader), *"release"* and *"entirely delighted"* by two others. The verdict of one,

"It was a horrendous life ... an overwhelming feeling of relief ... it was just so devastatingly awful to be an MP."

Another MP talked of,

"A massive relief ... going from black and white to colour ... getting my life back again, going back to being a private person."

Yet another expressed surprise at the extent to which s/he was relieved to no longer be seen as a public person. Most of the relief arose because of the constant, relentless intrusion of the media, especially the press. But relief was expressed too at no longer being at the (legitimate) beck and call of others, at no longer being under the conveyor belt pressure of casework and the dogged work that is inevitably required in seats that are far from safe.

In the immediate aftermath of having announced the decision to stand down, a former MP, quite comfortable with the decision, described an,

"Eerie after echo. The bomb had gone off and afterwards there was this silence.... it was sort of the aural equivalent of the question mark."

S/he went to refer to a couple of lines from a poem by Matthew Arnold, (Stanzas from the Grande Chartreuse),

"Wandering between two worlds, one dead
The other powerless to be born"

But the poem, as I checked later, goes on,

"With nowhere yet to rest my head
Like these, on earth I wait forlorn."

The verse as a whole is perhaps apt for this study

One former politician had little time to experience how life would be different because of standing down per se; s/he was shocked to learn of the diagnosis of a serious illness immediately after stepping down. Despite the challenges of medical treatment s/he faced, standing down was still described as dropping off a cliff and too abrupt a withdrawal. S/he was reluctant to get drawn into thinking too much about the emotional repercussions of standing down from office, but her/his partner clearly described a period of intense anxiety and depression, beginning even before the diagnosis of illness. There was a real sense of panic about how s/he would fill the void that had suddenly opened up. Even having known that s/he was to stand down, little thought had been given in advance to what s/he would do once not in elected office. It had been,

"Quite a rational way of looking at things but the actual experience of doing it was a whole different matter ... a bleak time ... became quite depressed."

And even at the time of the interview, there was the possibility that s/he might stand again at a council level.

Another former MP talked forthcomingly about events around the decision to stand down and the facts of what had happened but was notably reluctant to delve much into the emotional experience,

"I think I'd made my mind up and that was it, there we are ..."

Even a couple of years later on, s/he could aver,

"It's difficult because I haven't really stopped to think how the process occurred ..."

Yet, her/his partner was very clear about how devastating had been the impact on her/him no longer being an elected politician—a restless soul—unable to settle to anything, compelled to relentless physical activity. S/he had made no preparations for the future whatsoever despite having announced the decision to stand down long before the General Election,

"You have a few dustbin bags put at the door of your office and that's it, end of story."

Everything suddenly stopped—*"the water closed over ..."*—no mail, no telephone calls, nothing.

For most former politicians, however, there was considerable emotion expressed in recalling the period between having made public the announcement of decision to stand down and the immediate period post election. For some, it had been a turbulent time, despite the fact that standing down had been chosen. The misrepresentation of MPs and their expenses fuelled a raging anger both for a number of former MPs, with some deciding to stand down in the expenses' wake.

Welling up as we talked, one former MP remembered the tangle of expenses, the impact that it had had, the hurtfulness of being seen as prejudicial to the campaign, despite years of tireless work on behalf of the constituency, and its impact on the family. While her/his immediate reaction to the public announcement of her/his standing down had been almost one of elation, driven by the anger s/he had felt in being unjustly blamed, s/he could acknowledge that it was only now, in talking about it, how hard it had been at the time.

"I suppose I've always tried to keep emotions and politics separate … and therefore I have very much rationalised this whole transition from being an MP … had managed not to allow emotions that may be connect with it to affect me."

S/he came, however, to articulate a deep seam of anger and hurt and a profound, sad sense of rejection. S/he had come to recognise a number of different endings in her/his life at the same time as the ending of her/his parliamentary life; it had been indeed a turbulent time.

Another, one of the very few who had put a great deal of thought into thinking through the process of leaving, and had no regrets about the decision itself, talked with feeling about what a huge loss it felt when her/his decision to leave ministerial office was made public. It was the recognition of the end of her/his political career and that no further advancement was possible, that was so painful. This was the peak; s/he was never going to go any higher, feeling almost a sense of failure. Despite having achieved very high office, this former politician had still dreamt of a more senior post. S/he even occasionally found her/himself using phrases such as *"Of course, my life is over"* despite knowing rationally that this was far from the case.

The partner of one former MP had been concerned prior to the election that her/his partner might greatly miss the loss of status, no longer being an MP, and s/he was relieved to find that this had not been the case, despite some twinges at not being part of key discussions post election. S/he astutely observed,

"The fall away of people as they moved on to the candidate and moved on to the next person and all of a sudden, s/he is the past. That's an odd feeling."

A few former MPs may simply walk back into their previous careers, but most cannot,

"Being an MP is deskilling … one of the effects of the expenses crisis was this idea that MPs are full time, not allowed to do anything else … have no exit routes … it's Huis Clos … it makes people extremely vulnerable."

Two former MPs commented that a significant number of MPs feel trapped in the role, wishing that they could leave but feeling unable to,

"Certainly, when I talk to people in Parliament now, most of them, you know, feel a bit trapped."

Neither of these MPs had any regrets about having stood down, just a barely discernable occasional twinge, but they both recognised that their life had taken a very different turn from that which they had envisaged not many years before.

For those who had no previous career to slot back into, and even with having made a public decision to stand down, the future was more uncertain, unsettling and for some very precarious. That brought a sense of excitement for one, relishing the opportunity to do new things, as well as having the time and space for a much better quality of life. That sense of precariousness lingered long for one even after s/he had been offered a number of opportunities,

"The worry is that you can't fall on your feet that often without potentially falling off a cliff at some point."

For longer standing MPs, it should be remembered that it may have been many years since they were in the job market; they may well be unfamiliar with putting together curriculum vitae, unpractised in job interviews and even unused to doing their own research. Even having to deal with the practicalities of diary management, social media, or computer and internet networks at home may be a challenge, it all having been done on their behalf for many years.

Planning for the Transition and for the Future

Virtually all the former elected politicians in this study who had stood down had known that they would be standing down some time in advance. There were no last minute decisions, and many of the interviewees had a period of up to 18 months or two years in which to contemplate both the process of transition from elected office and what they would do in the future. While many—but certainly not all—made some preparation for what they might do in the longer term, only one had given careful thought to the process of transition from office. Just one.

The one politician who had reflected in depth about standing down had watched a number of leading parliamentary figures reach the most senior positions, some in government, and when they had left, had wondered,

"What would happen afterwards, and you know, would the rest of their life just be a kind of dark shadow in a blur, particularly if they disappeared from public sight, and how would they feel, and would they feel that what they were doing 20 years later was actually just as important and meaningful even if it was not this big thing?"

What happened to those who fell very publicly from grace, perhaps having cracked emotionally under the very considerable strains of senior ministerial office? What happened to former prime ministers?

"Good god, four years or whatever at the peak, and then that's it and then what do you do with the rest of your life?"

S/he was, therefore, acutely aware of the transitory nature of high office. Emotionally insightful, s/he readily drew parallels with loss and transition generally, getting older and mortality.

The decision to stand down from government office was taken over some time, in discussion with family, and planned with the utmost care— whom to tell, when and how. S/he had even arranged a farewell gathering although at the time it had not been billed as such, but it was, nevertheless, an important marking of the transition from office, and an opportunity for her/his work to be acknowledged. A ritual of some sort was necessary as, despite choosing to do so, leaving office was,

"Still a huge loss because, you know, it's what I loved doing and had always wanted to do, and there was also a sense of I will never again have such a big job."

S/he was clear that following stepping down from Parliament, s/he would not *"Hang around … I learnt that one really early – you move on. You know, you don't hang around and live with ghosts, and all of that."*

Planning for the process of leaving office with such care had helped enormously. S/he recognised the importance of endings and how to manage them. S/he had imagined, over a period of time and in detail, how s/he might occupy her/his days when s/he had no longer to travel to and from the constituency, how her/his days might be structured with a number of different activities. This had enabled this former MP to establish a new rhythm and structure to the week—after having slept heavily for three months such were the demands of office—that worked extremely well. Even so, having now time for leisure took some accommodating to after so many years at a much more furious pace.

It is curious, to the author at least, that no other former elected politician seemed to have given much thought to the process of transition except for the one former leader who decided to take on a ceremonial role very specifically as a transition to non-elected office. While a number of former MPs had disliked the role intensely and had not stayed for more than one or two terms, others had been an MP or leader for many years and it could have been predicted that the process of transition for this latter group might not be straightforward.

Despite finding no longer being in Parliament a great relief, another thoughtfully reflected on how the process of transition still needed some getting used to,

"It's sort of a big change to your identity, both how you think about yourself and how other people perceive you. So when you're a Cabinet minister, you walk into a room and people might hate you or they might love you but at least it's clear. You're not having to define yourself in that room and suddenly, that's all a lot more fluid."

A few had not even given any thought to what they might do when no longer in office. One former MP had made no preparations at all for stepping down despite having had a lengthy time in which to reflect. According to her/his partner, who was astonished at the lack of planning, the former MP did not think about post parliamentary life, did not want to think about it and did not prepare for anything. Another, a former leader, was adamant that s/he was just going to wait and see what would happen. These two, both long-standing former politicians, had since struggled to fill the void.

Others, however, had at least taken some steps to plan for the future, both in terms of work and family relationships. Luck played its part too for one; but it cannot be relied upon.

After having privately made the decision to step down, a former leader had, with her/his spouse,

"Started to piece together the components of the life we would have after I left office,"

S/he gave the impression that s/he had thought that the experience of transition would be simple and straightforward. With some surprise, s/he acknowledged that some months on it had been,

"Much less simple than I thought. The emotional impact is a lot less simple than I thought."

Perhaps this was partly because of an unforeseen local controversy that came to entangle the end of her/his leadership. It emerged however that s/he had planned some time before to join a longish trip abroad soon after stepping down and s/he acknowledged that this,

"Helped focus the mind in making the decision and it helped for there to be an element of calm after to sort of regroup."

For one former MP with no formal professional qualification or previous experience in anything other than the political arena, stepping down was a gamble not least with young children to provide for. Once it was known, however, that s/he was standing down, and now seen as less partisan, s/he had been asked to lead a policy review for the government. This both made very positive use of the period of transition and provided useful credentials for the future.

The process of transition was much more straightforward for one individual who had thought about standing down over many years, and fleetingly talked about it over a decade before. S/he remarked, with interest, how s/he had gone from being centrally involved in and *"obsessive"* about party strategic communications to,

"Immediately sitting on the benches and feeling like an observer and just thinking 'Oh, this is what it feels like to be a member of the general public watching politics.'"

By her/his own admission, s/he was not much driven by personal ambition and perhaps both this, the length of time that s/he had had to contemplate leaving office and strong family support led to a much smoother transition than for many others despite a lengthy tenure.

For those former MPs who are appointed to the House of Lords, there is a softer landing even if they choose not to be full-time working peers. While some council leaders may be appointed to the Lords during their term of office, few MPs can predict with certainty if they will later be appointed to the second chamber. The transition from elected office is gentler for those appointed as peers. The Lords permits a continuation of parliamentary life but without the demands of constituents and still the opportunity to influence,

"If anything, I get taken more seriously than I did when I was an MP" was the view of the one former MP and peer in this study.

As s/he pithily put it, MPs who find the Commons impossible to leave only doing so by,

"Kicking and screaming and nails screeching down the desk, which is partly why the Lords exists – to bribe people to leave."

S/he acknowledged that the Lords both provided a position,

"To still make things happen … to be honest, some reserve option in terms of if I got no other income, I could just concentrate on that."

The Lords does not, however, offer *"a clean break,"* commented one participant, but this is, of course, its attraction for many, although it is not invariably seen as a desirable destination.

Notably, even fewer former MPs subsequently stand for election at a local level than former council leaders stand for Parliament. With more directly elected mayors or, more recently still, with the advent of Police and Crime Commissioners (PCC) in England and Wales, this may change.

Of the PCCs elected in 2016, 5 of the 40 had previously been an MP, joining the Greater Manchester PCC and London Mayor (who acts in the role of a PCC), both former MPs. One Welsh AM from the fourth Assembly was elected as a PCC. Very few PCCs had been council leaders, although many had served as a councillor. The London mayoralty, seen now as one of the most high profile local government positions in the country, does attract MPs: its first three incumbents have formerly been parliamentarians. It is more straightforward for any candidate standing for election to such positions if they have previously stood down from any other political office rather than if they had been defeated. Unfairly or not, they are seen not to be tainted by the failure of electoral defeat, the subject of the next chapter.

REFERENCES

Simpson, J. (2014). Personal communication.
Weinberg, A. (2007). Your destiny in their hands: Job loss and success in Members of Parliament. BPS Annual Conference, York. *Proceedings of the BPS*, 15 (2).
Wright, T. (2015). Personal communication.

CHAPTER 7

The Experience of Losing Political Office: Defeated

Contemplating the Possibility of Defeat

Few former politicians who had been electorally defeated had prepared in advance for the possibility despite in many cases this having been a distinct possibility given the electoral cycle or more local factors. But even if defeat is objectively realistically on the cards, it is extremely difficult for any sitting candidate to admit either to themselves, or certainly to others working so hard for them, that defeat is a possibility. One former MP, speaking for many, was clear that despite representing a marginal seat,

"I never really thought about it, I gave no … because I had an absolute determination to get re-elected, I didn't prepare for this in any way, so I'd no idea of what it was going to be like."

One former leader, despite having thought a great deal about how s/he might shape the duration of her/his leadership and aware of the skill of knowing when to go, was nevertheless pipped to the post by the electorate.

A former MP did admit that s/he had recognised that losing her/his seat was a realistic possibility given the majority. S/he had given considerable thought to what might happen, but it was not possible to have an open conversation about what might happen after the General Election: MPs in such a position cannot afford politically for those conversations to become known. Candidates are seeking to persuade people to vote for them, encouraging people to come out in all weathers and campaign on their behalf, and they have to believe that they are going to win,

"Because otherwise you've got to be the most amazing actor."

© The Author(s) 2017
J. Roberts, *Losing Political Office*,
DOI 10.1007/978-3-319-39702-3_7

101

As one spouse put it,

"During the campaign, you can't ever think you are going to lose ... otherwise your strength runs out and you stop fighting."

While a conviction of electoral success is a political imperative, it does make any subsequent defeat all the more of a shock.

Council leaders go into elections defending both their seat and their leadership position. Depending on both the electoral cycle and the demographic composition of the authority's area, they may contemplate that their party might no longer be in control and hence that they might lose the leadership after a local election. They will much less often anticipate losing their seat as well, as reflected in this study. Any planning for the possible loss of the leadership role will therefore probably not take into account no longer being a councillor. The partner of one former leader described how, as leader, the former politician had given little thought to how long s/he might remain in post,

"Such was the kind of living day to day, week to week, dealing with the next crisis, whatever that might be."

S/he had mooted the possibility of her/his party no longer being in control and had some sort of plan but on the basis of still being a councillor. That s/he turned out subsequently to lose her/his seat as well was totally unplanned for and left both shell-shocked.

The Experience of Being Defeated

For those who were defeated at the ballot box, it was, inevitably, more shocking and more personally exposing than for those who had chosen to stand down. Usually, there had been little notice of such a momentous change in life: even if defeat was not totally unexpected, there had often been a desperate hope that he or she would somehow buck the national trend and just about hang on to the seat. A defeat takes place in the full glare of publicity, surrounded by family and those who have worked so hard for you, who have invested hope in you and who have, perhaps, depended on you for their job.

Shock, pride, a determination to steel oneself in front of the cameras and a crushing sense of failure and humiliation were dominant themes in most of the interviews. In just one—where the interview was more time limited than others—the focus was more on the political sequelae of defeat and less was revealed of the personal experience.

If de-selected, of course, a council leader or an MP has little choice of decision other than whether or not to seek selection elsewhere. This was the case for one of the interviewees in this study. As noted previously, there is in reality more of a continuum between standing down and being defeated, with varying degrees of voluntariness evident. I considered this former council leader as being on the cusp of having stood down (s/he had formally) but only as a result of having been de-selected as a result of a highly contentious local issue. S/he had not chosen not to stand else-where in the authority despite having been asked to do so. The circum-stances of her/his loss of office, defeat by a "selectorate," were therefore more akin to those who lost at the hands of the electorate, and hence s/he is included in this group. Given that such a defeat comes at the hands of one's own party, it comes as no surprise that feelings of hurt, anger and betrayal should run especially deep.

This well-regarded leader had been cut down by a group from within her/his party, and felt betrayed by a broken ministerial promise. Despite the contention, the de-selection had been relatively unexpected. S/he talked with what sounded like some under-statement of her/his sadness and anger at what had happened,

"I was not a happy bunny but as I keep saying to people, that's politics, you know. You've got to learn to live with it. If you can't live with it, then you're in the wrong job and it's not nice."

S/he later admitted that it had been,

"Awful, just awful … my big low … just unbelievable … embarrassment having to go on in the role for some time."

What had really hurt, and fuelled anger, had been that there had been no communication from the regional party and no acknowledgement of any sort. His/her partner was less restrained. It was humiliating and degrading to have been stabbed in the back, and by a supposed friend, and having to run through a gauntlet of party members at the selection meeting,

"They shouldn't have put anybody through that … it made me feel awful … I was very, very bitter with those people."

The choice, such as it is, to seek selection elsewhere, is inevitably tainted by the bitterness from the sense of betrayal by one's own side that comes with a de-selection.

WHEN DID THEY KNOW THEY MIGHT LOSE?

I was surprised by the number of those whom I interviewed who said that they had had virtually no indication before the election count of impend-ing defeat, or for some it was only in the 24 hours or so beforehand that the possibility of losing was even countenanced. Even by comparison with most redundancies elsewhere, electoral defeat is a remarkably sudden death.

A number of partners admitted to their private pessimism, or at the very least, caution about the election, almost as though they were the ones carrying the thought of the possibility of defeat. Perhaps this had then allowed the candidates the optimism that is necessary for campaigning. One reflected on her/his pessimism when it came to elections and acknowledged the anxiety pre-election, gearing up for the possibility of defeat. At the same time, however, the politician had a very different stance,

"Always an absolute optimist and wouldn't even talk about not winning ... wasn't interested."

But for a couple of others, both candidate and partner were taken by surprise at the unexpected defeat, having previously felt *"bullet proof."*

One former MP only realised her/his possible loss when the ballot boxes were turned out at 2 am; s/he had no period of anticipation. In fact, s/he had thought that the campaign had gone well and that,

"With a wing and a prayer, it'd be okay."

It was not. As the boxes were turned out, votes were piling up higher than expected for the opposing party in their wards. Similarly, another former MP in a marginal seat had never expected to lose. It was only when postal votes were added in mid-way through the count during the night that the balance tipped against her/him.

Another knew only from the first result—there were several recounts—although there had been a number of factors that arose in the year preceding that meant the parliamentary race had been going to be much closer than before. Factors included a boundary change and a (small) expenses issue that was effectively exploited by an opposing party both of which, in retrospect, might have foretold the result. S/he had known it was,

"Knife-edge" but again, *"you can sort of feel you can do it."*

These sentiments were echoed by others, often in a marginal seat. One said,

"I thought we might just pip the post, that we might just do it and you have to keep that sense because you've got to lead everybody else."

Another,

"It's heart and head stuff ... there's something in your heart that says I can beat this ... we'd worked incredibly hard, incredibly hard, we thought we could still nick it."

It was not until election night and hearing of the loss of a nearby parliamentary seat that,

"My heart really sunk and psychologically, I was kind of like at the depths of despair. At that moment I realised that the game was up."

A former council leader who had always held a fairly marginal seat acknowledged that s/he

"Hadn't wanted to see it coming, you don't believe it … but you could feel it, yes, as you went on the doorstep talking to people."

S/he recalled with despair of how entangled council candidates got with the expenses issue: people came to the door with the television on in the background talking about MPs' expenses,

"And it was just, 'you're all the same. You're only in it for what you can get. What about that lot?"

That same gut sense, about 48 hours before the election, warned another former leader of her/his likely but previously wholly unanticipated loss. A former big supporter,

"Couldn't look me in the eye … it suddenly felt wrong."

Similar forebodings were expressed by another former leader,

"In the last few days, people were averting their eyes."

But nevertheless, s/he had not expected to lose her/his seat, even on the night. And another leader who lost by a single number of votes had felt in the two weeks running up to the election that,

"The tide seemed to be turning."

Local politicians often develop a very finely honed sense of the direction of the electoral tide, albeit perhaps rather late in the day.

AT THE COUNT

Unsurprisingly, virtually all the defeated former leaders and MPs portrayed a grim determination at the count to keep themselves and their supporters together in front of the cameras. The descriptions, however, of their raw devastation are painful even to hear some time later, a far cry from the political banter that fills our screens and airwaves at election time. Humiliation of the most public kind is the common theme, rejected in the full glare of publicity by those for whom they have served.

On election night, most candidates are utterly exhausted having run themselves ragged for months—relentlessly canvassing, mobilising supporters, motivating the team, speaking, debating—prior to the election. MPs who have lost and to a lesser extent, defeated council leaders, are likely to have been in marginal seats and hence have come into the election period having been in campaigning mode for much longer than their former colleagues in safer seats. The intensity of the contest itself, under the national spotlight, will have been much more fierce. The final sprint may well have been punishing, lacking both rest and sustenance. In this state, candidates are pitched into the feverish melee of an election count, expectations on all sides raised, camera lens at the ready to shoot any unguarded moments.

One former MP was typical: s/he was going to the count knowing that many family members and party workers were going to be there,

"My nearest and dearest in the constituency, all the people who worked so hard and bust their guts and I had to put on a show because I did not want to be seen to be defeated in the local media."

S/he had seen how the press had covered the defeat of another former politician in the area,

"They ran it front page, big picture of him looking forlorn, a big picture of me behind him looking forlorn, his family members in tears, all that kind of stuff and I was determined to go out on a high, so I just put on a show. Inside I was smashed to pieces … I had to carry the party through it and that was incredibly difficult and it took every ounce of emotional strength … but you've got to hold it together and you know the second the mask slips, it's flashlight, flashlight, flashlight all over the place."

Another similarly reported a determination to put on a show, to keep laughing and joking with television crew, come what may but,

"It's the act … I was devastated, absolutely devastated."

Even worse, the loss was immediately attributed, wrongly, in her/his view, to the expenses issue. But worst of all was having had to tell her/his partner waiting anxiously at home that s/he had lost,

"Just feeling a complete failure, but not being able to show it."

But then the bravura kicked in and s/he delivered a defiant speech, confidently predicting success for her/his party in the soon to be counted local elections. But it was, undoubtedly, an act. *"A nightmare"* described the partner.

The determined focus on holding oneself together applied to all my interviewees who had lost and by and large, they put on a convincing enough act. The veneer threatened to crack only if and when people commiserated with them. One former leader who had known it would be very close, but still hoped s/he would win through, relayed,

"It was awful, awful. I was fine until people were nice to me. I had gritted teeth and then people came up to me and said, 'Oh, I'm sorry.' Don't be nice to me."

Another former leader who had only felt s/he was going to lose in the couple of days prior to the election could just about acknowledge how *"shitty"* s/he had felt. S/he acknowledged that s/he felt more comfortable taking a cerebral approach to her/his reflections on the defeat, rather than expressing much in the way of emotion—in common with a number of (male) interviewees.

"If you're going to take a beating, you just take your beating. There's nothing you can do about it."

This is, of course, true. It is the essence of our democratic system, that those whom we elect, we can and often will, later kick out of office. How individual politicians deal the impact of this is, however, another matter, and the focus of this work.

S/he had kept the looming defeat from virtually everyone until just before the count,

"Any successful leader has to have the ability to compartmentalise. If you do not, you will break and I've seen that ... and you break very quickly."

S/he instead focused on the last few hours of the campaign across the authority area, determined to do all necessary for her/his colleagues in the party group. Remaining in role as leader of the group helped carry her/him through: There had been no time to digest what was happening, caught up as s/he was, in the media scrum. S/he had had no time alone, no time to pause, for many days. Another former leader expressed very similar sentiments,

"You have a job to do now. You have a job to make sure that all of the ballots that have got your cross on come to you and there's no mistakes'. It was very mechanical and I stayed until the very last ward was declared ... after I'd lost my seat,"

S/he felt,

"Numb ... after losing my seat, I was dragged outside, broadcast live. Yeah, so I'd done my bit."

Few defeated MPs have similar responsibilities for their party colleagues; the closest parallel may be that of the Conservative Party Chairman who lost his seat in the 1992 General Election but even then, the Conservative Party was the victor, although Chris Patten was defeated as an MP. When council leaders lose their seat, it is the case almost always that their party will have sustained heavy losses and may well have lost political control of the authority.

For some, despite the devastation of a result that had gone against them, there was at least an ending to the uncertainty of many months, perhaps more, of not knowing what the future held. Life may have been put on hold, especially with children in a household, if, as an MP, they had lived in the constituency. In this respect, at least council leaders have less to juggle, being able to live and undertake their duties in closer proximity, with less disruption to family life.

A former MP, who struggled hard following her/his defeat, recalled the humiliation of election night but nevertheless recalled how the immediate reaction had been one of relief,

"Because it was over. One way or another, the decision had been made."

Many turbulent feelings assailed this former politician over the succeeding months, but s/he kept going initially by focusing immediately on the sense of relief that a decision had been made for the family and on all the practical issues that would need to be sorted. The period of limbo had ended, albeit if another was about to begin.

For one, the experience, while not easy, did bring with it a more positive sense of relief and some increased self-awareness. This former leader would never have walked away from the role, a combination of having loved it and of having felt an obligation to others, but s/he came to realise the toll that the leadership had been taking on her/him. S/he acknowledged that the role had to have been taken away rather than willingly relinquished. S/he admitted to intense anxiety at the count, and s/he had to stand just outside, smoking on the steps of the Town Hall throughout the night. S/he was devastated at the small margin of defeat initially, but then described a feeling of numbness at the result,

"The first 24 hours didn't really affect me. It didn't sink in."

THE IMMEDIATE AFTERMATH

A bravura performance, numbness, adrenaline and grim determination dominate the moments following a very public defeat. What then?

There are immediate worries about money, employment: what—if anything—does the future hold with fears that,

"Straightaway that you're going to lose everything."

But first, sleep. Sleep is high on the priority list in the immediate aftermath: interviews were peppered with phrases such as,

"Sheer exhaustion," "I slept for days, literally," "I hadn't slept for 30 hours," and *"I slept quite a bit, laid up sick for a week … it had been so hard going."*

All candidates are exhausted post election, but in this state, those who have been defeated have their belongings to collect, offices to clear and, worst of all for former parliamentarians, staff to be made redundant.

One former MP told how,

"Then it got worse … I had 48 hours to get your entire life bagged up and out and organised … to get back to London … given 48 hours and a shopping trolley to pile your stuff into so new people can come in. I didn't want to see my former colleagues who'd got re-elected or even those who had lost because you don't want to be treated as a leper."

Probed further, s/he went on to say how s/he did not want,

"Everybody coming up giving you cuddles saying, 'There, there.' You know, you're a proud person, you're a tough guy, you want to be able to shrug your shoulders and say, you know, 'C'est la vie. I'm going to get on with my life and do other things', and not be a wreck."

The clearing of the parliamentary office encapsulated for many the humiliation of defeat: the sudden and rapid sweeping away of years of work, people and memories; the takeover of what felt like a personal space by an unknown other; adjacent offices still occupied by colleagues who successfully contested the election and all potentially witnessed. One partner described how after clearing out the former MP's office, the police quietly let them out by a side gate as,

"They were taking photographs of MPs leaving [at the front]. You know, 'Ho, ho, look, he's packed his car up'."

Another described creeping into the Commons soon after the election to collect everything, deliberately choosing a Saturday to avoid now former colleagues as,

"The hardest thing I ever did … was I had to go in the weekend afterwards to clear my office out."

In that period,

"You feel that the whole world's against you … you learn who your friends are."

S/he had heard nothing, *"not a peep,"* from an allegedly very close friend. It was the sense of failure that was so devastating,

"There's nothing worse than a failed politician … it was a massive, massive loss."

Like so many others, s/he had never been seen to fail before. For this former politician, unlike a number of others, s/he was emphatic that it was not about shame but about failure.

A sense of personal failure and having let people down was a dominant theme in most of the interviews with those who had failed to win an election even if the electoral tide had been unstoppable. Many politicians have never experienced failure in their life before: they are, after all, mostly competent, bright, articulate people and used to success. A first experience of failure on a very public stage may well be excruciating. One former leader was frank: s/he had been afraid at failing at anything and even counted a relationship many years previously that had not worked out as a failure, despite having been happily married for many years subsequently. S/he acknowledged, therefore, that any election was a risk, a high wire act.

Most interviewees did identify feeling a deep and uncomfortable sense of shame, in addition to failure. One former leader had forced her/himself out every day despite the temptation to lock her/himself away and not be seen on the streets,

"The big over-riding emotion – and don't ask me to explain because I haven't been able to rationalise it yet and it still happens sometimes but less so now – is shame ... I just feel ashamed ... I want to know why and I can't process it... that's probably the number one emotion above all others."

S/he struggled to understand why s/he had felt such a sense of shame and wondered if it had been more about an almost unbearable feeling of having let others down. This party group had been an unusually close team of members, full of camaraderie. But this former politician was by nature a competitive character, and admitted that not winning was an unfamiliar as well as an unwelcome experience, both in a political context and more widely.

A sense of hurt, betrayal and resentment at having been rejected by the electorate was articulated by most interviewees. It was, however, infrequently readily volunteered, and often seemed understated. One former defeated MP described her/his resentment simply as a,

"Not a very elevated emotion."

After all, politicians know that politics is a rough old trade: the democratic deal is that the electorate can always turf any politician out of office and so it is inevitably discomfiting to acknowledge resentment, even anger, towards the electorate. But politicians are human too, with famously not so thick skins, as former Prime Minister John Major acknowledged.

Or, as one interviewee put it,

"Human beings aren't like taps."

They are not able to turn feelings off and on like a switch. For this former politician who had seen enough electoral results to know that people should not take a defeat personally, s/he had nevertheless done precisely that, acknowledging,

"It change the fact that you feel the way that you feel."

Her/his personal esteem had taken a nosedive. This former MP admitted to having felt her/his defeat as an injustice, despite always having known that an electoral loss could happen. S/he talked frankly about having felt,

"A sense of hurt. In some ways, it's like a bereavement, but at the end of the day, I think as a rational human being, you have to remind yourself of the real struggles and strife other people have in life."

It sounded as though s/he had been jostling understandably between a rational cognitive appraisal of her/his defeat and the less biddable affective experience. One leader, despite an unexpected wafer thin loss, did however manage to hold on to her/his pragmatism,

"I never shed a tear. I was devastated, but I was pragmatic ... I was very down on the Sunday, but by the Monday, I was up again. I just said, Well, the people have spoken ... move on."

In contrast, this former leader's family expressed fury at the electorate's perceived ingratitude.

One former MP dealt with her/his discomfort by chuckling at having been,

"Quite annoyed" with constituents, admitting that there had been,

"A little bit in passing of 'After all I've done'. I was a good local MP."

Some former constituents had come up to her/him to say how sorry they were, but s/he wanted to retort,

"It's no good being sorry now."

Her/his ire was directed internally: s/he blamed her/himself, in retrospect, for having not put in as much effort into the constituency. This former MP had always ploughed her/his own furrow, doing everything by himself, in order to advance on merit rather than as one who had been anointed by anyone else. S/he acknowledged that s/he had set her/himself a high bar and hence,

"That's why falling off was all the harder because ultimately, I've got no-one else to blame but me. That's the thing."

And the falling off for this former MP had indeed been very hard.

A former MP cautiously described the conflicting emotions that arose immediately after defeat. S/he could acknowledge that s/he felt,

"A feeling of ingratitude by the people you've represented for so long."

S/he and family had lived in the constituency for some years with many friends and neighbours in the locality. It was convincingly described as a double relationship, surrounded by acquaintances and neighbours who were at the same time electors. S/he would have no idea if they had voted for her/him but suddenly found her/himself asking,

"Well, why didn't you vote for me? You know all the things that I've done for this constituency."

Despite her/his caution, this time was described as her/his whole world having *"collapsed."*

Another was more forthright, admitting to having looked at people in the street in the constituency and thinking,

"'You didn't vote for me' with some resentment. Yeah, I think with a bit of resentment. It's like you've had your x years and then they haven't even said thank you very much. They've just literally kind of opened the door and said get out. No idea of what you're going to do, where you're going … a sense of anger and frustration and feeling humiliated and feeling a bit ashamed. And I know why I felt ashamed because I've nothing to feel ashamed of, but that sense that I didn't win."

One former leader identified having felt more hurt than angry, although s/he recalled family members having been enraged on her/his behalf, as was the case for another former leader.

"At the time we were doing a good job as we saw it. Some of the things were just beginning to work … and it's sad. So, you know the public decided for me, but it's not pleasant. It's not a nice experience. It feels very personal even though it's not … it was a kick in the teeth and however much you think you are prepared, it's still a shock."

S/he evoked the resonant image of Margaret Thatcher leaving 10 Downing Street on the day of her resignation in 1990, remembering how s/he would remind herself, "Well, all things end, you know. Look at her." Curiously, her/his daughter later evoked the same image as s/he described how the local press wanted a front page story with a photo of the just former council leader looking very upset,

"Almost like the media turned on Thatcher when she went and, you know, that upset me as well – that they wanted a photo of … looking sad, "Gone!""

Council leaders who lose at the ballot box lose their seats and their leadership position in one fell swoop. They are suddenly out from one day to the next: an immediate loss of position, job, status with no cushioning of transitional income; it all goes, office, allowance, everything. It is very, very cold turkey. As one partner put it,

"It just finishes, it just stops. There's not even that gradual, you know, if you retire from a job you've got that time to wind down and tie up all the loose ends and say goodbye to people … but suddenly to be like one day you're in the office and the next day, that's it, you're escorted from the premises and you don't go back and what do you do everyday?"

Yet the electorate is often unaware that this is the case, and the media, even if aware, are deeply unsympathetic. And for council leaders in this position, there is no constituency from which to flee.

Fuelled by the expenses issue and its distortions,

"You feel a sense of injustice. You know you can't be heard amongst the clamour. You feel a massive pressure on your family."

Former council leaders who lose their seats have often had to struggle against an overwhelming national electoral tide, irrespective of how well the local authority itself is seen to have performed, or how hard the local party has campaigned. This can both be a focus for anger and frustration towards the national party and/or its leader or, alternatively, a channel to defuse a more personal and bruising sense of rejection.

Both views were expressed in interviews in this study, with two leaders expressing very different attributions for their defeat. One made clear that s/he had no time for

"Whingeing like mad, blaming everyone but themselves … if you're going to defend a seat, you can get off your arse and do it yourself."

S/he took responsibility for having got both the local strategy and tactics wrong, blaming her/himself both in the immediate aftermath and since. Unsurprisingly, this former politician struggled hard over the next year. Another, of the same political party, had a very different view: S/he lost count of the number of local people who had told her/him that,

"Those people in London haven't done you any favours."

S/he acknowledged feelings of anger towards the party leader but had also struggled hard since the defeat. Even if a leader loses both their leadership position and seat as a result of an overwhelming national surge against their party, the initial sense of personal rejection is still strong.

For one leader, s/he went from a role that,

"Preoccupies all your time and all your effort and then all of a sudden, it's gone. It was a bit of a double whammy not only losing my position as leader which I'd anticipated, but to lose the seat as well meant that actually all of a sudden there was nothing."

At her/his former occupation,

"There'd been 'Oh, well, there may be a restructuring' and you thought 'Well, a couple of months down the line that does that mean?' but to have it there in front of you on a Friday afternoon, that was rather sudden … numbing"

Even another former leader who had adjusted to non-elected life with less difficulty was shocked at the suddenness of the transition,

"Life was very busy and then all of a sudden, it went bang, stop."

Most former MPs, even if they came to acknowledge the overwhelming odds later, initially blamed themselves,

"At the time, you think it's your fault … you're the candidate for goodness sake and this is a judgement on you and your party."

The reality is that both national and local elements matter: while local campaigning in tightly fought electoral contests is likely to make a significant difference and can sometimes buck a national trend, local views about national policies may still trump the best laid (and executed) plans. Furthermore, the same national issues may well affect different localities differently.

The struggle between what is deemed to be the rational approach—recognition that electoral defeat is an integral and desirable part of the political process—and the lived experience, of being crushed emotionally, was described very vividly in most interviews. One former politician quoted a recruitment consultant who had stressed how the way that defeated parliamentarians dealt with their defeat— *"having dusted themselves down"*—was a more telling test of their capabilities. It felt as though s/he was trying to persuade her/himself that this was so,

"I suppose that you've got to take that into the bigger picture."

But s/he acknowledged that this perspective takes time to be appreciated, long after the tumult of an election.

Another MP who had been defeated recalled how s/he had felt angry and frustrated at suddenly no longer being able to play a significant role in the political party in which s/he had been close to the centre of power and influential for so long,

"I found it a depressing time too because what was I to do in general? … I mean I was very dislocated."

"I was Desperate to Get Away"

For some former politicians who had been defeated—but not those who had chosen to stand down—the slap in the face of electoral defeat had led to an aversion to being in the constituency and a need, desperate for some, to get away and get some distance. This may be much more feasible for former MPs than council leaders.

Two former MPs who had been defeated described wanting to get away from the constituency as soon as possible. There was a real sense of urgency: wanting to leave the area; wanting to be away from former constituents; and not plagued by doubts and uncertainties about who may— or may not—have voted for them. Some expressed unease that their trust in those who they thought had voted for them might be undermined as perhaps they had not done so. Just a couple felt no ambivalence towards the constituency; it was not surprising that both of these former MPs were considering standing again for the same seat.

One former MP was clear that s/he wanted to leave the constituency as soon as possible, despite the long attachment to the area, friends, village, house and garden, all much loved by the former MP and her/his spouse.

"Sell up and call it a day ... turn the page."

This had been a very difficult decision for the spouse, with a career and domestic life rooted in the area. But the sense of rejection and hurt meant that s/he had been determined to leave.

As much as a former MP may want to get away from their constituency, it may not be easy to do so: not only may property be hard to sell but children may be tied, at least for a while, to schools in the local area. Former MPs in such a position may feel caught: wanting to move, but with no job in order to be able to get a mortgage and move; well known locally but now as the former MP, rejected, with no one knowing what to say to her/him directly; and an awkwardness about the changed relationship with the local party. One former MP described it as driving her/him mad. S/he would avoid people s/he knew in the town centre,

"I didn't want to see them. I didn't want to stop and have people say, 'Oh dear, I'm so sorry.' And you'd look at them and say, 'Are you really?'"

S/he was clear that,

"I didn't want any pity and therefore you had to, you know, pretend that you were quite alright and fine about it which anyone with any sense is going to know is not true."

Nevertheless, in order to defend against the often inevitable question from acquaintants, "What are you doing now?" s/he put on a brave face, spoke from a prepared script, and said, implausibly, that all was well. A former leader expressed a similar self-protective sentiment, that s/he,

"Hunkered down ... I want the fuckers to know that they'd got to me."

While one other defeated MP showed no aversion to their constituency, s/he had avoided the Commons, both to avoid former colleagues and the place itself,

"If you're in that place, you want to be there in own right. I don't want to be there as a tourist."

S/he thought it was partly about pride but more,

"I think it looks sad. I do think it looks sad. Ex-MPs clinging on to an ex-existence, I think, looks sad."

Only one was happy to return both to the constituency—the only place where s/he felt safe—and the Commons; it may be significant this was the only former MP determined to get re-selected.

Former council leaders cannot get away from the area in the same way, living only as they virtually always do in the local authority area, and often in the ward, that they represent. But even so, one defeated leader avoided going back to County Hall some distance away, for many months. At every election, s/he had emptied her/his office in order to avoid having to do so with a new incumbent waiting on the doorstep. Rather than meet with the Chief Executive immediately post election at County Hall, they had instead met elsewhere. But this meant that s/he had never been able to say goodbye to those with whom s/he had worked, fellow councillors who had been re-elected and officers including secretarial staff in the Leader's Office. S/he felt that now with no role, it would have been somehow inappropriate and awkward. S/he recalled how previously defeated councillors had sometimes come back to eat at County Hall and,

"Sit at a table and sort of pretend."

This former leader was having none of that. Nevertheless, not having been able to say goodbye was a source of profound regret, an important marker of transition that had not been possible.

Remaining in the area, still being known, brings constant reminders of what once was. A partner of a former leader described how,

"People still knock and ring and put things through the letter-box. The bottom line is as much as s/he might have wanted to walk away and think 'Sod the lot of you', s/he can't ... walk away ... it's an affliction in some ways ... you get recognised wherever you go, then you can't turn off. It's very difficult to turn off. You'd have to entirely move away to detach yourself from that."

None of the defeated MPs or council leaders in my study had been appointed to the Lords, although one interviewee had declined the pre-election offer of a peerage, in retrospect with some regret.

In essence, there appeared to be nothing systematic in place for MPs or council leaders who had lost their seats. Their job, their role, their identity, their social networks and their status disappeared overnight. A defeated MP summed it up,

"I don't think our establishment, our structures, our politics take any kind of notice or give enough support to people who are going to lose their seats or do lose their seats ... I just worry what kind of politics we are creating. We're creating a politics for the rich run by the rich ... It's becoming harder and harder and why would people take those kinds of risks with their lives?"

I consider one important element of leaving political office, especially in the aftermath of defeat—being acknowledged and marking the transition—in the next chapter.

CHAPTER 8

Being Acknowledged and Marking the Transition

"There Was No Acknowledgement from the Party at All ... Nothing"

Following an electoral defeat or a decision to stand down, there appears to be nothing systematic on the part of any of the three parties in terms of formal communication from the national party—a party leader, chair, local government spokesperson or party group leader in the Local Government Association. Candidates who are defeated at an election all lose at the same time, and hence it would be relatively straightforward for political parties to communicate effectively with them, although it is the case that extra staff hired for an election campaign are immediately let go once the election is over. It was not the courtesies alone that mattered, but rather that there had been some acknowledgement of the contribution that former MPs and leaders had made over, in some cases, decades; a sense that their work had mattered and been of value.

We saw in Chap. 3 how former Prime Minister and Conservative Party leader, John Major, had recognised, albeit somewhat late, how important it was to write letters to his former MPs after the 1992 General Election. But in this study, only a few interviewees, both leaders and MPs, had some communication from party leaders but only in two cases was this timely, personalised and experienced as helpful. In one case, a party leader had rung a defeated leader immediately post election and then again six weeks later, aware that a few weeks on might well have been a more difficult time. The thoughtfulness of this communication was highly appreciated.

J. Roberts, *Losing Political Office*,
DOI 10.1007/978-3-319-39702-3_8

On the other hand, a senior frontbench MP also rang this former leader, but he had not been briefed properly, wrongly thinking that s/he was still a councillor—an unfortunate but inflammatory mistake.

Often, however, there was nothing from the national party or party leader. For many of those who did hear from the party, it was experienced as too late, too insensitive and often both. One former MP, for example, felt offended that s/he had been sent key speeches from the General Election in which s/he had just been defeated. For most, the lack of personal communication was a source of considerable resentment, that after all their assiduous work over the years and a draining, exhausting election campaign, they had suddenly become invisible in the eyes of the national party. If the electorate was experienced as ungrateful, the national parties were experienced as more so. Even worse, especially for former council leaders, the national party might have had the major responsibility for their defeat, yet still not a word, even from a local government portfolio holder. Most felt abandoned by the party leadership, dropped from a very great height.

On the other hand, one former MP had a different view,

"When you're down on the dumps, you're quite cynical about it all and the last thing you need is a letter … and you were there yourself – you wrote the letters yourself to people that had lost in previous elections."

But even so, s/he went on to add,

"And okay, you get some nice, heart-felt ones as well, written in hand that aren't kind of like circulars."

This former MP gave the impression of having felt spurred on to frenetic activity to find alternative employment to support a family and,

"Relentlessly focused on not letting things fall apart financially – defeat doesn't buy you time."

The idea of spending precious time, *"sitting there feeling sorry for yourself reading letters about 'Oh, poor you' or be thinking, 'Poor me'"* and especially having people feeling sorry for her/him was an anathema.

For others, however, receiving appreciative letters, especially from former constituents and colleagues, had been very helpful—a reminder that they had been valued. One commented,

"People say sweet things and that does actually help. It's like a sort of bereavement, you know, when people write. It's rather kind to suddenly feel that you did leave behind some reputation somewhere that is appreciated."

This former MP had been deeply hurt by the lack of communication from the party leader. For another who had found defeat very difficult to adjust to, the support from those who had written was described by her/ his partner as very significant and important. For another, her/his partner remembered the postman staggering up to their home with many hundreds of positive letters following the loss of office from

"Really unexpected people ... it was very, very touching actually and made quite a difference."

One former leader who had stood down, but in contentious circumstances, was contemptuous of the national party,

"There was no acknowledgement from the party at all – not even a letter or an e mail. Nothing, which did hurt and looking back on it, I think that's outrageous."

Fellow leaders in the area and constituents, on the other hand, had been immensely supportive, a source of comfort in very turbulent times.

Another former leader described how insulting s/he had found the tone of the standardised letter that she and other defeated former councillors promptly received from the council, tersely asking for the return of identity card, phone and computer following their "resignation." No word of thanks for the work done, no acknowledgement of the possible shock of defeat. S/he had had no idea such *"horrendous"* letters had been sent previously and described her/his intense shame that letters of such an insensitive nature could have gone out under her/his leadership. S/he saw to it that was changed for the future, a last act of influence.

For those who chose to stand down, perhaps after considerable agonising, messages and communication from others are just as important in order for the work that they have done to be acknowledged. One former MP was more dispassionate,

"One of my axioms about it all was that if you ever expected anything from anyone, you were certain to end up disappointed, but if you expected nothing, you would be pleasantly surprised."

But few politicians are quite so detached, and recognition of the work that they have done, often over many years, and at some sacrifice to family life, is very important. Another former leader who admitted that s/ he had never sent letters to any others who had lost office previously was pleasantly surprised to have received tens of communications from a wide range of people (including the party leader) regretting her/his departure. Despite having not given before much thought to the transition from office assuming that s/he would *"just cease to be in office and that would be that,"* s/he had kept all these letters and acknowledged their importance.

A partner lamented how *"completely dead"* the party had been post defeat in terms of its former MPs but how much it had been appreciated that some people had written,

"It was really important that people bothered to write."

One other former MP who had given long notice of her/his intention to stand down primarily because of family factors at a time when there were significant boundary changes did not have an easy parting of ways with the local party. S/he attributed this to the party's disappointment that s/he had chosen not to contest the election, a sense that s/he had abandoned them, despite many years of hard work and dedicated service to the constituency. Resonating with the observation discussed earlier in Chap. 2 that elected politicians are in office not just as individuals but as part of a relationship with the electorate, the partner thoughtfully reflected on how,

"You become public property as an MP and in some ways, how dare you step away once all these people have put so much of their lives to putting you where you are."

S/he acknowledged a feeling of anger on the part of the local party at her partner going,

"So gratitude was about as far away from what they were feeling as you could possibly get."

The relationship between MPs and their constituencies is a complicated business.

"It Was Like a Bereavement … But There Was No Funeral"

Many former MPs and leaders in this study who had stood down had some sort of event that had marked their stepping down, but in only one case had this been organised and planned consciously as a rite of passage.

There was nothing from national political parties to recognise the contribution of MPs; it was people locally who stepped up to the plate both for some former MPs and council leaders. When they did, it was very much appreciated, whether a farewell party, a lunch or dinner in their name, Freedom of the Borough, a national honour or an honorary degree. In a number of cases, however, nothing of this sort had been organised and even if the former politician had received many individual messages of support, it is not quite the same as a specific event to acknowledge their contribution and mark their transition from office. All of the interviewees in this study, whether they had been defeated or had stood down, had worked incredibly hard on behalf of their constituents, often for many years and to the detriment of their families. That their contribution should simply be recognised was very important for virtually all participants.

For those who are no longer in office, the political juggernaut moves on rapidly. For a few defeated MPs and council leaders, there was an immediate, ironically named, in one instance, *"victory party"* or for another, *"a party/wake,"* but it was all too soon. For one former MP,

"The local party had a little social to thank people for working on the election and it was so soon afterwards that actually I was still fine. I was in kind of relief mode still ..."

Or for another, 36–48 hours after defeat,

"When you've just lost, you have to go to your victory party where you've got 150 to 200 people from your local party there and you have to make another speech and you have to lift them all and you can't be in tears."

But these are gatherings to thank party workers, not unreasonably, in the aftermath of an election, when emotions may still be high and the adrenaline coursing. But for defeated former MPs and leaders, there is often no opportunity later for their work to be acknowledged: their contribution and hard work recognised; no rite of passage. As the spouse of another former MP commented acerbically and understandably,

"We gave a party, they didn't."

In this case, a leading local player insisted on taking the former MP out to dinner, a gesture that was much appreciated.

Few former defeated MPs or leaders were able to mark their transition from office. Just one former leader, unexpectedly defeated, was given a surprise party, attended by local MPs, where s/he was presented with thoughtful gifts related to her/his period in office. This former leader went on to manage the transition from office remarkably smoothly, although a number of other factors are likely to have been significant.

For other former defeated politicians, nothing of the sort took place,

"It was just sort of, you were gone ..."

I was told however that a reception had been held for former Conservative MPs at Number 10 Downing Street after the 2010 election.

Despite that fact that one former leader had met with other defeated colleagues soon after the election, all to lick their wounds, there had been no formal way in which they had been able to acknowledge, and have acknowledged, the work, contribution and camaraderie of so many over the years. It was memorably put,

"It was like a bereavement, and it was, but there was no funeral."

S/he was clear that a specific ritual of some sort would have been immensely helpful. S/he had maintained close relationships with former colleagues and, prior to defeat, s/he had been appointed to a prestigious role that would remain as a testament to her/his contribution as council leader.

For council leaders who lose their seat, it is likely that the local authority will have changed political control, making it more difficult for the council rather than the political party to hold an event to mark their time in office. It should be remembered that the position of leader is a *council*, not a political party, position, and it is perfectly proper—and arguably beneficial—for such an inexpensive event to be held.

One former MP who had stood down, albeit with some ambivalence at the time, reflected thoughtfully on how helpful the award of an honorary degree and the ceremony that went with it had been,

"The point I'm making is that the weekend of this honorary doctorate was a real rite of passage for me, and it actually marked the end. It was difficult. Apart from the day when I made the decision to stand down and then the day of the election, this was actually the ceremony. This said, "That's it, so thank you actually," and it was the only sort of proper thank you that I got was the honorary doctorate, but it was the end of everything."

"Well, We'll Get Through It Together"

Coming together with others in a similar position was important for many who had stood down or who had been defeated, echoing Ebaugh's (1988) recognition of the protection afforded by a group exit, referred to in Chap. 3. There is something about coming together with others who have shared similar—perhaps bruising—experiences, a bond with others that can be very powerful. This may have been an informal grouping as, for example, for one former leader with others who had been de-selected in the area,

"So we've got a de-selection group, haven't we I suppose, I've never looked at it that way, but we are, aren't we?"

Another maintained close contact with others who had been defeated, averring that,

"Well, we'll get through it together."

Two other former leaders had had no opportunity either for their time in office to be marked, or to meet up with others in a similar predicament, although one had talked on the telephone soon after the election with other defeated leaders of the same political party, *"an exclusive group."*

One, an intensely private person, had hardly talked to anyone about her/his own distress. Instead, s/he had sought to check out how former backbench councillors from the authority were faring after defeat, carrying on a protective role,

"I set myself up as a little shop steward of the losers."

This was laudable but seemed to be at some expense to her/himself. Both these leaders seemed isolated, and they had struggled in the period following electoral defeat.

There is, of course, only one council leader in any one authority so that in their locality, leaders are very much on their own when they leave office. They are often standing down—for personal or political reasons—at a time when no other council leader is leaving office, and they may therefore feel even more isolated in the decision that they have made. If defeated, there is no mechanism for such former council leaders to share their experiences of leaving office.

MPs have some formal mechanisms for coming together. The Association of Former Members of Parliament (AFMP) was set up in 2004, and it has members from all political parties, including many of the former MPs in this study. It represents the interests of its members, holds events and links with other parliamentarians across the world. It is seeking to make the experience of former MPs more widely available as will be discussed in Chap. 13.

Former Labour MPs can also attend gatherings of the Parliamentary Labour Party (PLP)-in-exile, set up a year or so after the 2010 General Election. The PLP-in-exile does not include former MPs who have gone to the House of Lords in recognition that they have a very different status and perhaps that the Lords can be seen as a club itself. The group seemed to be much welcomed by a number of my interviewees but given a wide berth by one or two others. One former MP reflected that even at the PLP-in-exile,

"We don't spend a lot of time talking about the past. We do in terms of the politics of it, but not in terms of feelings and experience, no. I think there's sort of a common understanding that we've all been through something rather horrible as well as something brilliant."

There was a suggestion that it was only possible for some to go along to one of these gatherings once they had felt less vulnerable, had begun to find their feet and had a new role. One former MP admitted that when s/he had gone to her/his first meeting of the PLP-in-exile, it was *"fantastic,"* but by that time s/he had,

"Begun to find my feet by then ... I had a role, I had an identity."

S/he admitted that s/he might not have gone to a meeting of the group otherwise. For one other, according to her/his partner, attending a PLP-in-exile meeting would be tantamount to acknowledging that s/he would never again be re-elected, an unbearable thought.

Coming together with others who have been through similar experiences does not suit everyone. Some had kept well away from any association with former colleagues, determined to embark as soon as possible on a new chapter of their lives and not look back—more possible with strong family and social support. Some others, at the other end of the spectrum, hung back from such encounters because they did not feel in a robust enough state to do so.

Let us not forget that acknowledgement, affirmation, rites of passage and coming together in solidarity are fundamental human needs. Even exulted former heads of state have the Madrid Club, a group of 95 members of former presidents and prime ministers, created to promote democracy and change internationally. I would be surprised if it did not also serve a more personal need for those who had once strode the world stage.

References

Ebaugh, H.R.F. (1988). *Becoming an Ex.* Chicago: The University of Chicago Press.

CHAPTER 9

After Office: The Longer Term

How did individuals fare in the longer term following loss of office, whether they had stood down or had been defeated?

Over the course of the following year or two since the loss of office, the experience of former leaders and MPs varied. There was some predictable difference between those who were defeated and those who had stood down—with many of those who had stood down faring better than those who had lost—but certainly not in all cases, and it was far more nuanced than this simple binary distinction.

It might have been expected that age would have been be a factor in how former politicians experienced their transition from office given that for older politicians, their contemporaries in other occupations might well have been contemplating retirement and therefore that they might have adjusted better to the loss of office. In this small sample, this appeared not to be the case. There were certainly more anxieties about financial imperatives for younger former politicians, especially if they had a young family to support. But emotional adjustment was a different matter. Of course, the older politicians who had lost office were likely to have had been in office for longer.

While former MPs had much more polarised views about their experience of being a Member of Parliament, inevitably affecting their subsequent course, all the former leaders were unequivocally positive about their experience of council leadership. Many described how they might not have originally envisaged that they would have been elected leader

© The Author(s) 2017

J. Roberts, *Losing Political Office*,

DOI 10.1007/978-3-319-39702-3_9

but once they had been, the role had far exceeded their expectations. All therefore were very nostalgic about their time in office.

How Did Former Council Leaders Fare?

It was a mixed picture for former council leaders emotionally and, for some, financially, whether they had stood down or had been defeated. Those who had struggled most had been defeated at the hands of either the electorate or the selectorate. On the other hand, two others who had been defeated had seemed to adjust far more easily than at least one other who had stood down. For those who had to newly find paid work, it was often a struggle and two years on, a couple still were looking for employment.

With the higher allowances that council leaders now mostly receive, it may be possible not to have other paid work but there is no redundancy pay, no continuing pay of any sort to cushion their fall. On defeat, they may suddenly have no income whatsoever. They are suddenly out from one day to the next.

This sudden drop is not widely understood by the general public or even by many who are generally politically knowledgeable. There may be an assumption that council leaders, as politicians generally, are well paid, have handsome pensions, and perhaps, however unfairly, feather their own nests.

The theme of missing friendships and the camaraderie from their time as an elected politician came out much more strongly from former council leaders than from MPs: all but one of all the leaders interviewed volunteered how important the party group, other colleagues and wider social networks had been. With party colleagues, one reminisced how,

"The thing that brings you together is that political belief and understanding and, you know, I'd look at my group and I'd think, 'For all our faults, I'd far rather be with you. I want to be on your side'."

Another talked wistfully of staff within the authority whom s/he missed,

"The people and the contact virtually on a daily basis with lots of different people … all that wonderful group of people who made my life such joy."

It was often something about the wide range of different people that a council leader encounters on a daily basis that was greatly missed. Only one former leader had a different view that,

"Politics is a game you play on your own."

S/he had little time now for former party colleagues, perspicaciously instead commenting,

"My preference now is to feed and water all those friendships which I sort of neglected while I was in power rather than to cultivate the political network because I have a feeling that my friends will still be my friends even when the political network's forgotten all about me."

Whether having been defeated or having stood down, there was a hint from this very small study that female former leaders had fared better than their male counterparts: they had sources of identity other than as council leader to draw on following their loss of office. But with such small numbers, it is not possible to be confident about such a distinction.

COUNCIL LEADERS WHO HAD STOOD DOWN

Given the overwhelmingly positive experience of council leadership, even those who had stood down from the role acknowledged that it had been a major life transition. While the immediate lack of income was a consideration, it was much more: the sudden emptiness; the cessation of the ability to influence; no longer making decisions that had influence; the absence of relentless challenge; and often the disappearance of meaningful social relationships.

One former leader of approximate retirement age, had chosen when to step down with care after a lengthy tenure, but had made no plans for the future beforehand. S/he declared that s/he was glad to have finished and that it had been the right time to leave the leadership. Nevertheless, s/he had been through a significant period of anxiety, depression and low self-esteem. The spouse reported how worried s/he had been about her/his partner's bleak mood and negativity and her/his increasing dependency, s/he *"was just lost for a while."*

The former politician had been left with a void, nothing to fill the day, and had asked,

"What's my purpose?" "What am I here for?" "What am I going to do?"

The spouse thought that the experience had been much more difficult than expected,

"It was much bigger than had been expected … it hit very hard having this gaping length of time ahead."

Although the former politician described her/himself as a pragmatist and someone who had no time for regrets, there was a wistful quality to some of her/his musings. S/he missed,

"Those confidences that you know and knowledge is a power kind of thing."

Things had begun to improve after a few months as s/he had started to build some structure into the day—making sure that any activity was entered into the diary—but it had been a worrying struggle. S/he missed seeing the range of people that once s/he did,

"Yeah, seeing people. I miss seeing as many people on a regular basis."

There had been external recognition of the former leader's contribution to the area and some invitations locally in an elder statesman-type role, boosting self-esteem. S/he was nevertheless subsequently contemplating standing again as a councillor with some thoughts of regret at having severed her/his links so completely as the experience of leaving was as if,

"Dropping off the cliff … the intellectual and emotional abruptness."

Illness had intervened immediately on stepping down, tempering the experience at the time but later, feelings pulling her/him back towards office mounted.

Another, with other paid remuneration, had been less troubled by the loss of income and the loss of political office per se. There had been some anxiety about a future prospect of not having days full of activity, but on the other hand, s/he welcomed that there was now some space in the day for friendships that s/he had hitherto partially ignored. S/he had deliberately planned a very long trip abroad that had helped. S/he had not yet decided what new direction that s/he was going to follow. S/he was mildly curious to discover that s/he had not yet been very motivated to,

"Get off my bum and do anything about it … these things don't happen unless you do seek them out."

Despite the wealth of experience that this former leader had accumulated in different sectors, s/he thought that what people wanted was less the expertise but the contacts and the influence that came with the role of council leader—but that these fell away on exiting that role. S/he recognised the importance of context: that in the big city where s/he had been leader, s/he felt more of a pressure to be doing something different, still to be a "somebody." S/he quoted a colleague who had acknowledged that it was,

"The feeling of being nobody in particular that was bothering."

Away from the city, the feeling of being a "nobody" was much less insistent. Perhaps unsurprisingly, this former leader spent considerable time travelling abroad, both for work and for leisure where those nagging feelings diminished. But generally life was,

"More relaxed, more thoughtful, more time. Things that are important I have time to do … rather than being under the gun all the time."

Just the one older former leader had moved into formal retirement entirely contently and s/he had had more time to plan the transition with care. Even now, s/he was occasionally called upon, as an honorary alderman to deputise for the mayor, and retained both contact and some influence with the authority's longer standing officers.

COUNCIL LEADERS WHO HAD BEEN DEFEATED

There was a very wide range of experience even within this small group.

Two defeated former leaders, despite their initial devastation and the narrow margin of their defeat, had struggled less in the longer term since they had lost office. Both had strong wider family support that they described as having been crucial.

One had been devastated and deeply hurt by electoral defeat. S/he had, ironically, given considerable thought previously about when and how to leave elected office, but still had not been able to shape the ending. But as one of life's optimists, s/he had, after a period of devastation, been able successfully to move on. According to a family member, there was a point at which s/he was able to acknowledge that there would be other jobs and other ways in which s/he could make a difference, and it was then that s/he felt better about what had happened. S/he felt fortunate to have been appointed, very soon after the electoral defeat, to chair a local public sector body, at the time going through considerable challenge. The timing had been perfect. The role was also a source of a modest income, an important consideration with the sudden loss of allowance. Other local and regional mostly non-executive roles had followed and now, s/he felt that life was on more of an even keel. S/he had a better work–life balance, with more time for family commitments than when s/he had been leader. S/he was mindful however,

"Of the capacity to make a difference and to influence that you've lost."
S/he missed too the social aspects: at events,
"We were hosting as a council, then you'd always got friends around you."
S/he still regretted not having had the chance to say goodbye to all the people s/he had worked with over so many years. Nevertheless, s/he had moved on and found alternative satisfying roles. S/he was, furthermore, all too aware of the heightened financial challenges facing local authorities since her/his defeat and how difficult it would have been had s/he still been leader either of the council or the opposition. Opposition is a very different skill and, for this former leader at least, much less appetising.

Other former leaders echoed their good fortune to have led a council during more expansionary times than was currently the case.

Her/his daughter more readily acknowledged anger about her parent's defeat. She was angry at the ingratitude of the electorate after all the hard work her parent had done for the local community and to some extent at the party hierarchy. As she pointed out, her parent had lost her/his job but the party leader had kept his seat and still had his job. She described more vividly her parent's initial reaction to the loss of the seat,

"It just finishes, it just stops. There's not even that gradual, you know, if you retire from a job you've got that time to wind down and tie up all the loose ends ... one day you're in the office and you don't go back and what do you do everyday?"

Another leader who lost—and only by a whisker—at the ballot box had been initially devastated, but s/he had come to terms with the defeat remarkably quickly. Her/his spouse reported, however, that s/he had been numb in the immediate days after the electoral loss. S/he too seemed very optimistic in personality. S/he had come to realise how much stress the leadership had involved, the consequent effect of her/his health and how little time s/he had had for family. The big plus had been more time for family, partner, children and parents. Although this former leader had always had many interests outside politics that came to sustain her/him, the sudden loss of structure following electoral defeat was unnerving. S/he had soon found another party political role locally, thereby retaining political influence albeit on a smaller stage, in addition to a host of other sporting, community and family activities. It was the relationships that s/he had formed while leader that s/he missed most: the camaraderie with those with whom s/he had worked at the authority's offices and the interaction with groups of constituents.

S/he revealed a complex mix of emotions: optimism, determined positivity but also a lingering sense of failure; as someone who had never failed in anything before, s/he had always been fearful to attempt anything at which s/he might fail. She acknowledged, therefore, that an electoral contest was an inherently risky, high stakes act. S/he had been somewhat surprised and reassured that the actual experience of failure had not been quite as catastrophic as s/he had imagined. This itself had helped her/him to move on. S/he remained, however, hurt and very frustrated by how little use had been made of her/his skills since (considered more later in this chapter).

For two other former leaders, the experience of having been defeated had been much more devastating in the longer term. Although one had strong support from a partner, neither had much wider family support. For one, it was the loss of purpose that had been so difficult to come to terms with. The experience of the transition from having been a council leader with a bulging, impossible diary full of meetings and events, and nights spent reading and emailing into the small hours, overnight to nothing had been dreadful. S/he had thrown enormous energy, time and commitment into the role. Life for both her/him and partner had entirely revolved around the leadership, and the loss of office had led to a profound change in both their lives.

For this former leader, the role had been akin to ordination: the sense that this was what s/he had been meant to do with her/his life. It was very much wrapped up in her/his sense of identity,

"This is who I am, this is what I do. This is what gets me out of bed in the morning."

Without that sense of purpose, later months had been a hard struggle. Her/his experience had been that it had been difficult to gain employment despite having a well-regarded degree and having had a wide-ranging career previously. Having been a council leader had been seen as bringing unhelpful baggage. Her/his confidence had been shattered. By the end of the year, the effects on her/his health were evident,

"I'm a wreck. I'm unemployable."

The year following the election had been spent looking for jobs, spending as little money as possible. The last allowance payment had been just two days after the election count. Finances were a big issue and s/he had to rely on her/his partner to be the breadwinner, an unfamiliar situation, and one that inevitably changed the dynamic of the relationship. S/he much missed the buzz,

"The sense of you knew things before it appeared in the paper and there was always something going on …Yeah, I do like being out and about and meeting people."

S/he had become depressed, lacked motivation, and had found it very difficult to let go. S/he had held firmly on to documentation associated with the leadership, a manifestation of difficulties of letting go emotionally. Her/his partner was sympathetic and understood that in the circumstances,

"You'd question your own value, your skills and your abilities and the more jobs you apply for and the more knockbacks you get, it's very hard not to think, 'Well, maybe I am rubbish and not very good. I don't have the skills and abilities that people value and want to utilise.'"

S/he was initially reluctant to acknowledge any anger but then came to admit that there was indeed considerable anger directed towards the national party by whom s/he had felt abandoned. Her/his partner was much more forthright about how devastating the consequences had been of unexpected electoral defeat, and s/he expressed profound bitterness at how little attempt had been made to reach out to those who had lost. Her/his identity had, in the view of the partner, been almost entirely tied up in the role of leader. S/he still felt humiliated by the defeat well over a year later, described by the partner as a self-perception rather than concerns about what others might think. Finding paid work, despite good qualifications and a previous career, was a huge struggle,

"Being a leader means you are very good generalist and that's just the sort of job that companies are doing without at the moment."

To her/his immense frustration, s/he had been told by one of the organisations that s/he had applied to that she was *"vastly over-qualified"* and that in the view of another,

"'Oh, he's got too much experience and itchy feet'. Getting interviews is really difficult because you don't fit into particular boxes and then it's 'Sorry.'"

Nor were there many non-executive positions available to apply for. To rub salt in the wound, a number of quangos had been abolished by the same government as had, in her/his view, been responsible for the local defeat. On reflection, s/he wished that s/he had completed an additional professional qualification as restrictions on qualifications had been imposed in her/his previous professional role since her/his time away.

Her/his partner shared the anger,

"When you've sacrificed a lot, a career, to then have that happen to you and to get no recognition or apology or anything is unforgiveable really and that's where a lot of the lingering, continuing anger stems from."

Another defeated leader who had poured huge energy into the role had been through a period of depression some months after the election. S/he had initially not felt too bad,

"I didn't have a down time for quite a while. I end up getting a bit down when I struggle to find work."

But later,

"One really, really bad month, I locked myself away for a week. I didn't go out. I just didn't go out, I locked myself away."

S/he had managed to muddle through this time but s/he acutely missed the ability to shape events, and the intensity of the relationships with the close-knit group of councillors. They had been an effective team certainly but more a family. What had hurt most was a request from the new leader that s/he not attend a subsequent election count, despite the fact that s/he remained politically active in the party. The notion that s/he was seen as damaged goods was difficult to accept. This former leader had always been present at electoral counts, never distant. But on this occasion, s/he had been consigned to watching it on television, alone except for a bottle of whisky, feeling utterly betrayed.

My impression was of an intensely private person, very protective of others, but less so of her/himself. S/he described her/himself as very optimistic about life although s/he had experienced some periods of low mood in the past. There had not been anyone in whom s/he could have confided and this interview had been virtually the only time that s/he had talked about the experience of what had happened. S/he had found it very difficult to access the course that s/he had wanted to do or to find work, a source of immense and understandable frustration. Savings had been run down and s/he had to live off credit for a while. S/he had picked up bits and pieces of work but clearly nothing satisfying in the longer term, nor very financially rewarding. The time since the election as described as *"a mess."*

Another former leader in the defeated group had had a shorter period as leader but longer as a councillor. S/he had been able to secure a job initially, but only on a fixed term contract. Living in an area of high unemployment, s/he had not been able to obtain continuing employment subsequently. This had been a time of enormous financial and emotional stress for her/him and the family in addition to coping with the bitterness of the betrayal by the local party. There had, of necessity, been more time for family, much welcomed, and some continuing involvement and influence in local community matters. S/he had later started a small local enterprise, a far cry from politics, which was a focus for additional activity. But it had been an exquisitely difficult period for a couple of years or so, before more recently both s/he and her/his partner had felt that they had *"got life back."* S/he could acknowledge, despite the difficult circumstances of her/his loss of office, that s/he missed meeting a wide range of people, both locally and across the country and,

"Knowing what's happening … you don't know the ins and outs of things … I think there is a frustration there that I'm no longer leader."

For those former council leaders who had been defeated, asking about any previous plans they might have had for planning their succession might have felt somewhat hollow. It is important to understand that going into what might be a hard fought electoral campaign requires knuckling down and concentrating ruthlessly on what needs to be done in order to win, and often not allowing thoughts of personal or party defeat to get in the way of their determination. Justifiably therefore, any thoughts council leaders might have had about planning for their succession would have been low down on their priority list.

Nevertheless, one had former leader had previously, relatively early in office, given some thought about the need for succession planning. S/he had thought that s/he would probably step down after four years because,

"I think you become too blasé and you just expect … I think you can be in a position of authority for too long … you start to think it's a god-given right to be there and I think if you were to get a challenge, you'd find it difficult to face up to that challenge."

In the same vein, another commented,

"You can maintain the momentum for only so many years and then you just become part of the machinery and you're not delivering anything new. It's very reactionary, very defensive."

Neither former leader was able to put their plans for limiting their term in office to the test.

WHAT HAPPENS TO COUNCIL LEADERS' SKILLS ACQUIRED IN OFFICE?

Council leaders, like MPs, accrue a wide range of knowledge and skills in their leadership position. A unitary authority will, after all, be responsible for around 700 different functions across a wide span and the complexity of the role of the leader of the council being at the interface of the many different actors on the local, regional and often national stage is not to be underestimated. Clarity of leadership and skills in communication with a wide range of players, relationship building, decision-making, priority setting, policy analysis and governance are just some of the attributes needed by effective council leaders. A number of former leaders commented that they had learned other specific and more nuanced skills, for example,

"You don't always have to decide. Sometimes in business people say, 'Well do you want to buy this or not?' whatever it is, and they're putting a case to your organisation. In politics sometimes you can say, 'Hmmm, okay, that's

*interesting, I'll tuck that away and I'll think about that'. In business ...
it's always binary, whereas in politics there's another way ... so you hold the
uncertainty until that moment arises.*"

Not dissimilarly, another reflected,

*"I used to be a lot more black and white than I am now. Politics is about
shades of grey, not absolutes."*

Another talked of how learning effectively to deal with different organisations across private, public and charitable sectors was,

*"Almost like being bilingual or trilingual in seeing each organisation's
strengths and weaknesses."*

Despite this wealth of learning, however, former council leaders' skills
were rarely made use of. A few were school governors, a couple had been
appointed as Deputy Lord Lieutenants, one had successfully applied to
chair a local health trust and another working was part-time in a different capacity for the party. But hardly any had been approached by their
political party, local government institutions or local stakeholders to share
their experiences. This was a source of considerable frustration to many.
Instead,

*"Nobody seems to want to know you after and you just like fade away ...
perhaps they tried to contact me on the old council e mail system which you lose
on the Sunday anyway ... I really don't know because there are those skills that
could be used to encourage other people."*

S/he felt strongly that s/he had much still to contribute to encourage
those coming on behind. Given the amount of training that s/he herself
had benefited from, it was a foolish waste of resource not to capitalise on
such a potential contribution. S/he, like others, had not been asked, for
example, to mentor other less experienced council leaders.

Another, with an impressive range of experience not only as council
leader but also in senior positions in other sectors, wistfully reflected on
the contribution that s/he potentially could make,

*"I would love to be able to be in a position to contribute experience of the
political world to people who don't really understand the political world. That
would I think be a valuable contribution be it by teaching, writing, whatever
... To businesses that deal with politicians, everybody from property developers
to major infrastructure suppliers ... people know very little about how politically led organisations behave differently from others."*

None was engaged in any programme to promote public understanding about politics, local government or governance more widely.

How Did Former MPs Fare in the Longer Term?

The experience of former MPs was mixed and divided more obviously into those who had chosen to stand down and those who had been defeated but nevertheless still not neatly. All those who had been defeated in this study had unequivocally enjoyed being an MP although that they had enjoyed different aspects of the role. Those who had stood down varied more in their views about the experience of having been an MP and hence had fared starkly differently since.

Whether they had stood down or had been defeated, all had had to deal with crafting a new role and identity for themselves. One reflected,

"It feels a bit like being 22 and sort of thinking, 'What shall I do with my life?' But on the other hand, you're not taking anonymous tiny little footsteps; you're taking sort of semi-public, big footsteps. So the experimentation is a bit harder and it's sort of a big change to your identity, both how you think about yourself and how other people perceive you."

A number of former MPs had turned to writing in different forms, both to set the record straight or to draw on their experience in Parliament and government to inform future policy. While it was undoubtedly cathartic for a couple, writing in whatever form is a means by which people come to reflect on what has been, what might have been and what might still be—a reflective space.

MPs Who Had Stood Down

Of my interviewees in this group, two had stood down under some pressure, either personal and/or political, and five had come to their decision entirely of their own accord without there having been any external pressure. Within the latter sub-group, three had found the job of an MP uncongenial personally or, at the very least, unsatisfactory politically; one was keen to do other things with her/his life; and another had very much relished the role but had reflected long and hard on when might be the best time to bow out.

One who had *"enjoyed every minute of time"* as an MP had nevertheless decided to stand down. The expenses issue raised its head here too such that this former MP had been seen as damaged goods, although it turned out that s/he was blameless. The context of having been unjustly pilloried in the media inevitably influenced her/his course following standing down from elected office, with a specific project to set the record straight.

Although s/he had always previously sought to separate politics from emotions and think about the transition from being an MP in a wholly rational manner, made easier by how hard s/he had worked—*"Eight or nine days a week … I was a moving bus before"*—s/he could admit now that this pattern had left little room for emotions. Having more time subsequently had allowed her/him to reflect more and to make significant changes in her/his life.

Looking back, this former MP thought that her/his decision to stand down had been correct but still not an easy one. Having publicly announced s/he was standing down some months in advance of the election, there had been an opportunity to consolidate contacts in order to set up a business consultancy later. There had been many positives including fewer obligations,

"I don't have to be anywhere if I don't want to be there."

S/he was more in charge of the working day having set up the business; no major financial anxieties; and a number of changes in family relationships. S/he had come to realise the damage that such immensely long hours, especially with the nature of her/his former constituency, had done to members of the family.

What was needed now was a new chapter in life, both working and personal. It was a time when s/he could be more in control of any commitments entered into. And this included no longer being active in the party that s/he had represented in Parliament, having felt somewhat let down by the party in its reaction to expenses,

"I don't want to be part of the structure of it … I've never really thought about this but I suppose there's an element of feeling a little bit let down by it and there's an element of going backwards as well."

This was not an uncommon reaction in this study: a number of former MPs and leaders whose working lives had previously been consumed by party political work now had virtually nothing to do with the party of which they had been a long-standing and loyal member.

This former MP conveyed a sense to me of having started on a new journey that had involved more emotional turbulence than s/he had bargained for, but nevertheless with some optimism. S/he recognised that,

"There's lots of senses of endings in my life in the last couple of years and the things that have started haven't yet filled on the spaces."

Nevertheless, the transition from political office had been enormously helped by the acknowledgement and the ritual provided by the award of an honorary degree.

In the new chapter of this former MP's life, s/he had found a new "family" from the charitable networks within which s/he was engaged, enabling a move on from the former political party "family."

One other former MP who had stood down had struggled to regain the same degree of meaningful structure and activity since. S/he was clear about the reasons for going, a combination of reasons including some personal distress, and that no other decision rationally could have been possible. Nevertheless, s/he conveyed a deep sense of frustration, longing and sadness about being out of the mainstream so completely, despite the welcome positive changes in her/his personal life.

Despite having chosen to go in good time, s/he had made little preparation for the future, nor for thinking how her/his skills could be best used. S/he felt an intense frustration at not being in a position to influence the course of events, seeing instead a lack of serious, grown-up politics,

"The worst thing is you see things happening and you think, 'God, I wouldn't half mind being able to get in there and tell them to stop being so bloody silly.'"

S/he however denied missing day-to-day politics, telling me that s/he had no desire to be back in the Commons, and s/he had been *"bored rigid"* by the tea room—all later flatly contradicted by the spouse who was adamant that s/he would not have gone unless s/he had *"had a knife held to the throat."* S/he did admit a profound ambivalence that,

"Whatever else you do after politics, it can never really compensate in a sense because politics has got this sort of gladiatorial element to it."

The real crushing disappointment had been not getting into the Cabinet, despite clear intimations of likely promotion, with speculation that a backstairs deal had been cut. This had left a lingering sense of having being unfairly excluded from higher office. The rawness and intensity of that "failure" had diminished little—the episode was described by the spouse as an *"absolute catastrophe"* following which s/he went into a period of minor depression from which s/he had never recovered, even now. Once again, this former MP had never failed in anything before.

As if to console her/himself, s/he pointed to the role of luck in politics,

"It's not merit, it's accident ... there's no point in making your whole life hinge upon being Prime Minister before the age of Pitt. You know, you've got to have a sense of perspective about it."

Unlike many others, this former MP certainly did not miss the constituency,

"The grinding tedium of surgeries ... The only thing that is worthwhile is being a minister, being a backbencher is shit and being a backbencher on the government side is the shittiest of all, quite frankly."
This was a view shared more decorously by others from different political parties. The timing of election to Parliament within the electoral cycle is a key determinant of longevity on the backbenches but not one usually under any individual candidate's control.

Given this former MP, as many others, had always wanted to go into politics even as a tiny child, it might have been expected that s/he would have found the transition from elected office very difficult. S/he was described by her/his spouse as engaged in incessant, restless physical activity that could never quite compensate. S/he was all too aware of her/his restlessness, making clear that s/he would advise any aspiring MPs,

"To have something beyond politics when you feel you've got energy to spare."
All five who chose without any constraints to go had flourished, certainly personally. A small sample, of course, but they were of different ages, gender, political party, and had experienced very different levels of seniority within the House of Commons. Only one, both within this small sub-group but also the wider group of former politicians who had stood down, had given considerable thought and attention to the transition from office, both when and how. This may, of course, have been less of an issue for those former MPs who had not taken to the role since they had been relieved simply no longer to be subject to the constraints of office. But others, who had had far more positive experiences of life as an MP or as a council leader had not given much thought either to the process of transition.

The careful thought that just one former MP and, to a lesser extent, one leader had put into planning for the transition from office and for the future had paid dividends. It had enabled them to acknowledge and mark the inevitable pain of leaving a richly enjoyed role and move on to new chapter. The former MP had gone on to have a busy, varied and challenging portfolio career post politics. There was, importantly too, more time for family, a very big plus. Leaving politics had been wholly positive for family relationships. Not that there was nothing s/he missed: the camaraderie with close colleagues and friends, and the intensity of policy discussions on key issues.

Another former MP, who stood down after a limited number of terms, demonstrated an interesting mix of detachment, dispassionate curiosity and thoughtfulness. S/he had experienced much less of a cliff edge to her/his transition. Having made what was in the end a very straightforward decision to stand down, there began a gradual transition while still elected back into a role related to her/his previous career. S/he readily admitted that luck had intervened at the right time in order for such an opportunity to be available. Unusually, the new role carried with it as much, if not more, influence in the political arena, status, and proximity to the Westminster village. S/he admitted that,

"It's completely different and it's completely the same."

It was almost as if s/he had been able to retain all the more congenial aspects of being an MP, without the more tiresome elements. This was highly unusual. No other former politician I interviewed was in such a position except the individual who had been appointed to the Lords. Unsurprisingly, the rest of the group found themselves with considerably less influence, mostly not involved in politics.

This former MP had quite enjoyed the constituency work but recognised both the increasing constraints and demands on MPs. S/he had never come into the role with high expectations; there was more a sense of curiosity about what it would be like. And s/he was very aware of how political ambition almost inevitably ends unhappily,

"Then you'll want to be in the Cabinet and then you'll be fired because everyone is fired sooner or later and then there'll be this hole you can't fill. So, I have always had a pretty solid sense of the sort of limitations of political life."

S/he was, nevertheless, pleasantly surprised at what a relief it had been to cease being a Member of Parliament, and at how positive a difference it had made to family life. S/he acknowledged that this must have meant a level of discomfort as an MP previously of which s/he had not been aware. S/he admitted just to a mere itch at no longer being in a position directly to change policy in which s/he had strong and informed views.

In contrast, another former MP had had much higher expectations of being a Member of Parliament. S/he had, however, increasingly come to dislike intensely the deeply unpleasant experience of being an MP and had thus sought well in advance of the General Election to return to her/his previous career. S/he had been able to do so without a great deal of difficulty—acknowledged to be both fortunate and unusual. It was not, however, all plain sailing. With a number of years away, s/he understandably was anxious that the loss of skills would be of such an order that s/he was no longer capable of carrying out the responsibilities of the post to the required standard. Being a parliamentarian, in this former MP's view, was very de-skilling. It had taken a good deal of persistence and application over many months to feel assured that s/he had still the ability to carry out to a sufficiently high level the professional role to which s/he had returned.

S/he had never had any doubts about the wisdom of standing down; the relief had been overwhelming. S/he had had just a few occasional tinges, missing some of the more constructive elements of the legislative process, and some of the social relationships from the Commons. And, in any case, s/he had been appointed to a commission that brought her/him into contact with the Westminster world and former colleagues. This appointment had itself been a pleasing acknowledgement of her/his contribution to the workings of Parliament.

Another was flourishing despite having initially been anxious about future employment and being able financially to manage. No doubt these anxieties had been allayed to some extent by her/his appointment to the House of Lords but membership of the Upper House had not been her/his prime focus. Rather, s/he was driven still to bring about policy change and to campaign; the Lords was therefore a useful platform. S/he was wary nonetheless of its increased political partisanship with former MPs treating the Lords as if it were the Commons,

"It's a faint echo of the Commons played out by people who either were in the Commons or want to be in the Commons but no audience ... a phantasmagoric version of the Commons."

Since stepping down as an MP, there had been more time for her/his young family and, by choice, s/he had successfully sought a number of part-time senior non-executive roles. S/he was, however, considerably less financially secure than when s/he had been an MP but nevertheless,

"Being able to concentrate on family, still run my own life and still be taken seriously is all enjoyable."

It is also perhaps a rare combination.

A former senior minister who had stood down having come over time to dislike being an MP had no regrets either. For her/him,

"It became very much you had to pay quite a big price to get to the really good stuff which was the big decisions."

Her/his quality of life now was unequivocally better with more time for family, friends, and new projects to try out, new things to pursue. Life previously had been swallowed up. Family relationships, as with others, had improved with having more time. Both s/he and one other former senior minister talked about a sense of guilt in the first year or so at not being hard at work at a weekend, or having the temerity to spend time on a leisure activity during the week.

Although employed in consultancy and with non-executive work, this former MP conveyed a sense of excitement about the still continuing uncertainty, and about what the future might hold. In the early days, s/he relished to challenge of the new,

"There was a lot of picking up new things and going, 'Oh, this is a nice toy to play with' and then putting it down again … and I think in a way that I'm still in the middle of that phase."

That the longer term was still very fluid felt a little unsettling, but not unduly so. More immediately, life was much more richly textured with a much clearer sense of individual purpose even if s/he had not yet found a job with the same major opportunities to effect change,

"I miss the big purpose of it. That's the big thing … and I miss the adrenaline of doing things to deadlines and getting things right and exciting moments and being at the heart of big decisions, definitely."

There had never been any doubt, however, that the decision to go had been right.

Looking back, s/he felt that s/he had a much better sense of perspective about the larger political picture, about what was important and what was not. S/he commented of former colleagues,

"They think they're in the Truman Show and actually no-one is watching."

Memorable words.

MPs Who Had Been Defeated

Defeated MPs, unlike council leaders, have a severance pay package: before 2015, they received a Resettlement Grant, the amount dependent on age and how long they have served, and a Winding-up Allowance. There have been changes since the start of the 2015 Parliament (see Chap. 14) and a Loss of Office Payment has now replaced the Resettlement Grant. But most MPs still nevertheless experienced a time of considerable anxiety, especially if they had a family to support financially. Loss of ministerial office may mean an even more significant drop in income, quite aside from its steeper political fall. Defeated MPs knew that they would have soon to find alternative employment and hence did not feel that they could relax and reflect on future options over the summer months. There was a frenetic, anxious, driven quality for the younger, defeated MPs. What could they do? What job could they possibly get? Would anyone want them?

One relatively youthful MP talked powerfully of how difficult it had been to come to terms with the loss of identity and structure after a number of terms in Parliament, by far the major part of her/his working life to date. S/he had no clear focus of where and what s/he wanted to do, let alone what s/he might be able to do,

"The big thing for me was the identity issue about what I was there now to do and what was my focus."

S/he felt under enormous pressure suddenly, both in terms of her/his own expectations and those of others,

"To find a new sort of hole, a new sort of place for me to be."

It was an immensely unsettling time, plagued by anxieties about what work might be possible and plagued by feeling of restlessness at home. A job was essential for financial reasons *"and for sanity reasons."* But what could s/he offer?

S/he missed the power and the influence, the ability to,

"Pick up the phone and say 'I want this done' ... the decision making ... being in the middle of the political powerhouse where you know what's going on."

S/he missed,

"My own team, I miss the people I worked with. I think that most of the MPs I speak to, what they miss is the people. They miss that sort of structure of the people they had."

It was easy to ruminate on the loss of opportunity and dwell on what might have been and,

"You think, 'well, is that it?' Will that ever happen again?"

The loss of a possible future featured strongly here as elsewhere.

Looking back, s/he thought that s/he had got quite depressed,

"I felt as if I'd had the confidence kicked out of me ... I had no kind of real sense of where I was going to go next. So I think you actually need somebody to be there and just help you manage through that because it isn't just about the job. Being an MP isn't just a job. You have to adjust every aspect of your life to it."

S/he avoided going out, avoided any engagement with people, and did not want to be asked any questions, having had,

"No sense of where I was going."

S/he acknowledged over the succeeding six months,

"Mourning, missing the job and a sense of anger and frustration and feeling humiliated and a bit ashamed."

Having had some distance over the course of the next few months, s/he later felt more able to pick her/himself up but only at the insistence of a friend, shocked at how rock bottom her/his mood had become. The friend, with experience in the field re-worked her/his curriculum vitae. The CV subsequently re-appeared in a much more positive light, filling this former MP with renewed hope and more confidence, which slowly led to an increasing number of opportunities over the course of the next year. But it had been very hard. One of the key problems s/he had found, echoed by some others (but not those who had attained senior ministerial rank), was that potential employers had no idea of what an MP (or council leader) did, what their skills were and how these might translate into another role. A number had been told that they were either over-qualified for a position, that their skills did not fit or that they may not be able to cope with being line-managed—all a source of great frustration.

Things were much better two years on, but still *"not quite there"* for this former MP, with some unfinished sorting of family life and relationships with the party, still to address.

For another relatively youthful former MP, the weeks following the electoral defeat were frenetic with activity to find another job and a source of income. A myriad of job applications resulted in only a few interviews; her/his sinking morale subsequently was hardly surprisingly. S/he was spurred on by anxiety about what might happen, compounded by hearing of how many former colleagues in the Commons were,

"Running around like mad trying to find something ... former Cabinet members who had applied for so many things and got nothing."

The determined persistence of this former MP had resulted in pieces of work within days but secure employment in a field related to politics by three or four months post-election.

S/he acknowledged how hard the first months had been, struggling between the initial devastation and worry about future insecurity on the one hand but on the other hand, trying to keep a grip on a wider perspective. The rational side pressed on,

"You have to remind yourself of some of the tough times and the difficult times you've had in your own life and that can help you through it, and you think, 'Well, actually, is that really so bad? Is this the worst thing that could have happened?'"

The role had been exhilarating, at least to begin with: s/he enjoyed so much of the work of a constituency MP, including the casework; making a difference to the local patch; and the sense of powerfulness. The bond with the constituency had been strong,

"The sense of loss is partly the kind of sense of connection you have with an area and with people and that bond is broken in some ways."

S/he could honestly recognise that s/he liked the attention and status too. But the demands of a marginal constituency are of a wholly different order from safer seats and the demands grew, on both the individual and her/his family.

S/he later came to appreciate that for all the early devastation post defeat, there were some positives to be gleaned after the long-term pressures of representing a marginal seat,

"Learning to have a different kind of life and be more relaxed has in some ways been a challenge but actually it's quite a happy challenge because as you learn to do it, you do actually realise that there is another world out there and it's quite a healthy world."

It was almost a voyage of discovery. S/he went on to describe how,

"You start to settle down and your body finds and your mind finds a sense of equilibrium and all of a sudden, there are benefits and advantages – space, weekends, opportunities to do things that you just could not do either as a Member of Parliament or as a minister. So that helps to temper things and make things easier over a period of time."

S/he had paid more attention to her/his health, as well as her/his family. But it took time. And the temptation to go back into the fray has remained. Perhaps in readiness, this former MP was consoling her/himself,

"It probably helps if I am going to do politics again, to have tasted defeat as well ... that's what I tell myself anyway."

The period of uncertainty had gone on for much longer for one other former MP who had had less of a financial imperative to find work immediately. Her/his experience of being an MP had been unambiguously positive in every respect. Losing ministerial office had been deeply galling, a first slip in a previously smooth ascent, but not at the time seen as a prelude to defeat at the hands of the electorate.

Since electoral defeat, this former MP admitted that s/he had not been doing a great deal other than moping: reading, some bits of writing, a few media appearances and meeting up with former colleagues or journalists. There was little sense of meaning and s/he found it hard to get motivated and instead, ruminated over what had gone wrong. Most of all, s/he was angry for not having worked harder in the constituency: if only s/he had been more assiduous; that was why s/he had failed. It was the sense of failure that permeated,

"Ex-MPs are like rotting fish. Failed politicians are the worst of the worst. That's what I feel and there's an unspoken feeling that the failure is conta-

gious. I don't think people say it but ... it's not de rigueur to hang about with politicians who have lost because it's a fish without gills."

Her/his partner was even more direct: s/he had become very depressed following defeat, incapable of doing anything, and had not done any meaningful activity since. S/he had had no hinterland, nothing beyond politics. It sounded bleak.

Perhaps unsurprisingly then, this former MP was determined to get back. This was acknowledged to be a potentially dangerous strategy, given the possibility that it might fail. And a second failure might be even more personally utterly crushing. Despite the risk, this former MP had immediately been back on the stump, canvassing and campaigning with evangelism on behalf of the political party locally. In contrast to a number of other defeated former MPs, the constituency felt one of the safest places to be and not somewhere to be avoided. Despite having lost there and the initial feelings of resentment, it was still somewhere where s/he would be recognised and affirmed. The importance of affirmation—from people in the constituency, from the party and from some media appearances—came over strongly. As her/his partner commented, it is,

"Really, really important all of that, s/he really likes it when people phone."

The threat otherwise was that s/he would completely disappear off the political map, an almost intolerable thought. On a more positive note, however, the time since defeat had enabled her/him to take steps to improve her/his physical health.

The sudden lack of structure and activity following defeat was well described by one former MP,

"Events don't come at you ... as an MP, you are incredibly busy simply by standing still, whereas, as a civilian you have to make your own weather ... that takes a while to sink in."

But it was all too clear that,

"Nobody was interested in my views any more. Why should they be? ... Suddenly the phone doesn't ring anymore, the invitations don't come in and it's all different ... like a sort of bereavement, you know."

S/he determined that this was a new chapter in life and s/he was keen to re-locate as soon as possible, and turn the page. But other than the determination to get away and start afresh, s/he had had no idea of what s/he might do. In retrospect, the experience had been worse than s/he might have anticipated. The family had indeed left the area, not at all a straightforward task given their deep roots in the area.

S/he was fortunate to be able to continue with business appointments, held while an MP, but even so, s/he had wanted to go on to other things. At the same time, s/he was still regretful at not still being in the House of Commons, and s/he could acknowledge the internal struggle: the recognition of the need to move on, yet still wistful, regretful and to some extent, angry about elements of the election campaign. An air of wistfulness—not depression—was very evident, perhaps stirred to some extent by our conversation. Despite taking on a number of roles and projects, including writing, s/he was nothing like as busy as s/he had once been,

"You learn immediately that the market for ex-MPs is a very low one."

With more MPs now being full time professionals, it was,

"More difficult to have a part-time career as well like a lawyer or journalist or businessman."

Picking up a former career again if political office were lost was therefore more problematic.

For this former MP, there was a sense of a lack of fulfilment, despite all the activity. S/he missed the whole business—and busyness—of being an MP and although s/he tried to persuade her/himself that s/he would not have enjoyed a very different Commons, s/he acknowledged,

"Actually, I think I would."

Unlike redundancy elsewhere, former politicians cannot usually seek similar alternative employment in the short term: there is simply nothing equivalent, except of course for the relatively few who may be appointed to the House of Lords. As one former MP pithily put it,

"There's no way of getting back into politics ... I mean the big after care treatment is the House of Lords ... that escape route keeps you in politics."

One former MP focused far more on political experiences following her/his loss of office, more the cognitive rather than affective aspects. I thought that this arose from a personality style, a clear and forthright view about what should be important, and a reluctance to delve into the less well-charted waters of affective experience at least with me. S/he nevertheless reflected on a sense of dislocation following the loss of senior ministerial office, which was by far the most significant loss for her/him. As difficult and complex as it might be to effect change, even at the most senior levels, this was at the core of what engagement in politics was all about. For her/him, the loss of government office was a far more shocking transition than the defeat at the hands of the electorate. S/he could go as far as to say that,

"The loss of the ability to be able to do that still remains difficult to deal with at a certain level."

Her/his partner was more direct that this former MP had been profoundly perturbed by having,

"Lost a sense of who he was ... lost a sense of having a future ahead, a political future ... somebody whose past was now sealed off ... the death of a future."

Apocalyptic stuff but this was the felt experience.

Once again, this politician had had a very successful path in life until this point. Succeeding months were pre-occupied with both setting the record straight and seeking to put forward a positive policy agenda for the future, but inevitably from a less authoritative position. It was a depressing time, with disappointment and immense frustration at not being able to influence policy decisions for the first time in many a year. S/he had some contact with a few former colleagues but not as much as s/he would have liked. It was the policy discussions with the most senior political thinkers and commentators that s/he most missed.

The frustration at not being able to effect change was even more difficult having experienced high office as,

"You read the papers and you look at what's going on, all the events, you understand the potential of what you could have done differently from what is now being done ... there's a kind of perpetual reminder of the possibilities of office, and you're confronted with the reality you don't have that."

There was some suggestion of recurrent thoughts of "what if?" with regard to specific decisions that had been taken previously, but such thoughts did not appear to be intrusive.

S/he articulately summed up what many other interviewees had voiced,

"The power to really decisively change things goes with political power ... and that is what you can't replace by some other thing."

For this interviewee, political power meant senior government office, and it was impossible not to confront squarely its inevitable and irrevocable loss. But it is a tough ask when this thoughtful former MP, as a number of others, had sought so hard to be in a position to effect change. For the most senior ministers especially, having been at the core of government, what then? It is stark,

"It's something that once you've tasted, there's no going back."

Nothing can quite ever substitute.

Her/his stance was to move resolutely on,

"You have to throw yourself forward in life rather than backwards."

And have no truck with symbols of a past life as an MP, such as a Commons pass. If the electorate boots out an MP, so be it.

This former minister appeared to have had less difficulty in being put forward for a number of executive roles post defeat than other interviewees but s/he was not persuaded that this would have been the right course. Even a very senior executive position would have been subject to the constraints of a new government and inevitably involve operating at a very different, less strategic level. S/he had opted, therefore, for the more varied portfolio route, and had crafted over time a number of engaging, thought provoking areas of contribution and activity. A couple of years on, s/he had, according to her/his spouse, developed a narrative of what s/he was doing, something that brought some coherence, explanation and meaning to the areas of interest. The inherent frustrations of a portfolio career were however acknowledged: different portfolios offer variety certainly, but each position inevitably is more peripheral compared with being in the thick of high politics. It could never be quite the same.

WHAT HAPPENS TO MPS' SKILLS ACQUIRED IN OFFICE?

MPs may come into Parliament with different skills but once there, most acquire over time an impressive set of skills from their time in the House, the constituency and, if they become senior ministers, their departments. These skills are not dissimilar to those of council leaders but MPs are in the media spotlight to a much greater extent, they run their own office—akin to a small business—and, for senior ministers, the stakes are higher, the demands are more complex and a finely developed strategic sense is even more important.

But note also the cautionary words of one interviewee that,

"Being an MP is de-skilling in rather a radical way."

This former MP was aware of how difficult it had been to keep up with previous professional skills and all the more so after rules were introduced in 2009 in the wake of the expenses' controversy to increase transparency about any additional work that MPs did, whether they were paid or not, by Gordon Brown's government. The effect of this had been, in her/his view, to see anything other than work strictly in role as an MP as shameful and stealing from one's constituents.

In this study, the first imperative for nearly all the former MPs of preretirement age was to find paid employment but it was far from plain sailing even for some of those who had stood down. As one said s/he had learned,

"The actual truth is it's very, very difficult for ex-MPs to get employed because no-one understands the skills set and no-one wants to employ an ego-maniac."

This highly skilled former MP was unequivocal,

"I cannot tell you at the point when I first started to canvas jobs how quickly and powerfully it became apparent that having 20 odd years as an MP on your CV, however impressive the roles you had and the functions that you had, and in my case, the communications skills at a very high level that I had, almost no interest, no understanding."

S/he thought that it had become more difficult for former MPs that once it had been both because the reputation of MPs had diminished and because appointments were now more likely to be made on the basis of skills (ill-understood of MPs) rather than "*big cheese-based,*" that is on the basis of having been an MP alone.

All but one of those MPs who had stood down had come in time to find rewarding roles in employment or non-executive roles although not necessarily ones that were financially lucrative. Those who had been defeated were mostly able to find roles that held some meaning and reward, albeit over a longer time and having struggled much harder. That their confidence had been battered had been an additional challenge. The political parties however and civic society made little use of what former MPs had to offer.

For those who had stood down, they had had time to plan what they might do in the future during the last few months of their time in Parliament, although not all took advantage of that time. But whether they had chosen to go or had been defeated, there were similar dilemmas about the future and similar challenges in how their knowledge, skills and experience could be best used.

One relatively young former MP articulated the dilemma of not knowing whether s/he should follow the pull of finding something that uses her/his political skills but was not politics or turning to something completely different that would be more of a challenge. And how might this be reconciled with the possibility that s/he might seek to go back into politics, either into Parliament or some other role one day?

There was a wide range of roles that had been taken on: a few were able to return to a previous career; a couple found an academic berth; a few others turned to writing; a couple found (after much effort) new executive roles; others picked up roles either in consultancy or as a non-executive in not-for-profit organisations, or less often, in the private sector, that used the knowledge of a particular sector that they had acquired as MPs. Unsurprisingly, the skills and experience of having held a senior government position were more readily recognised than that of having been a backbencher alone.

But one former MP with long government experience, who had stood down was explicit about feeling that her/his skills had not been made use of as they might have been,

"I'd like to think that perhaps I would have had one other job as it were ... running a housing association or running an organisation ... where you needed somebody who was able to not try and run things on a day to day basis but who could set a strategic target and knew where the politics were."

The advice that s/he now would give former colleagues was clear,

"People should enter politics with practical experience from a job in the 'real economy'. Why? Well, at the start of a Parliamentary career, you need to establish a reputation for speaking with authority on a limited number of subjects and building from that base. Secondly, politics is hugely about luck and accident: lucky the MP to enter when your party is one election away from winning power and you can aspire to the red box. Having another activity means that the dependence on luck for career satisfaction is mitigated. Finally having an outside activity makes it easier to decide to quit because there is a life beyond it – when people hang on in Parliament for too long they can easily end up as picturesque parts of Westminster architecture."

The political parties made less use of former MPs, even of those who had ministerial experience, a point corroborated by some partners (in the next chapter). One interviewee related how s/he and a former colleague, both former MPs who had stood down, had been invited to meet with a senior figure in their political party *"to tap into our wallets."* But they pressed further,

" We felt it would be useful to have occasions where it would be possible to meet shadow ministers and particularly if you have been a minister yourself or a PPS in the department at a certain time, then it might be useful to talk to some of the Shadow Ministers who weren't even in Parliament at that time. But that's never actually happened. There's a feeling amongst some of us that we are a political resource that the party isn't using properly."

Another former MP from a different party lamented how her/his skills had been laid to waste despite having offered her/his (considerable) services to a high-ranking party insider but,

"I think I was quite low down his list of priorities ... the party could perhaps more systematically think, you know, 'What has this MP done and what

could he do to help us?' There is nothing really done there in a very concerted way."

Only one might have been described as having been engaged in activities that sought to enhance public understanding about politics, political leadership and the political process—and this was very much as a result of her/his own efforts. Mostly, it seemed that MPs' knowledge, skills and experience were squandered by their political parties and left untapped by civic society, a finding that echoes the work of Theakston's Leeds group (Theakston et al. 2007; Byrne and Theakston 2015).

REFERENCES

Byrne, C. and Theakston, K. (2015). Leaving the House: The Experience of Former Members of Parliament Who Left the House of Commons in 2010. *Parliamentary Affairs* doi: 10.1093/pa/gsv053.

Theakston, K., Gouge, E. and Honeyman, V. (2007). *Life after Losing or Leaving: The Experience of Former Members of Parliament.* A report for the Association of Former Members of Parliament by the University of Leeds.

CHAPTER 10

Partners and Families

All my interviewees had partners at the time of loss of office, even if this subsequently changed. Three former political office holders were no longer in a relationship with the partner with whom they had been at the time of their defeat. In a couple of cases, the defeat seemed to have played a significant part in the separation. One commented that s/he did not think her/his then partner *"could cope with me ... morose, down ... very hard to be with."*

While this study did not attempt to pursue in depth the effects of holding political office on family relationships, there were plentiful hints of the effects on marriages, couples and children, as well as the wider family. This was particularly the case for former MPs who represented constituencies some distance from Westminster, and all the more so if constituencies had been marginal. One thoughtful former MP reflected that s/he *"probably didn't worry enough about damage to the family"* while in office. Weinberg's work has illustrated the effects of the long working hours and the constant demands of MPs' job on family relationships (Weinberg 2012, 2015) or, more anecdotally, Linda McDougall (1998). Of life as an MP, Sarah Champion, elected as an MP in 2012 and who has vowed to serve only two terms, is reported to have said (Pidd 2015),

"It destroys your personal life. You can't have a personal life. You can't ... the job is fabulous. The lifestyle is a living hell."

While council leaders do not generally have the same geographical disruption to family life, they not only have intense demands on their time but they carry ultimate responsibility for all that their local authority does,

© The Author(s) 2017
J. Roberts, *Losing Political Office*,
DOI 10.1007/978-3-319-39702-3_10

and, in addition, they may continue in their previous employment. This inevitably impacts not only on their individual wellbeing but also on that of their families. And if there are political conflicts, especially conflicts within a political party, its effects spill over. One former leader recounted the major impact of the internecine political conflicts on her/his family. Her/his spouse had often gone to bed in tears and the children were said to have been beside themselves with anger. After de-selection, the spouse was described as never having ever been so angry, and it was s/he who some time later suffered the most severe ill effects on health as a result of what had happened.

THE PERSPECTIVE OF FORMER POLITICIANS: THOSE WHO HAD STOOD DOWN

From the perspective of former politicians who had stood down, the changes in family relationships following leaving office were almost wholly positive, sometimes to a degree that had not been anticipated. For example, it made an,

"Enormous difference, the biggest difference … didn't appreciate it at the time what a big difference it would be … the biggest, unexpected plus."

Relationships between couples were much improved, commented on by most of the participants: the decision to stand down had, after all, been taken mostly in concert with partners, all of whom were supportive. One summed it up for many,

"They see me more, they see me more relaxed, more time for them and that's all a good thing."

Another former office holder was more forthright,

"Bliss-bliss-bliss. No media. No bloody press intrusion … we got our marriage back."

Time was clearly the most significant factor but it was not the only one. The intensity of political office can sharpen any political differences there may have been between couples, and the nature of the couple relationship may have changed with the transition from office. One former MP, who had experienced the unwelcome intrusion of paparazzi into a former partner's travels abroad, talked of a very welcome sense that the couple relationship had become,

"More ordinary, less buzzy, less of that adrenaline."

More often, it was the partners rather than the former leaders and MPs themselves who voiced changes in the couple dynamic. It was almost as though this was too difficult and sensitive an area for the former politicians themselves to pursue. More practically, spouses might have come to have fewer constraints on their own career and life, no longer subject to the demands of their partners' political office.

In one case, the loss of office had led to a reappraisal and recalibration of family relationships, and subsequently to a profound and perhaps overdue, change in the marriage. This former politician acknowledged that, *"I'm only now appreciating this idea of ending."*

The positive effects were not confined to the couple relationship. The effects had spread wider: children, not just younger ones, but children who had grown up and left home; elderly parents; and siblings too. This was partly again because of time but for children, even if older, it was partly because of a happier dynamic between parents. For one former politician, the wider family had been relieved no longer to be associated with the perceived tawdriness of the expenses scandal, even though their relative had had absolutely no culpability at all.

There was a suggestion, ruefully made by some older former politicians, that they were glad to be able to spend more time with their grandchildren, having not having been able to spend as much time years before with their own children. That their families may have taken the brunt of their absence while they were distracted from home life and immersed in Parliament was acknowledged, one for example, talking explicitly about having not previously realised the harm that had been caused to her/his partner and daughter.

The Perspective of Former Politicians: Those Who Had Been Defeated

There was again a more mixed picture for those former MPs and leaders who had been defeated. While there was more time available for family relationships, this was not always seen in a positive light for the couple relationship. Defeat had been mostly unexpected and even if the partner had entertained the thought of the possibility of defeat, it was not something that had been easily openly discussed or prepared for between the couple before the election with regard to either the possible emotional or practical consequences.

In the immediate aftermath of defeat, partners and families rallied to console the politician. It was often the partner or children who more visibly expressed anger at the perceived ingratitude of the electorate. The (grown-up) children of two council leaders were angrier on their parents' behalf initially than the politicians themselves: one was said to have cried all night in fury.

Following electoral defeat, it was a very sudden and unwelcome transition from a couple relationship where at least one, and possibly two partners, had been busy, earning money, and often out of the home, to one where one person had been defeated, quite possibly having felt exposed and humiliated, before being thrust immediately into an enforced period of unemployment with its possible effects on identity and status. The dynamic between the two individuals was wholly different.

In this study, there had, not unexpectedly been some difficulties between couples post defeat and there had been a need to renegotiate the way in which they functioned together. Couples often suddenly saw more of one another, not always a bonus. One former MP admitted that her/his social life had been wrapped up with work—no need to explain where s/he was or with whom—and that had all suddenly disappeared. There was evidence of tension between some couples focused on more practical issues about what next to do, for example, about whether or not a home in the constituency should be sold, about money, and, crucially, about future work. Childcare may suddenly have become an issue with a steep drop in income in a way that it had never been before with consequent effects on job hunting, and even going out socially.

In the immediate term, if the partner had been in paid work, they suddenly become the sole wage earner, bearing an additional responsibility for the household's financial affairs. Those pre-retirement age MPs and leaders who had been defeated recognised this change of affairs acutely, perhaps frenetically active in attempts to find work or in other cases, deeply despondent and lacking motivation.

For one former MP, it had been something of a surprise how much the more relaxed atmosphere and time to play with children had improved the quality of family life after defeat. S/he had come to realise—in retrospect–quite what the risks and the costs to family life had been. Even with older children, the effects on family relationships may be very positive: one former leader described the consequences of losing on the immediate family as wonderful; family members were less anxious now that the intense demands on her/him had been lifted,

"*The pinched look on me had gone.*"

They all saw much more of one another at home: domestic arrangements were less fraught; and both spouse and children had become a lot happier. Former politicians may be simply more physically available than they had been before. However much time they might have come to have, former politicians still may not be emotionally available: one former MP relayed how her/his irritability and snappiness with the couple's younger children had only compounded the sense of depression and guilt.

It was not just on the immediate family where effects were felt of defeat. Many elderly parents had been drawn in, whether because of their unease at press treatment of their politician offspring, or at times directly when they may have been pulled into questions about an MP's expenses. Or, in one case, there was an unspoken but nevertheless changed relationship with siblings arising from a perception of their reluctance to help with the re-election campaign.

THE PERSPECTIVE OF PARTNERS

Pride featured prominently. Many spouses volunteered how immensely proud they had been of their partners' achievements when they were in office and the differences that they had made to the area. Partners of leaders especially talked of how the former leader may have forgone the opportunity of a higher paid job in the past but a passion, a vocation, had driven them on despite the costs—on finances, health and family.

With regard to the loss of office, partners were, by and large, much more direct in terms of the consequences for the former MP or leader, both for those who had stood down and those who had been defeated, and the consequences for family relationships. From partners, there was less qualification and often a much more intense and raw portrayal of the effects on the politician of the transition period, as described previously. Partners were, in this small sample, willing to describe in more vivid terms the effect on the couple dynamic and on the family.

The grown-up daughter of one former council leader acknowledged how angry she had felt at the electorate's ingratitude: why had they not taken their anger out on the national party rather than on local figures that had done so much for the area? She felt strongly that,

"If you are going to be at the very top one minute and then the very bottom the next, there does need to be something in place that supports you or helps you deal with that."

On the other hand, she welcomed the fact that her parent had subsequently not needed to work as hard and that s/he could see more of the children and the grandchildren.

All the partners I spoke to had been very much drawn into the effects of the loss of office both because the relationship between the couple had been affected, but also, to varying degrees, because their lives themselves had been directly affected by the change. Some partners may be highly engaged in the political world even if they have not sought election, while others may be totally uninterested in politics. Even if not a political animal, a partner is likely to have been very involved in the work of their partners in office and to have organised their lives around its demands, both emotional and practical.

For some leaders' partners especially, the political office of their spouse had been a positive boon, particularly the opportunities to meet new people and to make wider friendships. For others, determined efforts were made to keep partners and children well out of the spotlight, for example,

"We all had discussions about politics around the table but as far as anybody outside was concerned, nobody was entitled to any piece of us."

One partner memorably likened the pressures of ministerial office and its impact on the family to,

"This feeling of being inside something. It was like being tossed around inside one of those big plastic clear balls that you sometimes see children playing on lakes in."

The destructive impact of the press on politicians, their partners and children was once again searingly described,

"The feeling that everything you did was examined through the wrong perspective."

There was an almost palpable sense of powerlessness felt by many partners in the face of the outside world.

Partners of Politicians Who Had Stood Down

The number of partners interviewed in this group was very small, just four, so even more caution is necessary in drawing any conclusions. While for two partners the experience had been wholly positive, for a couple of others it had not been plain sailing despite many perceived advantages. All four former politicians had discussed standing down in advance with their partner. If circumstances in the public domain had influenced the decision to stand down, the partner had been affected as well.

One partner was unambiguously positive on the effects of the loss of office on the marital relationship and on her/him. S/he was direct and straightforward in describing how bad an experience it had been for her/him—and for the children—for many years while her/his spouse had been in Parliament: a painful, very lonely life, as if s/he were a single parent. The former MP would arrive home exhausted on Sunday with other things to think about and would then disappear. S/he made clear that,

"The price the family pays for ambition is far too much … you are asking everybody around you to pay a terrible high price for something which is a mirage, a dream."

Leaving office as an MP,

"Is horrible … you leave with your tail between your legs and your ears flat … it ends with a sour taste in your mouth. You are sacrificing your life to it, sometimes your health … and probably your marriage and damaging your family life."

From this partner's perspective, despite the considerable difficulties previously in the marital relationship, once the politician had stood down they had come to have,

"A very good life … for me absolutely charming and delightful."

This spouse was much happier with the current situation; s/he had,

"Waited for this for years, a companion, I had nobody to talk to before … a big change, wonderful."

Despite all this partner's disappointments and pain over the years, s/he was very clear that s/he had no regrets about how their life had turned out and would not now change anything. But s/he reflected on MPs' careers asking,

"What have they got at the end of their long careers? How many very satisfied, happy politicians have you got at the end?"

Another former MP's partner had been keen for her/him to have some experience outside parliamentary life, aware as s/he was that her/his spouse had been both consumed by its heavy and often immediate demands but increasingly less personally fulfilled by it. S/he was very reflective about the pressures on politicians and how those pressures can subtly influence their individual wellbeing and relationships at all levels. The practicalities of family life shuttling between Westminster and a distant constituency had been a major consideration. Leaving office had eased those pressures but the lack of a regular income brought a different pressure and necessitated still some days working away from home. The partner initially said that her/his life had been unaffected by the transition from political office but then went on describe how her/his spouse was more emotionally available for the family and more able to attend to the children since leaving office. This partner was adamant that s/he missed absolutely nothing since her/his partner had stepped down: MPs and their families are,

"Always careering along the edge of this sort of precipice ... these people are humans. They're just working bloody hard and they have to be kind of super-human, angelic, all these things and at the same time they're trying to be, a lot of them, family people and it's really very hard."

Standing down, the partner thought, had allowed an opportunity for the former MP to re-evaluate how s/he lived life, having always before looked at what s/he should do as a politician rather than having lived life for himself in any other way—and having ended up feeling somewhat unfulfilled. The personal and the political had been very entangled.

Spouses of council leaders may experience intense pressures but they do not experience their partner disappearing off to Westminster for the week. Their close proximity to the area where political office is held can bring its own difficulties. More than one spouse, for example, found comments that had been made in the local press very hurtful and upsetting, especially knowing many of them to be untrue. It is also easier for leaders' partners to engage with the more social aspects in the local area of the leadership role, even if they have their own career. It can be a means by which they themselves get to meet a wider range of people, enjoyable in its own right but perhaps also enhancing their self-confidence. They get very used to the absence of a partner in the evenings, and their sudden reappearance when political office ends changes the couple dynamic, as when any one individual in a couple retires, or is made redundant. It may take consider-ably more getting used to if the loss of office occurs well below retirement age and/or there has been little or no warning.

Even if the politician had been around retirement age, the change in the couple dynamic can be profound. One spouse reported how her part-ner not only became anxious and panicky about what s/he was going to do but s/he started depending much more on the spouse, for example saying,

"'Well, you will have to do this so that we can do things together' ... when I was getting home from work, I couldn't even get my coat off where I would have to sit down and he'd have to tell me what he'd done during the day how-ever menial it might have been ... as if hungry for me to get home."

This was very different from when the politician had formerly got home from council meetings and would have had to unwind before being able to converse. S/he now would ring anxiously for her/his spouse to get home. It was a worrying time for the spouse. There had been a definite change in their roles and in their relationship. S/he felt that s/he had to be far more sensitive than previously, aware of the now enormous void in her/his partner's life with no other focus other than family. Things had picked up to some extent after a few months and s/he felt more optimistic for the future particularly when s/he retired and the couple could share activities.

For another, the transition had been considerably smoother and the impact more straightforwardly positive both for the former leader and spouse. Following stepping down, s/he was noticeably more relaxed and more continuously emotionally available than before. But this former leader was well past retirement age and was seen to have fulfilled the sense of purpose that had driven her/him for many years.

PARTNERS OF POLITICIANS WHO HAD BEEN DEFEATED

It was notable that seven of the nine partners of politicians who had been defeated (compared with four out of eight who had stood down) agreed to talk with me. It is a small sample but, nevertheless, a high response rate especially for a request for a significant amount of time and possible intrusion into sensitive areas. I came to understand that this was most likely because of the intensity of feelings that had been provoked by the defeat and what had happened since.

During the election campaign, as discussed earlier, a number of partners had been worried about the potential loss of the seat even if their politician spouses had not appeared to countenance the possibility. For the partners of politicians who had been defeated, the change in life circumstance is abrupt and shocking, even if they (and not the politicians themselves) had anticipated a possible electoral loss. Said one,

"It is a shock. It's a loss as well because it did feel like a bereavement because it was the end of something that we'd both thrown ourselves into ... I actually sat up in bed crying and said 'This can't be over. We've thrown our whole lives into politics. This can't be over."

This partner was aware that s/he had initially conceded a supportive role to console the defeated spouse for a short while, given the shock. S/he estimated that it had taken her/him a good two years to get back on to an even keel.

Another described being at the count as,

"Terrible. Emotionally it was just draining and I wouldn't go through it again. I don't think I could ever go through it again ... It's like you'd lost somebody, lost something and it was never going to come back. I think the closest thing you could put against it would be like a death, if that makes sense."

Anger was a common but not constant theme on the part of the seven whom I interviewed. The majority of partners of those who had been defeated voiced intense, at times very bitter, anger mostly towards the national or the local political party of which they had also been members. All of these left the party as a result.

For those in local government, a defeat at the hands of a big national swing is especially hard to take. As one partner described,

"I was angry. I was angry and upset ... how can people be so ungrateful really? You know, how can people not realise what's been done for them and just take anger at the wrong people really."

S/he went on to fume that the Prime Minister had,

"Still got re-elected in his constituency and he still had a job to go to. He could still go about business and do what he loved, whereas suddenly ... had a pile of papers on her desk one day and the next it's someone else's."

S/he recounted how someone had stopped the former leader a week or two after the defeat asking for a local issue to be taken up. With some glee, the partner relayed how the response simply was,

"I think you'll find that's someone else's problem now."

In a similar vein, another acknowledged her/his anger towards the electorate,

"I don't think people are educated to understand what local politics is all about because it's completely different to national and if they realised the difference between the two, then you wouldn't lose good councillors ... I think it's a crying shame when these people lose their seats, it makes me angry."

The spouse of one former MP had geared all her/his life and work to the constituency and it had been an enormous change to dig up those deep roots. It had been exquisitely hard to leave a much loved home, built up over years, and the local community. Leaving had involved considerable personal grief: it had necessitated a huge upheaval both to her/his career, family and social life,

"I really minded ... Yeah, I really miss it ... and it's being part of a village, a community, my friends ... my life was there."

The electorate had to some extent not just slapped the former MP in the face but her/his partner as well. S/he too avoided now going back to the area, it was simply too painful. It was like bereavement but people had seemed not to understand the sensitivities. There was undoubtedly a sense of anger in the interview but s/he made clear that s/he did not want to pursue this avenue,

"I really don't want to go there ... I'm just putting it into another part of my brain."

Speaking personally but in the second person,

"I mean you gave up your life. You know, a big part of your life just cut off."

S/he conveyed bitterness at the ingratitude of some who had wrongly judged her/his spouse during the campaign especially after all that both of them had done over the years in the constituency, and then to add insult to injury, they had given a valedictory party for local party workers rather than anyone organising a party to thank them.

What had rankled most was how the national political party had ignored her/his spouse completely after the electoral defeat, as a result of which s/he had withdrawn her support from the party. It had taken nearly two years to re-organise their domestic and working lives elsewhere.

For the partner of a council leader who had lost but who had had little warning of defeat, anger was much more explicit. As a couple, both working, their lives had revolved around the leadership role and the loss of office had suddenly led to a profound change in their lives. S/he was clear that anger was,

"The over-riding feeling because, and without wanting to sound selfish, it felt as much my loss … given the effort and time and everything that had been put in … I felt it was very much a joint effort."

The partner felt utter fury at the national political party leadership that had taken decisions at a national level that had had devastating effects locally, and that had then abandoned the now former leader. S/he was furious that there had been no attempt whatsoever to reach out to those who had lost their seats despite their unceasing hard work and commitment. Anger had turned into bitterness, intensely felt by both of them nearly 18 months post defeat,

"It's seeking vengeance against people within your own party."

In this case, rather than leave the party, the partner had remained a member but was active in finding common cause with like-minded others,

"A focus for anger and for a need to seek redress somehow."

While the partner had gone on with day-to-day activities, it had been difficult for the couple to move on, suspended in a kind of limbo since the electoral defeat. The partner was concerned, caring and supportive but frustrated too, telling me,

"There's a very surreal air and it's a fine balance between being supportive and dictatorial and sympathetic, but it's intensely frustrating … trying to hold on to something that's not there. It's gone and there's nothing we can do about it."

A couple of partners of those who had been defeated had left in fury the political party of which they too had been a member as a result of how their spouses had been treated. Their goodwill and activism had been lost as well as that of their spouses.

For another partner, there was a similar sense of frustration and a quandary about the extent to which s/he should pressurise the spouse to do something meaningful. Her/his anger was directed less at the electorate or anyone else with regard to the electoral defeat itself but more a frustration at the appalling waste of former politicians' skills and expertise which remain untapped by the political parties after a defeat. This could, s/he maintained, be a free good and a win-win both for any financially constrained political party and for the individuals' self-worth. But instead, former MPs were out of the fold, their considerable experience unused, cast aside,

"The waste of the loss, really … the fact that there's all of those years of experience, knowledge, expertise particularly in a party that's in opposition but hasn't got the sense to use it in some way for free … The individuals concerned would feel so much more self-worth that they haven't got all these years that are just dumped and finished."

Was it, s/he mused, something about the association with loss that parties found so unappealing? But why not, s/he continued, use them in a back office capacity? Or was it just poor organisation? S/he thought,

"Nobody really thought about what it might use … it is really stupid not to be using them more sensibly and in a more focused way for the future."

S/he was outraged that the party instead could stand idly by while, in one reported example, a large number of former MPs had applied for a very junior job within the party pitched at a level far too low for most of them.

As her/his partner had not yet gained meaningful employment following electoral defeat despite the time that had elapsed, s/he acknowledged resentment at being the sole wage earner despite some positives in domestic arrangements. S/he bore the brunt of the financial stress in the household, and expressed frustration at seeing an able individual essentially fritter away her/his considerable talents. S/he had repeatedly suggested possible avenues to explore but so far to no avail. There were significant implications for the couple dynamic.

The effects of the loss of office fell especially hard on another spouse, arising from a sense of anger and bitterness at how the loss of office had occurred through de-selection. S/he described how,

"I don't think it affected me at the time, I think it was kind of delayed shock. It affected me about a year, a year and a half later … depression."

As a result of the severe financial stress,

"I didn't know what we were going to do and I just got lower and lower and in the end I just cried at everything. I even cried in the job centre because I didn't know what we were going to do."

S/he slowly got better with treatment and became more positive, with the couple subsequently starting their own small business. S/he had however left the political party, having been a loyal member for very many years, and would not speak to the prime mover in the back-stabbing of her/his partner.

Given that many politicians will have got used to success, perhaps in other fields and certainly by having won at least one election, a significantly changed demeanour post defeat may introduce an unfamiliar element into the relationship of the couple. A partner may never have seen their spouse having failed at anything before, realising for the first time that they were not right on top of everything as once they may have thought. One former office holder was described as,

"A changed man, a different man."

This will inevitably impact on a partner.

The confidence of politicians inevitably takes a hard knock with defeat, however accomplished they might have been. One was said to have been,

"Terribly knocked by it … been knocked off a big perch."

Despite the initial anger, upset and humiliation, there came a sense of unaccustomed freedom,

"You know, we were private citizens and that was a really big liberation."

No longer would s/he have,

"To keep my head down. I was so vulnerable. You'd drive everywhere at 30 miles an hour for fear of speed points. You know, it's just you're so law abiding because everything is so terrifying that you'd end up …You just see Daily Mail front pages wherever you go"

There was a strong sense of the loss of a joint, deeply meaningful enterprise, a wistfulness of no longer being in the know of what was going in Westminster, but on the other hand, s/he was able to pursue her/his own interests,

"Do something of my own … so it wasn't entirely negative."

S/he had observed with pleasure the children becoming closer to her/his spouse partly as s/he was more available but perhaps also because they had come,

"To realise your parents have got feet of clay after all."

This partner had perceptively reflected on wider changes from the loss of office. While in office,

"People don't talk to you properly. They only see the office, they don't see you and they certainly didn't see me. They never saw me".

After the loss of his/her spouse's seat however,

"You become an ordinary person and a whole set of relationships change. It's really quite curious how that happens. People think you're more available perhaps … so a lot of relationships became easier and you could be a bit more selective and you could say no to things. You didn't have to go to gruesome things that you didn't want to go to."

S/he estimated that it had taken two years for both of them to get over the defeat,

"You know, you just have to accept it takes about two years to get over this and then you just can move on and it's just history. You just have to let it go."

S/he volunteered that there had been a number of MPs they had known for whom,

"It's been a real struggle … there is nothing as ex as an ex-MP. That kind of feeling. There's lot of wives who had such a terrible time that if you bump into them, they're really quite glad to be out of it. It's such a vile life."

On the positive side, the partners of those former defeated office politicians who had found meaningful employment—not of those who had not—welcomed the extra time that there now was for them and for the wider family. One who had initially been furious on his partner's behalf at the time of the close defeat was now glad that it had happened. This former council leader had been unlikely to stand down despite the toll that the office was taking on her/his health, something that greatly concerned the spouse. S/he was not only partner to describe a sense of losing their spouse when they had held political office,

"It's like the lights are on, but there's nobody in."

S/he was delighted at regaining the spouse, finding them now "in." S/he had a sparkle in the eye, was generally healthier, and the additional family time was much appreciated by spouse and (older) children.

This research demonstrates that the holding of political office has a profound impact on partners and families, both positive and negative, and so too does the leaving of that office, again both positive and negative. Yet that impact is often not recognised or acknowledged. Partners and children are not elected to public office: they are not in any sense fair game either when their spouses are in office or when they leave it. Partners' lives may well be directly affected by their spouses' exit from political office. But indirectly too, they are affected: they hold the emotional intensity of their spouses' leaving especially if it follows an electoral defeat. Perhaps as a result they are more likely than their spouses vigorously to voice the consequences of political exit.

REFERENCES

McDougall, L. (1998). *Westminster Women*. London: Vintage.

Pidd, H. (2015). The people's Champion. *The Guardian* 10 February.

Weinberg, A. (2012). *Should the job of national politicians carry a government health warning? The impact of psychological strain on politicians*. In A. Weinberg (Ed.), *The Psychology of Politicians*. Cambridge University Press: Cambridge.

Weinberg, A. (2015). A Longitudinal Study on the Impact of Changes in the Job and the Expenses Scandal on UK National Politicians' Experiences of Work, Stress and the Home-Work Interface. *Parliamentary Affairs* 68 pp. 248–271.

CHAPTER 11

Key Themes

Summary of the Findings

In terms of individuals' handling of thoughts, emotions and behaviour, there were not only some commonalities of experience of leaving political office but, inevitably, given the widely differing personalities, backgrounds and experiences, many differences. The manner of exit—voluntary or involuntary or varying shades in between—accounted for some of the differences but by no means all. The picture was more nuanced. I shall summarise my findings here.

While a few of the politicians in this study were only too pleased to be relieved of the chains of office (for that is what they were felt to be), most, including many of those who had chosen to go, grieved in some way. Even if the decision to go was the right one, all missed some aspects of the role and most missed what came over as the intoxicating brew of being in the centre of things and mattering: having some influence; the ability to effect change at some level; making a contribution to thinking on policy; being seen to be on the national or local stage; and even simply being busy and in demand, the less definable "buzz." Former council leaders especially missed the camaraderie and the friendship groups.

Assumptions may be made that those politicians who had chosen to go had planned and prepared themselves for life after elected office but, in many cases, curiously, this turned out not to be so. And even when plans had been made, the actual experience of no longer being in office was

© The Author(s) 2017
J. Roberts, *Losing Political Office*,
DOI 10.1007/978-3-319-39702-3_11

often not as had been expected. The process of transition from office had, by and large, been given little thought.

There was a small sub-set of four MPs (no council leaders) for whom the experience of transition from office was unequivocally positive. For them, the experience of being an MP had become increasingly uncomfortable, albeit in different ways, as previously described. Two had been able to return to their previous profession, each in its way a "club" in terms of close collegiate working, while another was young, able enough and with fewer domestic commitments to be justifiably more excited rather than anxious about the future. One had come to find the role uncomfortable but only after a number of years and changed personal circumstances, and s/he had subsequently found a berth.

Most of the former politicians, however, whether they had been defeated or had stood down, had much more ambivalent experiences: a rational and ready acceptance of the consequences of what had been chosen or dealt by the electorate but a yearning and sense of dislocation at the same time. Most acknowledged a profound loss—a loss not only of what had been but also of what might have been, a future as well as a past. Even if they had chosen to go, some could admit a sense of grief. Constituencies were avoided, sometimes people too. No longer did it matter to others what they thought, what they did—no one knew, much less cared. The buzzy world of which they had been a part had moved on without a backward glance. The sense of irrelevance and impotence was hard for some to deal with and a small minority seemed depressed.

Those who were defeated had other issues to contend with in addition: shock often at an unanticipated event; a crushing sense of failure, humiliation and, for some, shame. Whether by defeat at the hands of an electorate or a selectorate, feelings—sometimes sheepishly acknowledged—of betrayal, hurt and anger were common. Many had little or no acknowledgement from their parties of their diligent, immensely committed work over many years, further rubbing salt into the wound.

In the longer term (over a couple of years or so), most but not all of those who had stood down had accommodated well to their change in circumstances. They had found other sources of employment, interest and social networks, although they still missed the ability to have significant influence, to matter politically, and, for council leaders especially, the camaraderie. There was more time for partners and family, much welcomed. A couple of interviewees had however struggled, one with finding work as well as with the emotional aftermath. The one interviewee who had planned both the transition from office and the future with care had flourished both in his/her working and personal life—but still could acknowledge the profound life changes.

There was a more mixed picture still in the longer term for those who had been defeated. Social networks had almost inevitably changed, for some very significantly. One felt as though s/he had lost her/his family, and former council leaders missed the friendships and camaraderie within local government. Two had flourished—personally and with a range of political and civic activities—after an initial period of devastation. Some others had struggled to move on in their personal lives and in finding employment, while two others were only just coming out of a period of profound low self-esteem and were beginning to find their feet. And a couple of others remained in an unhappy, fairly withdrawn and angry state.

That someone was of retirement age or beyond did not necessarily mean in this study that they would adjust more easily to the transition from office. On the other hand, the imperatives for younger former politicians to find alternative employment and build a new narrative were undoubtedly stronger. Nor did length of tenure seem to make much difference: leaving political office was exquisitely difficult for both some who had been in office for a relatively short time and some for much longer.

There was just a suggestion that women had adapted better to their exit from office but numbers are so small that great caution is necessary.

All the partners interviewed had been very involved with a decision to stand down or with support in the aftermath of defeat. They were the ones who held the anxiety about possible electoral defeat and acted to contain the intense emotions as their political spouses had left office, whether by standing down or defeat. The effect on the couple relationship when the politician had stood down was largely very positive even if this meant on one occasion that refocusing on the marital relationship had led to its end. The couple dynamic in another case had become more unsettled with one partner now at home alone so much more.

Where the politician had been defeated, the effect on the couple relationship was more complicated. All the partners had been very supportive up to and through the election. Some of those who had lost at the ballot box felt guilty and a sense that they had failed their partners as a result of having been defeated. With more time available for the couple, some found that there were unexpected benefits for the relationship between them while there was a number where the couple dynamic had got much more difficult, usually where the former office holder had remained very troubled.

Partners themselves often expressed a rawness and intensity about the experiences that they and their politician spouses had undergone. Whereas the former politicians themselves were often somewhat coy about what they perceived to be negative feelings, their partners were much less restrained about their fury and rage—mostly towards the local and/or the national political party—at the abandonment of their spouse. A number had left the political party as a consequence. There was fury too at the lack of recognition and use of their partners' skills and knowledge—that it had all been left to waste.

How Can the Findings Be Explained?

Leading on from the findings of the study, can we make sense of the range and intensity of experiences described by former MPs and council leaders? And can we explain some of the differences in their experience and suggest factors that might lead some individuals to find the transition from political office especially difficult? How do we understand the impact on partners and families? Can anything be done to mitigate the consequences?

Thinking About Politicians as Individuals

That it was unsurprising that there were many differences in the experiences of those leaving political office has already been highlighted. Unemployed and retired workers, after all, respond very differently to the loss of work (Warr et al. 1988; McKee-Ryan et al. 2005; Gabriel et al. 2013; Wang 2013; Vough et al. 2015), as do athletes (Cecić Erpič et al. 2004). Byrne and Theakston (2015) found a range of different responses to exiting parliamentary office in their recent study. Nor will there be one standardised way in which the transition from political office is best managed. Even in the intense world of psychoanalysis where received wisdom has been that termination of therapy should be managed in particular ways, it is now recognised that,

"*No one phenomenon characterises endings, nor is there any one particular way analysts should manage termination*" *(Kantrowitz* 2014).

For politicians who leave office it is an ending. Few will regain political office. A minority of council leaders become MPs but most will not. Either way, it is an ending of their council career. Not many defeated MPs return to the Commons and even fewer now than once did with less frequent bye-elections (Riddell 2013, personal communication). And those who have chosen to go do precisely that.

There are nevertheless some commonalities of experience that can helpfully point the way to a better understanding of the process by which our elected representatives return to life as ordinary citizens.

ENDING AS A TRANSITION

Exiting political office is undoubtedly a process, as are all transitions. It has long been recognised that retirement, for example, is a process that takes place some years before the actual event with planning and decision-making, and that it is not complete for a number of years (Beehr 1986; Kiefer and Briner 1998; Wang 2013). Athletes coming to the end of their sporting career go through a "termination process" (Cecić Erpič et al. 2004). So too, despite the drama of a one-off election defeat, is leaving political office a process over time.

Murray Parkes (1971) was one of the first to use the term "psychosocial transition" for a period during which affectional bonds have to be severed and old models of the self have to be given up. He wrote extensively about bereavement, a powerful transition for us all, and I discuss bereavement and grief in the context of political office below.

Considering transitions more generally, Schlossberg (1981) defined a transition as,

"An event or non-event that results in a change in assumptions about oneself and the world and thus requires a corresponding change in one's behaviour and relationships."

Her paper presents a model to understand human adaptation to changes of different kinds and analyses both individual characteristics and external occurrences. The inevitable changes in adult life, Schlossberg writes, require a new network of relationships and a new way of seeing oneself. Different individuals will adapt differently to similar transitions depending on the characteristics of the particular transition: of the pre- and post-transition environments, and of the individual.

Bridges' (2009) later work on transitions from the perspective of the management of change in the workplace suggests that there will be three transition phases: ending, losing and letting go. First, an ending of what had been; secondly, an in-between time, a "neutral zone" when the old is gone but the new is not yet operational; and only then, coming out of transition and making a new beginning. The neutral zone is described as,

"A kind of emotional wilderness, a time when it wasn't quite clear who you were or what was real." (p. 8)

As discombobulating as this sounds, it is, Bridges writes, when crucial psychological realignments can take place. Only then can transition move on to a new beginning when people can discover a new sense of identity and purpose. He writes,

"Transition starts with an ending and finishes with a beginning."

The "neutral zone" is similar to Ebaugh's (1988) notion of a *"vacuum,"* a period of feeling anxious, ungrounded and not knowing where one belongs; and the notion of *"liminality."* Liminality is described (Ashforth 2012, p. 136) as a psychological concept referring to a,

"Betwixt and between state, of being roleless."

These descriptions are reminiscent of many of my interviewees and their sense of dislocation.

Ashforth (2012) describes four phases of transition in organisational life: preparation; encounter; adjustment; and stabilisation. He paints a picture of a more rapidly changing and turbulent organisational landscape and sees change has having become the norm and stability the exception. Perhaps so, but there remains a great deal of work to do in any transition between the ending of one role and the beginning of another.

I shall draw in more detail on two frameworks—from Ebaugh (1988), subsequently amplified by Ashforth (2012), and later in this chapter, Marris (1993)—from the disciplines of sociology and psychology to inform an understanding of transition specifically from political office. Together, they offer a rich understanding of the interaction between attachment, meaning, loss, role and identity.

Ebaugh's Model of Role Exit

The decision to stand down taken by former MPs and council leaders in this study can be usefully informed by the best developed model of role exit, that suggested by Ebaugh (1988) whose work was highlighted in Chap. 3. Ebaugh's model was described with voluntary exits more in mind, so it may have limitations with regard to politicians who left office having been defeated, although she acknowledges that voluntariness should be regarded as lying on continuum. Her model outlines four stages: initial doubts; seeking and weighing alternatives; the turning point; and creating an ex-role. Ashforth (2012) later expanded Ebaugh's model to take involuntary exits into account.

The process of voluntary transition from the role of MP or council leader begins with initial doubts. There may be a precipitating event: in this study, for example, an episode of uncomfortable media intrusion, or an expenses issue raised. Or, the doubts may be less about what is disliked about the office but rather because of external factors or family commitments pulling the politician away from office.

The sub-set of four MPs who had come to dislike their role made clear their doubts about the job itself, their push factors. There may be "*an epiphany*," as for one of them, or a more gradual and growing sense of unease. One of the four had for many years gained much satisfaction from the role only subsequently finding both the attractiveness of the job diminishing and the pull away to his/her family strengthening.

Escalating doubt and uncertainty may understandably provoke anxiety. Ebaugh suggests that in such circumstances individuals contemplating leaving a role may seek to *share their doubts* with others who may validate or alternatively weaken them. This option is, however, much less open to political office holders: talking to anyone but those whom they trust completely is fraught with danger. Should any hint of their standing down become known before a decision is made, then the decision would be taken out of their control. They would be unable to control the timing, crucially important for any politician; less able to change their minds and stand again should they decide to do so; and, especially for council leaders, be seen as a lame duck. None is an appetising prospect.

Ebaugh's second stage in voluntary role exit—*seeking and weighing alternatives*—is also more constrained for politicians. They may well agonise in private about the relative advantages and disadvantages of standing down—most of the interviewees in this study did—but before any decision is made public, it is not realistically possible for them to pursue the possibilities of alternative employment. Alternatives to established political office will be strongly influenced by pragmatic issues such as income security, pension considerations (for MPs not council leaders)—"*sidebets*"— accumulated over time. Ashforth (2012, p. 122) describes the possible "*role entrapment*" as a result,

"*The longer an individual spends in a role, the more the sidebets accumulate, and the more aspects of his or her life become intertwined with the role … creates strong inertia such that it takes a powerful stimulus to provoke role exit.*"

The parliamentary expenses issue of 2009 provided just that powerful stimulus, resulting in a much higher number of MPs standing down in the 2010 General Election than is normally the case and having a powerful effect on some of the former MPs in this study. Yet there was the suggestion from interviewees in this study that a significant minority of MPs had come to feel trapped in their role, discussed later.

A *turning point*, the third stage, and the final push to trigger the explicit act of leaving, is described by most role exiters interviewed by Ebaugh. A public announcement by a politician underlines their final decision—there is no going back—causing *"a veritable soup of emotions, most notably relief at having resolved the issue"* (Ashforth 2012, p. 127). Many of my interviewees described precisely that, a huge sense of relief at a decision having irrevocably been made, come what may.

This third stage, the turning point, is suggested by Ashforth (2012) to be the first stage for those who exit a role involuntarily. An involuntary exit is more destabilising: often unexpected and hence with less time for any preparation and more threatening to an individual's sense of identity and control. But Ashforh argues that the issue is less the voluntariness of any exit but rather what the loss is perceived to mean and what the expectations of the future are. He neatly re-orders Ebaugh's stages and, applying his suggested model to politicians who are defeated, informs our understanding. Politicians' summary dismissal by the electorate is the turning point following which attempts need to be made to make sense of what has happened. Politicians will attribute their defeat differently—perhaps with escalating doubts—externally to the national party or government or possibly more internally on to their own shortcomings. They make seek to distance themselves from their previous role to minimise distress at the loss. At some point, former politicians will have to seek and weigh alternatives before progressing on to Ebaugh's (and Ashforth's) fourth stage, *creating an ex-role.*

All politicians leaving office, whether they have stood down or have been defeated, will need to *create an ex-role*. The imperative for all former MPs and council leaders is to articulate a new narrative for the future—who they are and what they are doing—to themselves and to others, whether they are leaving voluntarily or not. Creating an ex-role, Ebaugh (1988) argues, is a challenging process for many, involving a tension, at least initially, between an individual's past, present and future. Any previous role has to be taken into account and integrated into a future identity. The more that an individual's identity has been equated with their previous role—as often is the case for politicians—the more that it is likely to remain a significant part of their evolving identity. This "role residual" (Ebaugh 1988) may remain as a consuming nostalgia (as for at least one of my interviewees) or, more productively, over time it may become an integrated part of a new narrative underpinning the ex-role.

THE PRESSURES ON POLITICIANS

The marked relief on ceasing to be in office experienced by the sub-set of four former MPs takes the discussion—a brief discursion here—into the experience of holding political office. The impact on partners and families has been discussed earlier. The discomfort of these four former MPs as a representative in the Westminster Parliament raises a number of important questions about the role of an MP in the modern day, how MPs are perceived, and their working environment. Perhaps because there is a steady queue of people clamouring to get into the Commons, it may be easy to avoid such a debate at a time when public indignation over expenses and cynicism in politicians remain a powerful force.

These questions will however not go away. Are MPs to become ever more professionalised, divorced from the world of work outside the Commons? Are MPs elected constructively to build legislation (the determination of one interviewee) or simply as gladiatorial representatives between competing interests (the view of another)? In the wake of the Scottish referendum and demands for more devolution, what is the remit of Westminster MPs vis-à-vis other elected representatives in our system of governance? With the degree of media intrusion and at times entrapment into the lives of MPs and their families, and the political becoming ever more personal, what sort of psychological defences may be required in order to withstand the pressures? Are we constructing a system in which narcissistic defences are increasingly necessary?

It may be co-incidental, but these four former MPs appeared very reflective, thoughtful and perhaps on the more introverted side of the personality spectrum. Might there be less place for such characteristics in our future parliamentary representatives? We know that both MPs and councillors score highly on extroversion scales (Weinberg 2010; Local Government Association 2012). From the USA, Cain (2012) writes of a cultural over-valuation of extroversion. As one of my interviewees commented,

"For centuries, it was possible for introverted type people to be MPs and I don't think it's possible now. I think that's the problem – there used to be a mixture, used to be a more well-balanced reflection of the variety of human personality than it is now."

One former MP in this study reflected on the effects of the pressures on MPs' wellbeing and highlighted the amount of alcohol that both s/he and colleagues had drank in the Commons,

"Just extraordinary ... in fact, when I go back there, I just realise how much ... I haven't stopped drinking but I just don't drink like that, it's just other people around you ... drunk, abusive, self-abusive behaviour, self-medication I think."

Weinberg (2012) has led studies investigating the pressures on British MPs and their working environment. One study (Weinberg 2010) investigated MPs' personality traits, looking at the relationship between personality factors, psychological strain and sources of pressure at the interface between home and work in 30 MPs from a wider longitudinal study. He noted an increase in psychological strain and a strong relationship between levels of emotional stability and MPs' view both of the job and their ability to carry out it following the expenses row. It should be noted however that some of the questions raised by interviewees in this study are wider than simply the pressures of the job. James et al. (2016) have illustrated the extent of the harassment and stalking of Westminster MPs, experienced by 81 per cent of their 239 respondents with a significant proportion of these reporting psychological ill-effects. Even worse, tragically, in 2016, one MP, Jo Cox, was murdered as she was going about constituency business.

The pressures of the media and public scrutiny do not arise to the same degree for most council leaders. Those interviewed for this study were all unequivocally positive about the role (including one who had been both a council leader and, less happily, an MP). Yet the immensely rewarding and challenging aspects of council leadership are barely recognised within political circles or beyond. On the other hand, some argue for a similar spotlight on to an expanded number of directly elected mayors. The London Mayoralty now has a very high public profile and similar considerations of the pressures of office will apply.

I return now to the experience of the majority of those whom I interviewed.

Loss, Grief and Change

For the majority of the rest of the former MPs and council leaders interviewed (16 out of the 20), loss was a strong theme even if the decision to go had been entirely voluntary and consistently felt to have been right. In varying degrees, interviewees expressed a loss of structure, identity, income, purpose, status, activity, social relationships, attention, influence, relevance, authority and of what might have been. All change involves loss of some sort, even positive change,

"Whether change is sought or resisted, and happens by chance or by design ... the response is characteristically ambivalent. The will to adapt to change has to overcome an impulse to restore the past which is equally universal." (Marris 1993, p. 5)

Even the four interviewees for whom leaving office was a great relief could acknowledge some loss, albeit minor in the overall scheme of things, and far outweighed by the positive aspects of leaving.

It has long been understood that a fundamental aspect of our being as humans is that we grieve—feel intense sorrow and distress that interrupts our normal relationship with the world around us—when faced with a significant loss. Grief in response to the death of someone close is seen in all cultures throughout the world (and in mammals). But any significant loss can precipitate similar feelings. Freud recognised a century ago that mourning took place in response to the loss, but not necessarily the death, of something that was loved, what he called "a loved object" (Freud 1917). From Freud came the idea of *cathexis*, a process by which we invest mental and emotional energy into a person, an object or an idea that is very important to us. If that loved object is lost, it must be *de-cathected*: the investment of energy into that object must be withdrawn, as in the process of mourning.

Freud made a distinction between mourning and melancholia (or depression as we would now call it). In mourning, the ego gradually withdraws from that which has been valued but lost: this is an intensely painful process but, over time, the person finds ways to connect with other "objects" of value. In contrast, in melancholia, the ego clings desperately on to the object in order to prevent the loss of part of itself. Melancholia is not an ordinary sadness, Freud makes clear,

"The distinguishing mental features of melancholia are a profoundly painful sense of dejection, a cessation of interest in the outside world, loss of capacity to love, inhibition of all activity ... a lowering of the self-regarding feelings to a degree that finds utterance in self-reproaches and self-revilings."

Klein had a more complex conception of an individual's internal world than Freud. She viewed the process of mourning as one in which the loved lost object could be re-instated internally, strengthening rather than depleting the ego in its task of forming new attachments (Klein 1940).

Kübler-Ross (1969) later developed a now well-known but subsequently contested five-stage model of classic grief—denial, anger, bargaining, depression and acceptance. Grief can however manifest itself in many different guises, perhaps re-emerging and re-asserting itself over time in a less defined pattern.

But questions remained about grief. Although the loss of someone or something loved might be naturally seen as painful—something deeply valued is no longer present—love does not adequately explain grief. Neither was it understood (even Freud was puzzled) about why grief should be so painful and last so long. What possible function could it have, not least because it plunges the bearer into a state in which replacing the lost relationship is characteristically more difficult?

Marris' Understanding of Loss and Change

Grief can be better understood if it is recognised that the fundamental crisis of bereavement and any significant loss arises not from the loss of the other, but from the loss of self (Marris 1993). Marris, drawing on Attachment Theory (Bowlby 1988), argues that loss disrupts our ability to find meaning in experience and grief represents the struggle to retrieve this sense of meaning when circumstances have bewildered it. He sees grief as a process of psychological reintegration,

"Impelled by the contradictory desires at once to search for and recover the lost relationship and to escape from painful reminders of loss." (p. vii)

Attachment Theory posits that humans have a fundamental need for security, both physical and emotional, and that how these needs are met will profoundly influence our development and relationship with others. In our earliest years we are dependent on at least one attachment figure, usually a parent (or two) in the first instance, to provide the consistency and predictability necessary in order safely to organise our experiences. In this way, we can make coherent sense of our world and our relationships within it. It is a prerequisite for our understanding of what is going on around us and for stable personality development. As we grow within the context of warm, stable and loving relationships, we develop a more coherent sense of ourselves and of others and of the relationship between the two. We develop the capacity to trust and we become more resilient and better able to manage our thoughts, feelings and behaviour. Marris writes,

"The organisation of meaning depends on a maturing power to conceptualise the relationship between feelings, purposes and actions." (p. ix)

Even so, the need for some thread of consistency remains throughout life. Marris notes how profoundly disruptive experiences of change and transition can be. He observes how a wide range of significant transitions—from bereavement, divorce, re-housing or even unfamiliar new business ventures—evoke similar patterns of response as we struggle to find meaning within much changed circumstances. He makes clear that such a crisis can arise just as much from voluntary as involuntary changes: in either,

"The anxieties of change centred upon the struggle to defend or recover a meaningful pattern of relationships." (p. 1)

Our purposes and expectations come to be organised around a set of relationships that are then crucial to the way we construe the meaning of our lives—how we understand the world, who we are, and how we live with others. With the loss of any important relationship, the structure and meaning that was based upon it disintegrates, provoking a characteristic anxiety, restlessness and despair that is the manifestation of a profound threat of the loss of meaning.

Marris argues that the task of psychological reintegration is essentially similar whether the structures of meaning fall apart from a physical bereavement, a broken personal relationship or because of profound social disruption. It is about the change, loss of a relationship and hence meaning. Reintegration requires that the purpose and feeling that have been lost in a change be extracted from its previous setting and reformulated in the present in order to infuse the evolving future with new meaning. Couched in psychological terms rather than sociological, the concept of reintegration nevertheless sits well with Ebaugh's notion of creating an ex-role.

LOSS AT WORK

While much has been written on unemployment and job loss, especially from a sociological perspective, with the economic turbulence internationally since the 1980s (for example, Jahoda 1982; Stokes and Cochrane 1984; Fineman 1987; Warr et al. 1988; Latack et al. 1995; Kiefer and Briner 1998; McKee-Ryan et al. 2005; Strangleman 2012), only relatively recently has thinking about grief been applied to the workplace and redundancy (Vickers 2009; Gabriel et al. 2010, 2013). Vickers interviewed middle- and senior-level executives who had been made redundant and explored their *"journey of grief."* She was struck by a pattern that emerged from her interview data showing a phased passage into grief that was central to respondents' reported experience of redundancy: something changed; loss commenced; loss confirmed; and afterwards.

She argued that in these cases of redundancy, unlike retirement that is usually well known about and often planned in advance, the process of grief still had started before the certain knowledge of the redundancy. Respondents talked (in retrospect) of something having changed in the workplace before any talk of redundancy; something was "*not quite right.*" There was an echo of this in some of my interview data from a few who had been defeated, for example, of eyes being averted in the last few days of the election campaign, of something being not quite right.

Hartley (1987) extended understanding of the psychological impact of job loss to the spouse, recognising that unemployment affects not just the individual but also their family. From interviews with the wives of former managers interviewed in her study, she noted that they were not passive witnesses to their husbands' unemployment but they were directly involved. They provided enormous practical and emotional support with some consequent strain on themselves. Yet a number felt unable to draw support within their neighbourhood. A more recent and very different study from Australia (Bubonya et al. 2014) examined the mental health of spouses and adolescent children after involuntary job loss from survey data. They found that wives', but not husbands', mental health was adversely impacted by their spouses' job loss if financial strain had followed or if there had been relationship strain prior to the loss. Adolescent girls, but not boys, resident in the household were also negatively affected.

Gabriel and colleagues examined the effect of job loss on a group of middle-aged professionals (a mixture of managers in business, charities and local government) immediately after the trauma of the loss (Gabriel et al. 2010) and again two years later (Gabriel et al. 2013). In their first paper, they proposed the term "*narrative coping*" to describe the unemployed professionals' struggle to construct a story that offered meaning and solace. In their second paper, they describe the trauma of job loss for their interviewees and their consequent "*fragmentation of identity.*" Three different behavioural responses to unemployment were seen,

"*A feverish search for a new job, resigned downshifting to a low-skill, part-time job and a positive re-invention of the self in doing many different jobs, some paid, some unpaid. Each subject related to a different type of narrative identity – wounded, fragmented or flexible.*"

The authors commented on how limited was their ability to predict the paths that each of their interviewees were to follow from the first interviews. They were struck by the usefulness of the qualities of opportunism and flexibility in their sample, not documented previously, in terms of being able successfully to reshape their lives. Whatever other skills and resources their interviewees had possessed, the willingness to be flexible in order to maintain some control and to discover a new chapter in their lives was very significant.

Much has been written on loss associated with retirement and ageing, and the consequences of retirement and ageing on physical and mental health (Beehr 1986; Atchley 1989; Kiefer and Briner 1998; Kets de Vries 2003a; Calov et al. 2009; Adams et al. 2011; Damman et al. 2013; Wang 2013). Many facets have been examined including planning for retirement; the degree of control; the loss of structure and meaningful activity; discontinuity and continuity; changes in social engagement; the need for role replacement; loss of purpose and identity; the opportunity for accomplishment; work-role centrality; and attachment to the work or to the organisation. It is a complicated picture. Retirement is now conceptualised as a process over time, just as any transition, and more is understood about its impact at a more finely grained level. Wang (2013) demonstrated that,

"Over an eight year period of retirement adjustment process, about 70 % of retirees experienced minimum psychological well-being changes; about 25 % of retirees experienced negative changes in psychological well-being during the initial transition stage but then showed improvements afterward; and about 5 % of retirees experienced positive changes in psychological well-being. These findings suggest that retirees do not follow a uniform pattern of retirement adjustment."

More recently, attention has been paid to the importance of the experience of work pre-retirement and post-retirement work on the retirement process. For example, workers in jobs with high levels of complexity are less likely to retire while workers who are dissatisfied with their job are more likely to choose retirement (Wang 2013). Jobs that do not allow much personalisation are easier to leave behind than those that do as they offer little reinforcement to a person's sense of identity (Atchley 1989). Vough et al. (2015) propose a more nuanced model still. They use a "sensemaking" lens to focus on the subjective meanings that people attach to the factors that trigger the retirement decision rather than simply the factors themselves, in order to understand the impact on their interviewees' evolving identity.

That retirement is not just a matter for the individual has been increasingly recognised. For example, a spouse's employment and involvement in decision-making will influence satisfaction in retirement (Szinovacz and

Davey 2005). Kiefer and Briner (1998) go further: they suggest that the way in which retirement is managed has significant implications for the organisation that the retiree is leaving, so that retirement is seen as a reciprocal process.

Kets de Vries (2003a) brings psychological insights into his analysis of the difficulties that leaders in particular face in letting go at the end of their career. He considers the financial, social and psychological barriers to *"letting go"* and comments how,

"For leaders, the relinquishing of power is especially difficult ... for them, the retreat into the private sphere represents an enormous reversal. They are suddenly deprived, at retirement, of what to them are essential nutrients: identification with an institution of great power; influence over individuals, policies, finances, and the community; and constant affirmation of their importance as individuals and of their role as leader to others."

He suggests that leaders feel *"the assault"* of ageing more than most because they tend to be more narcissistic, as a result both of predisposition and position,

"Narcissists are more aware of decline – after all, the realization of one's mortality is the ultimate narcissistic injury – and thus decline has a greater psychological impact on them than it has on other people."

Whether or not leaving political office is perceived as a decline will be dependent on a number of other factors. But a loss of some degree it most certainly is.

LOSS IN THE CONTEXT OF POLITICAL OFFICE

For the overwhelming majority of my interviewees, their political role had much valued and one into which enormous passion, energy and commitment had been poured. For many, it had been a role that they had cherished from an early age and had been seen as akin to a vocational calling. It was an occupation in which their values were deeply embedded and from which they had derived identity and meaning. For some, it was virtually all consuming: personal sacrifices had been made; strong relationships had been forged. In elected office, the boundary between the personal and the political is hard to maintain.

The influence and authority that come with political office further compromise the personal–political boundary. Politicians are much in demand; constituents bombard them with requests that only they, it seems, can deal with; and their pronouncements command the ready attention of the media. They occupy a *"valued social position"* (Warr et al. 1988), albeit one that is perhaps less valued than once it was. In such circumstances, it is dangerously easy for the distinction between the political role and the individual occupying that role to become further blurred.

But my interviewees had been (sometimes forcibly) cast out from the political tribe, or even, for one interviewee, what had felt like her/his family. Political office powerfully offers psychological motives for identity, meaning, control and belonging (Ashforth 2012).

In this context, it is to be expected that the transition from political office should have presented challenges for many participants in this study, whether it had been chosen or not. It had been a world in which their values had indeed been at the core, where they had derived purpose and meaning, and in which their status, group and individual identity continually had been affirmed. Its loss inevitably led to profound changes in their world and hence to their sense of self. Each struggled—in varying ways and to varying degrees—to come to terms with a new set of circumstances within which they could craft coherent meaning.

There are additional complexities of the process of transition from political office when it is involuntary and at the hands of an electorate. It was notable how many of those who had been defeated described, sometimes hesitantly, feeling as though they had been bereaved—echoing Shaffir and Kleinknecht (2005) and Kwiatkowski (2015). They were acutely conscious that no one had died and often were somewhat embarrassed at having made the comparison. But that was how it felt for many, and worse, *"there was no funeral."*

In defeat, the exit evidently has not been chosen and the politician has had no control over his/her demise; s/he has had little or no time to prepare for such a drastic disruption to their life—indeed, the exigencies of campaigning demand that all thoughts of defeat are banished; and for many of my interviewees the defeat was unexpected even until after the count had started. The bad news had come in under the full glare of a baying media and at a time when candidates were run down and exhausted. In addition to the wholly unwelcome new set of circumstances into which the (about to be former) MP or council leader had been plunged, they had to contend with having their previous expectations, hopes and calculations dashed. What had seemed to make sense shockingly no longer made any sense. In such circumstances, the challenge to an individual's self-concept is all the greater.

As one former bewildered council leader said about his/her leadership role,

"It was who I was, what I did… it was what got me up in the morning."

Or the partner of an MP who had been unexpectedly defeated said s/he had,

"Lost a sense of who he was."

Unlike those who have chosen to stand down, politicians who have either been defeated at the ballot box, or worse, been de-selected by their own side, have to deal with their feelings of hurt, resentment, anger and betrayal—all making more complicated the process of coming to terms with their loss. It is recognised that the process of grief is more challenging where there had been an ambivalent relationship with that which has been lost. How much more difficult might this be when a politician tries to reconcile the virtually irreconcilable: on the one hand, appreciating and valuing that democracy depends on the electorate being able to kick out an elected representative but, on the other hand, feeling hurt, ingratitude and anger that the electorate has done pre-cisely this after all their hard work. But the wrestling between these two conflicting responses is dangerous to articulate: the democratic deal, after all, is clear. No room for whingeing. No wonder that many of those who were defeated could not bear to go back to either the constituency, the party, or the county hall where once they had held sway: the painful conflict that it evoked was simply best avoided. No wonder some went into retreat.

REINTEGRATION AND A NEW NARRATIVE

Following a significant loss or disruption, the task is to re-organise our experiences in very changed circumstances and to create sense and mean-ing out of them. And so it is for politicians leaving office. One of my interviewees, quoted in Chap. 6, reflected on how helpful s/he had found going away after standing down and for there to have been,

"An element of calm after to sort of regroup."

The task of psychological reintegration—or to create an ex-role, in Ebaugh's (1988) terms—is an imperative for all politicians leaving office, however voluntarily or involuntarily. Even for those in this study who were champing at the bit to leave and for whom transition was almost inevitably going to be more straightforward, the actual experience of no longer being an MP or council leader would be unfamiliar.

Marris (1993) suggests four conditions that facilitate the process of reintegration:

i) Past experiences of warm and consistent relationships in childhood that strongly influence how we interpret the world, our capacity for trust, emotional resilience, and how we in turn relate to others;
ii) The less conflicted or unresolved the meaning of what has been lost;
iii) Time to prepare for the loss;
iv) Events after the loss may support or frustrate process of recovery, including the ability to feel in control of your destiny after the loss and to find common endeavour with others facing a similar predicament.

These conditions are helpful in considering the transition from political office and I will return to them when I consider more fully the factors that might help or hinder the transition in the next chapter.

Contemplating leaving political office is almost inevitably linked to the idea of someone else taking on that role, a successor. The ease with which an individual may be able to embrace such a notion is both political—whether your party remains ascendant, perhaps—and personal. Kets de Vries (2006) considers the relationship between individuals' power orientation and their personality structure in his extensive studies on leadership and leaders. He argues that narcissistic personality traits, including poor self-esteem and a desire for admiration and prestige, are more prevalent in leaders than followers. Political leaders are no exception, and moving out of the sunlight thus is especially challenging for some.

Notably those who had found the transition particularly troubling had not felt able to voice how they had been feeling, either privately or more widely. It was simply not a subject that they felt comfortably could be raised. This is unsurprising given the dearth of public acknowledgement of their predicament. Former MPs scatter to the wind and it is hard even to identify former council leaders. Echoing Keane (2011), our system rightly demands that politicians return to life as an ordinary citizen, but with more understanding and support for the personal task that they face, it might be easier for them to construct over time an ex-role, a new narrative of who they are and what they do.

One partner summed up the journey that had been made by his/her partner over the two years since electoral defeat: despite the initial devastation, over time,

"He got what is important for him, which is a narrative about what he's doing … he feels he's got something that explains who he is."
That is precisely the task.

WIDER RIPPLES BEYOND THE INDIVIDUAL

The interview material in this study demonstrates the extent of the impact, both direct and indirect, on the partners of former MPs and council leaders both during their time of office and at the time of leaving and since.

That partners of politicians are drawn into the demands of political office is no surprise: demanding jobs of any sort have a similar sort of impact. But the discomfort and the degree to which most partners felt that their lives and careers had been constrained by the public scrutiny arising from their spouses' role are worth highlighting. Partners are not elected.

Linda McDougall, the wife of the Labour MP, Austin Mitchell, has documented accounts from both female MPs and MPs' wives of the effects of parliamentary life on partners and children (McDougall 1998). She notes with approval a Parliamentary Partners' Support Group having been set up in the late 1990s but she makes no mention of parliamentary exits. Resonating with a couple of the interviewees in this study, she reports how one MP had only come to realise how little time he had previously spent with his children when his first grandchild was born.

The impact on partners of their spouses' exit from political office will depend on the experience of office of both partners, the experience of the politician leaving office, and the dynamics of the couple relationship. Relief, pride, loyalty, delight, anxiety, impatience, frustration, guilt and anger were all in the mix. Hartley (1987) noted similar emotions in her study of wives of unemployed men. Inevitably, these will impact on the couple relationship, as with any major life transition.

For those who adapted badly to standing down or who were defeated, their partners were centrally involved. It is normally part of the marital deal to offer understanding, support and consolation to the other at times of stress. But partners may well not have been prepared for the intensity of their own feeling or that of their spouses, nor how long it was to last. It is not, as we have seen, something that is much remarked upon. Partners were the ones often to hold the pessimism and anxiety prior to an electoral defeat, and, with less restraint, to articulate hurt, anger, outrage at ingratitude and lack of acknowledgement afterwards. Often they had left the political party, not their spouses. It was as if they were the receptacle for such intense feelings and that it was somehow more permissible for them and not their spouses to hold and to articulate them. Democracy has, after all, dealt a perfectly proper hand. Relationships with local and national political parties were beyond repair for a number.

With so little thought having been given to those departing political office, political parties risk losing the allegiance and goodwill of those who hitherto have been unstinting in their commitment to them. Political parties may lose the activism, knowledge and understanding of long experienced and loyal people. Given the currently parlous state of all the main political parties, it seems foolhardy to squander such a potentially useful resource.

That the ripples of leaving office had spread widely throughout the wider family and further still, to the political party, is readily understood through the prism of systems thinking. Family systemic thinking (e.g. Campbell and Draper 1985; Dallos and Draper 2010) draws on wider systems theory to understand the nature of any system. Instead of considering an individual in isolation, it looks at the family as a unit albeit one embedded within ever widening systems (such as here, the political party, the electorate), and the relationships within them. It stresses the interdependence of action within families and in other relationships. Family systemic thinking is less interested in the intra-psychic but in the interpersonal. It is interested in the relationships between family members and how those relationships each impact reciprocally on one another. It offers a theoretical justification for the approach taken in this research to interview the partners of those who had left political office.

So, there are implications for individuals, their families and political parties in terms of what can be done better on a human level—but are there any wider implications? I consider this in Chap. 13.

REFERENCES

Adams, K.B., Leibbrandt, S. and Moon, H. (2011). A Critical Review of the Literature on Social and Leisure Activity and Wellbeing in Later Life. *Ageing and Society* 31 pp. 683–712.

Ashforth, B.E. (2012). *Role Transitions in Organizational Life: An Identity-Based Perspective*. East Sussex and New York: Routledge.

Atchley, R.C. (1989). Continuity Theory of Normal Ageing. *The Gerontologist* 29 (2) pp. 183–90.

Beehr, T.A. (1986). The Process of Retirement: A Review and Recommendations for Future Investigation. *Personnel Psychology* 39 pp. 31–55.

Bowlby, J. (1988). *A Secure Base: Clinical Applications of Attachment Theory.* London: Routledge.

Bubonya, M., Cobb-Clark, D.A. and Wooden, M. (2014). A Family Affair: Job Loss and the Mental Health of Spouses and Adolescents. *IZA Discussion Paper 8588* October 2014.

Byrne, C. and Theakston, K. (2015). Leaving the House: The Experience of Former Members of Parliament Who Left the House of Commons in 2010. *Parliamentary Affairs* doi: 10.1093/pa/gsv053.

Cain, S. (2012). *Quiet.* London: Penguin Books.

Calov, E., Haverstick, K. and Sass, S.A. (2009). Gradual Retirement, Sense of Control, and Retirees' Happiness. *Research on Ageing* 31 (1) pp. 112–135.

Campbell, D. and Draper, R. (1985). *Applications of Systemic Family Therapy.* London: Grune & Stratton, Ltd.

Cecić Erpič, S., Wylleman, P. and Zupančič, M. (2004). The Effect of Athletic and Non-athletic Factors on the Sports Career Termination Process. *Psychology of Sport and Exercise* 5 pp. 45–59.

Dallos, R. and Draper, R. (2010). *An Introduction to Family Therapy: Systemic Theory and Practice.* England: Open University Press.

Damman, M., Henkens, K. and Kalmijn, M. (2013). Missing Work After Retirement: The Role of Life Histories in the Retirement Adjustment Process. *The Gerontologist* doi: 10.1093/geront/gnt169.

Ebaugh, H.R.F. (1988). *Becoming an Ex.* Chicago: The University of Chicago Press.

Fineman, S. (1987). *The middle class: Unemployed and underemployed.* In S. Fineman (Ed.), *Unemployment Personal and Social Consequences.* London: Tavistock.

Freud, S. (1917). *Mourning and melancholia.* In James Strachey (Ed.), *The Standard Edition of the Complete Psychological Works of Sigmund Freud* Vol. XIV. London: The Hogarth Press.

Gabriel, Y., Gray, D.E. and Goregaokar, H. (2010). Temporary Derailment or the End of the Line? Managers Coping with Unemployment at 50. *Organization Studies* 31 (12) pp. 1687–1712.

Gabriel, Y., Gray, D.E. and Goregaokar, H. (2013). Job Loss and Its Aftermath Among Managers and Professionals: Wounded, Fragmented and Flexible. *Work, Employment and Society* 27 (1) pp. 56–72.

Hartley, J. (1987). *Managerial unemployment: The wife's perspective and role.* In S. Fineman (Ed.), *Unemployment Personal and Social Consequences.* London: Tavistock.

Jahoda, M. (1982). *Employment and Unemployment: A Socio-Psychological Analysis.* Cambridge: Cambridge University Press.

James, D.V., Sukhwal, S., Farnham, F.R., Evans, J., Barrie, C., Taylor, A. and Wilson, S.P. (2016). Harassment and Stalking of Members of the Unitied

Kingdom Parliament: Associations and Consequences. *The Journal of Forensic Psychiatry and Psychology* doi: 10.1080/14789949.2015.1124909. Accessed 24.1.16.

Kantrowitz, J.L. (2014). *The Myths of Termination*. East Sussex and New York: Routledge.

Keane, J. (2011). *Life after political death*. In J. Kane, H. Patapan, and P. `t Hart (Eds.), *Dispersed Democratic Leadership*. Oxford: Oxford University Press.

Kiefer, T. and Briner, R.B. (1998). Managing Retirement – Rethinking Links between Individual and Organization. *European Journal of Work and Organizational Psychology* 7 (3) pp. 373–390.

Kets de Vries, M.F.R. (2003a). The Retirement Syndrome: The Psychology of Letting Go. *European Management Journal* 21 (6) pp. 707–716.

Kets de Vries, M.F.R. (2006). *The Leader on the Couch*. Chichester: John Wiley & Sons Ltd.

Klein, M. (1940). *Mourning and its relation to manic-depressive states*. In *The Writings of Melanie Klein* Vol. 1. London: The Hogarth Press.

Kübler-Ross, E. (1969). *On Death and Dying: What the Dying have to Teach Doctors, Nurses, Clergy and Their Own Families*. New York: Scribner.

Kwiatkowski, R. (2015). Our House. *The House* 37 no.1513 27 March 2015.

Latack, J.C., Kinicki, A.J. and Prussia, G.E. (1995). An Integrative Process Model of Coping with Job Loss. *Academy of Management Review* 20 (2) pp. 311–342.

Local Government Association. (2012). *Politicians and Personality. A Guide for Councillors*. London: LGA.

McDougall, L. (1998). *Westminster Women*. London: Vintage.

McKee-Ryan, F.M., Song, Z.L., Wanberg, C.R. and Kinicki, A.J. (2005). Psychological and Physical Well-Being During Unemployment: A Meta-analytic Study. *Journal of Applied Psychology* 90 (1) pp. 53–76.

Marris, P. (1993). *Loss and Change*, London: Routledge.

Murray Parkes, C. (1971). Psycho-Social Transitions: A Field for Study. *Social Science and Medicine* 5 pp. 101–115.

Riddell, P. (2013). Personal communication.

Schlossberg, N.K. (1981). A Model for Analyzing Human Adaptation to Transition. *The Counseling Psychologist* 9 (2) pp. 2–18.

Shaffir, W. and Kleinknecht, S. (2005). Death at the Polls. Experiencing and Coping with Political Defeat. *Journal of Contemporary Ethnography* 34 (6) pp. 707–738.

Strangleman, T. (2012). Work Identity in Crisis? Rethinking the Problem of Attachment and Loss at Work. *Sociology* 46 pp. 411–425.

Stokes, G. and Cochrane, R. (1984). A Study of the Psychological Effects of Redundancy and Unemployment. *Journal of Occupational Psychology* 57 pp. 309–322.

Szinovacz, M.E. and Davey, A. (2005). Retirement and Marital Decision Making: Effects on Retirement Satisfaction. *Journal of Marriage and Family* 67 pp. 387–398.

Vickers, M.H. (2009). Journeys into Grief: Exploring Redundancy for a New Understanding of Work Place Grief. *Journal of Loss and Trauma* 14 (5) pp. 401–419.

Vough, H.C., Bataille, C.D., Chul Noh, S. and Dean Lee, M. (2015). Going Off Script: How Managers Make Sense of the Ending of Their Career. *Journal of Management Studies* 52 (3) pp. 414–440.

Wang, M. (2013). *Retirement: An introduction and overview of the handbook.* In M. Wang (Ed.), *The Oxford Textbook of Retirement.* Oxford: Oxford University Press.

Warr, P., Jackson, P. and Banks, M. (1988). Unemployment and Mental Health: Some British Studies. *Journal of Social Issues* 44 (4) pp. 47–68.

Weinberg, A. (2010). Too hot to handle? MPs' personalities and their experience of stress and controversy. BPS Annual Conference, Stratford upon Avon. *Proceedings of the BPS,* 15 (2).

Weinberg, A. (2012). *Should the job of national politicians carry a government health warning? The impact of psychological strain on politicians.* In A. Weinberg (Ed.), *The Psychology of Politicians.* Cambridge University Press: Cambridge.

CHAPTER 12

What May Help or Hinder the Transition from Political Office?

As we have seen, the experiences of leaving political office shared some commonalities but they differed too. The previous chapter explored how we might better understand the process of transition from political office, and thus better understand the differences in the experiences of those exiting office as well as the experiences that may be shared.

The interview material suggests the following factors all had a bearing on how transition from political office was experienced and I draw on both the material from this study and insights from the academic literature considered in earlier chapters to address each in turn:

(i) *The experience of office*
   The journey of transition was much more straightforward for those MPs who had come to dislike the role. Not surprising, but it underlines Marris' (1993) second facilitative condition for re-integration, discussed in the previous chapter, and the importance of understanding the meaning of what has been lost. These MPs were clear that Parliament was no longer for them and had long before started the process of withdrawal. For one, far from losing a sense of purpose in leaving Parliament, it was the opportunity to regain a sense of meaningful purpose, a very different outlook compared with most other interviewees.
   It was less straightforward for those council leaders and MPs who, although they were clear that they should stand down, still had relished and much valued their time in office. This was true even if

© The Author(s) 2017
J. Roberts, *Losing Political Office*,
DOI 10.1007/978-3-319-39702-3_12

the decision to go had been entirely voluntary. As many said, nothing can quite replace the challenge, the excitement and the buzz of political office. For those for whom there had been external or family pressures to stand down, feelings were more complicated still and difficult to resolve, depending on the circumstances.

Marris' emphasis on the meaning of what has been lost chimes with insights from the academic literature on factors that facilitate adjustment to the loss of work in a range of occupations. One of the most useful—borne out by this small exploratory study—is the importance of the experience in work before the loss (for example, Wang 2013; Vough et al. 2015).

(ii) *The manner of leaving and the degree of voluntariness*
In standing down, politicians will have at least some degree of control over their decision to leave office, and it would be expected that such politicians would fare better in making the transition. The manner of exit—having chosen to stand down or having been defeated—did make a difference to the experience of leaving political office, but as we have seen, it was far more nuanced than this alone. Indeed, two former office holders, both unexpectedly and narrowly defeated, had adjusted well and flourished within a relatively short time, while two who had stood down, albeit with some degree of involuntariness, had struggled for a long time subsequently. The picture is evidently more complicated as Ashforth (2012) suggests, with the meaning of the loss being the key issue.

Any degree of involuntariness in the loss of political office—whether because of de-selection, electoral defeat or a wish to avoid personal or political embarrassment—will complicate and make more ambivalent the meaning of what has been lost. Feelings of anger, hurt, betrayal or guilt may all cloud the picture.

(iii) *The degree of planning and preparation for leaving and the future*
Planning for both the immediate transition from office and the future had helped considerably. This is not surprising: Bridges (2011, p. 8), resonating with Weinberg (2007), states clearly,

"The failure to identify and get ready for endings and losses is the largest difficulty for people in transition."

Planning for a very different life—a different status, different social networks, a different identity, no longer mattering to others in the same way and a different purpose in life as well as the practicalities of income and structuring time—is a challenge. But it is important. Just *"waiting to see what happens,"* as one interviewee in this study had done, is a dangerous strategy. The one former MP who had planned leaving office with assiduous care had flourished, while s/he was still able to acknowledge how much the loss of office had meant personally. The journey from a role hugely valued was recognised as having been deeply unsettling and painful, but s/he had emerged positive and confident of the decision to stand down and of her/his new direction.

Planning does not necessarily entail a fixed view about the future, rather a broad proactive stance to try out different possibilities, as one of my interviewees who had enjoyed *"playing with different toys"* and another who had been able to find more equanimity after a very difficult period, having set up a small business in a very different sphere than the one s/he had originally envisaged. There was a suggestion that inflexibility about the future was unhelpful. One interviewee had struggled to move on with her/his life, having only one set and very determined goal that s/he would regain political office.

Planning was, of course, much more difficult for those who were defeated, often unexpectedly. There was little, if any, time to prepare for the loss of office. Not only were candidates in marginal seats consumed by campaigning in the months before an election, but, psychologically, it was very difficult to admit to themselves, let alone to others who were campaigning hard on their behalf, that defeat was even possible—hence the importance of partners holding the pessimism.

Electoral defeat takes office away so very suddenly and at a time of exhaustion and frayed hope, neither condition conducive to beginning a process of psychological re-integration. And in such circumstances, politicians feel responsible for others—their campaign team, fellow defeated councillors and their staff—rather than attending immediately to their own needs. Furthermore, far from winding down as the election approaches, recognised as facilitating the process of retirement in other occupations (and possible for politicians standing down), the pace of work ramps up enormously.

(iv) *Personal resilience*

My study did not attempt to explore personal resilience in any depth, but it did seem to influence the journey of transition from office among my interviewees. The idea of personal resilience echoes

Marris' first facilitative condition for the re-integrative journey—past experiences of warm and consistent relationships in the childhood. I did not probe the backgrounds and personality development of those whom I interviewed: that was not the deal in terms of my research. There were nevertheless a few hints in some of the material volunteered of earlier difficulties that might have impacted on how individuals had been able to manage their transition from office. This would hardly be unexpected: we know that personal resilience is derived from a number of factors including our early experiences.

(v) *The degree to which the individual's identity was wrapped up in the political role and the degree to which other sources of identity, professional and personal, were present.*

It was very apparent that those whose identities were almost entirely wrapped up in their political role and whose social networks were exclusively centred around politics had suffered most. Politics was all consuming with little time, interest or energy for anything else. As discussed earlier, Ebaugh (1988) and Ashforth (2012) are very clear that role exit is more difficult for those whose identity is submerged in that role.

(vi) *Being able to finding a new role (or return to a previous profession).*

Finding a new role, whether to earn income—an imperative for those under retirement age and a breadwinner—or to begin to acquire a new identity, made a considerable difference to the journey of adjustment from political office. Those who had languished at home struggled most, confidence and self-esteem lowered further. As observed earlier, with the increased pace of change in many professions, it may be more difficult now to return to a previous job.

Whatever is the new role(s)—paid, voluntary, whatever it may be—it brings different social networks, different opportunities, a structure, the possibility of purpose—a new source of identity, key to developing a new narrative about who a former MP/council leader is and what they do.

(vii) *Family and social support*

Family support made a great deal of difference to those leaving political office in this study, but it was not always available: family relationships might not have been tended to as they might owing to the demands of office; the effects of the loss of office might have brought about significant difficulties in the couple relationship or the "family" of most value was the political party that the politician felt most abandoned by.

Meeting others in the same position did help some, finding a common endeavour with others in a similar predicament, described by Marris. Many interviewees had taken solace from meeting with others in a similar situation, whether a group of de-selected or defeated councillors, former Labour MPs (the "PLP-in-exile") or the AFMP. In the early days, however, some had not felt robust enough even to meet; they needed first to have begun to find their feet, to construct a new narrative about who they were and what they would do.

Notably, those who had found the transition from political office particularly troubling had not felt able to voice how they had been feeling, either privately or more widely. It was simply not a subject that they felt could be comfortably raised. Politicians are not supposed to complain about the proper exercise of a democratic choice.

(viii) *Acknowledgement by others of their value in office*

Acknowledgement of the contribution that the former council leader or MP had made was enormously valued by those who had experienced it. And its absence made things significantly worse. Letters and events to mark their transition from office—whether a private dinner, genuine and personal letters of appreciation, an honour—had meant a great deal: not quite a funeral, but something akin to it, and certainly a significant rite of passage in the journey of transition. It helped the ex-politician to have recognition and appreciation of their contribution. These so-called "*transition bridges*"— something to preserve a sense of personal continuity on the journey of transition—are known to be helpful (Ashforth 2012).

An opportunity to say goodbye to valued others in an unrushed manner was especially an issue for council leaders. Local government officers are employed by the council and will immediately serve the council leader's successor, whereas MPs employ their own staff and may instead be more troubled by feelings of guilt for their staff.

(ix) *Recognition of their skills after leaving office*

That the skills and experience of both former MPs and council leaders were little recognised, much less used, compounded the diminished sense of confidence and self-worth of a significant number in this study. For some former politicians, the recognition and affirmation of their skills and experience in this way may help to assuage difficulties in adjusting to life after office. Over half the former MPs in both Theakston, Gouge and Honeyman's study (2007) and Byrne and Theakston's (2015) study stated that they did not feel that enough use was being made of their skills, knowledge and experience.

These findings resonate with what has come to be understood from research into the impact of redundancy and retirement, already discussed, but the nature of holding political office introduces constraints on the availability of some protective factors. The introduction of fixed five-year term Parliaments in the UK by The Fixed-term Parliaments Act 2011 that took effect for the first time at the General Election of 7 May 2015 does now allow for more certainty for MPs, at least in terms of when an election will be fought. Council leaders are long used to the date of elections being known well in advance.

Length of tenure did not seem to be a factor influencing adjustment to loss of office with the possible exception of those MPs who stood down having found the role uncongenial. Three of these four chose to leave after one or two terms, the other after much longer. That length of tenure was not otherwise a factor may be understood by a number of factors each counter-balancing another. For example, the longer the duration of office, the more that an individual's identity may be wrapped up in the role to the exclusion of other identities versus the salience of the loss of "what might have been" as well as what had been for those who had been in office for a relatively short period.

Neither was age a factor in this study. Young and older former MPs and council leaders struggled alike. It might have been expected that middle and older age would be a protective factor: older politicians may be more financially secure; peers in other occupations might be approaching retirement; and individuals may have had longer to establish a more robust sense of themselves through a variety of life's vicissitudes. This was not however apparent. The imperative for younger former politicians to find alternative employment and build a new narrative was undoubtedly stronger. If and when they did find a new role, then the opportunity to build a new narrative was that much more straightforward.

There was just a hint in this study that women had adapted better to their exit from office, but numbers are too small to be confident about this.

Only one former MP was adamant from the moment of defeat that s/he was determined to find another parliamentary seat and remained absolutely set on this outcome. It may be that this lack of flexibility did not serve her/him well, given the importance of flexibility following job loss, suggested by Gabriel and colleagues (Gabriel et al. 2013).

Attribution of blame for having been defeated—a personal failure for not having worked hard enough or that it had been because of a national tide that had been very difficult to counter—did not seem to be a factor in adjusting to life after office in this study, but the numbers are very small. A cohort effect when many MPs of one political party are swept out of office, such as for some councils mid-electoral cycle or at the UK General Elections of 1997 or 2015, may be protective, as in the notion of group exit (Ebaugh 1988).

Although the precipitous loss of income and financial strain arising from the loss of office undoubtedly added to the psychological pressures on individuals in my sample and their partners, financial security on the other hand did not of itself prevent difficulties in making the transition from office, echoing work on redundancy more generally (e.g. Stokes and Cochrane 1984).

These factors listed above come together in different ways for different individuals and seem to influence how a politician leaving office tackles the task of re-integration and creating a new narrative. As Ebaugh (1988) makes clear, an "ex"-role is very different from a "never," not having ever been in political office. Her valuable insight should be held firmly in mind in the development of that new narrative especially as our democratic system understandably but firmly squashes any notion that former politicians have any continuing formal status. Recognition by others, perhaps even members of the public, that an individual had previously been in political office and a public figure—a transition bridge—can be helpful to strengthen the new narrative in which having been an MP or a council leader is a key part.

While it may be possible to predict the risk factors for those who may find leaving office especially troubling, it should be stressed that the nature of political office, its visibility and, for most, the magnitude of the transition of relinquishing it means that even the most resilient and well supported former politicians may struggle. However well planned the exit may be, leaving political office involves a profound, irreplaceable loss for most, whether they have stood down or been defeated.

As one former MP sagely reflected,

"The power to really decisively change things goes with political power ... and that is what you can't replace by some other thing."

PRACTICAL STEPS THAT COULD MAKE A DIFFERENCE

This study has given voice to a range of experiences of politicians, former MPs and council leaders who left office in recent years and some of their partners. It is clear that we treat exit from political office very differently from exit from any other role. When politicians leave office, they simply go. Democracy demands that those whom we elect, we can at another time deprive of office. Quite right too. But at a personal level, why is it not possible simply to acknowledge and empathise with the turbulence that this may provoke for many?

It is not difficult to do better. Doing better does not mean that we have to compromise the fundamental tenets of our democracy. Nor does doing better necessarily mean spending money.

WE ALL SHOULD:

- Simply acknowledge and talk openly about the human consequences of politicians leaving office. Celebrate that we can turf politicians out but leave salaciousness aside. We should normalise the sense of dislocation and understand the need to find a new narrative over time.

Individual politicians could usefully:

- Before exiting office, think about and plan—not always possible—for the future. But take care about whom you confide in, given the political risks.
- Despite the time pressures of office, do not neglect close family members and friends—important to nurture anyway but you will need them later—and maintain other interests. Carve out the time and safeguard it jealously—and unapologetically.
- If you are standing down, plan for the time leading up to leaving, the immediate transition and the longer term, accustoming yourself as

far as possible to a different life. Anticipate how it might be in some detail.

- Even if contesting a marginal seat, get someone else to do some planning on your behalf, just in case. Better something than nothing.
- Do be flexible. Try different avenues. Do not hold out only for one thing.
- If someone else does not organise an event suitably timed (if stepping down, at the time of exit; if defeated, later), to mark your leaving, do it yourself—or again, get someone else to. You need a rite of passage.
- Recognise that this is a journey, maybe two years at least, in which your task is to craft a new narrative of who you are and what you do. You may not know what that is. This time may well be anxiety provoking and/or exciting. In the early stages especially, it is entirely understandable that you might feel uncertain, bewildered and disorientated.
- Recognise the many skills that you have acquired in office. Seek support with writing a CV/being interviewed. Ask others for advice—remember, you have the Upper House next door (very) full of people from many walks of life. Ask even if you feel so much less confident than you did.
- Do not hold back from talking with others in the same predicament if that would help you. You do not have to be all sorted before you go—they have been there.

Partners and family could usefully:

- Understand and anticipate what may be coming with the loss of office, including its intensity, both the direct and indirect impact on you.
- Your partner will need support—but you may well too.

Political parties (local and national) could usefully:

- Acknowledge—in timely and personalised manner—the contribution made by the departing politician and their family. This needs to be thought about in advance so that someone has the time, space and thoughtfulness to write genuinely and meaningfully. This is not costly.

- Organise an event to celebrate their contribution. It will help.
- Put to good use the departing politician's knowledge, experience and skills to energise and build the party at grassroots and coach less experienced politicians. It will help them and you.
- Think about the flow not only into but also out of political office. Political parties should engage—and be seen to engage—with the conditions that may make our democratic system more robust.

Parliament, Local Authorities and the Local Government Association (LGA) could usefully:

- Recognise the potential difficulties for politicians leaving office.
- Acknowledge—in a timely and personalised manner—the contribution of the departing politician. Do this even if there has been a change of political control.
- Signpost former MPs and former council leaders to helpful employment and career advice including help with CV writing, interview technique and the use of social media to help find employment.
- Recognise the increasing impact of the loss of office that will face full-time council leaders and directly elected mayors and its potential consequences.
- Track what happens to former council leaders. The LGA could do this. Currently, we have no idea.
- Put to good use former MPs' and council leaders' knowledge, experience and skills, for example, incisively condensing complex material, ruthless priority setting; political judgement and decision making; and effective communication in a wider range of settings.

REFERENCES

Ashforth, B.E. (2012). *Role Transitions in Organizational Life: An Identity-Based Perspective*. East Sussex and New York: Routledge.

Bridges, W. (2011). *Managing Transitions: Making the Most of Change*. London: Nicholas Brealey Publishing.

Byrne, C. and Theakston, K. (2015). Leaving the House: The Experience of Former Members of Parliament Who Left the House of Commons in 2010. *Parliamentary Affairs* doi: 10.1093/pa/gsv053.

Ebaugh, H.R.F. (1988). *Becoming an Ex*. Chicago: The University of Chicago Press.

Gabriel, Y., Gray, D.E. and Goregaokar, H. (2013). Job Loss and Its Aftermath Among Managers and Professionals: Wounded, Fragmented and Flexible. *Work, Employment and Society* 27 (1) pp. 56–72.

Marris, P. (1993). *Loss and Change*, London: Routledge.

Stokes, G. and Cochrane, R. (1984). A Study of the Psychological Effects of Redundancy and Unemployment. *Journal of Occupational Psychology* 57 pp. 309–322.

Theakston, K., Gouge, E. and Honeyman, V. (2007). *Life after Losing or Leaving: The Experience of Former Members of Parliament*. A report for the Association of Former Members of Parliament by the University of Leeds.

Wang, M. (2013). *Retirement: An introduction and overview of the handbook*. In M. Wang (Ed.), *The Oxford Textbook of Retirement*. Oxford: Oxford University Press.

Weinberg, A. (2007). Your destiny in their hands: Job loss and success in Members of Parliament. BPS Annual Conference, York. *Proceedings of the BPS*, 15 (2).

Vough, H.C., Bataille, C.D., Chul Noh, S. and Dean Lee, M. (2015). Going Off Script: How Managers Make Sense of the Ending of Their Career. *Journal of Management Studies* 52 (3) pp. 414–440.

CHAPTER 13

Why Losing Political Office Matters to Us All

Losing political office is a major life transition for the individuals involved and the ripples spread wider, to family members and beyond. But are there further implications for our democratic system? Other than at a human level, why should we care?

In the first part of this chapter, I briefly review the rippling effects of the exit from political office from individuals on to partners, families, political parties, employers and wider civic society. I then go on to reflect on the relationship between those who are elected and those whom they represent, to consider concerns about a political class that is seen to be increasingly separate from ordinary citizens, and to make the case for more "fluidity" in our political system in order to strengthen our representative democracy.

POLITICIANS THEMSELVES LOSE OUT

The research presented in this book illustrates the extent to which politicians can be affected by leaving office. Having seen colleagues struggle, it is possible that politicians in office may be fearful of stepping down or, at least they may be anxious about what lies ahead. They may end up staying too long as a result which could compromise the effectiveness of their representative role, and lead to a narrowing of personal options.

Let us dismiss the widespread notion of former politicians in the UK generally breezing into well-paid jobs or corporate directorships. As we

© The Author(s) 2017
J. Roberts, *Losing Political Office*,
DOI 10.1007/978-3-319-39702-3_13

have seen in Chap. 3, this is simply not the case (Gonzàlez-Bailon et al. 2013; Byrne and Theakston 2015). Byrne and Theakston found that nearly a majority, 42 per cent of the former MPs in their study who were seeking paid employment, were still out of work three months after leaving Parliament; and 27 per cent of these (or 11 per cent of the total) were still out of work 12 months after leaving. The struggle to find employment was evident in this research. Of course, in austere economic times, former politicians will find it harder to get a job just as many people will, and there is no reason why former politicians should be immune, but their skills and experience could at least be recognised and taken into account.

Partners of Politicians Lose Out Too

Electoral defeat especially places enormous demands on politicians' partners. I have demonstrated that they are the ones often to contain the anxiety in the run-up to the election; supporting their spouses' hurt and devastation immediately after defeat and holding and supporting their grief and dislocation in the ensuing months—while struggling themselves to make sense of their very changed circumstances too. No mean task—and largely unrecognised.

Political Parties Lose Out

Kiefer and Briner (1998), as we saw earlier in Chap. 11, suggested that the way in which retirement in general is dealt with has implications for the organisation from which they are retiring. In a similar vein, I argue that there are implications for the organisation—the political parties—from which exiting politicians come.

Through their dismissive and thoughtless treatment of those who step down from office and especially those who have been defeated, political parties risk losing the goodwill, activism and even membership of committed and knowledgeable people. By not recognising what their former colleagues, whether they have stood down or been defeated, have to offer, parties lose out on the skills, wisdom and energy that could bring much to the party and the mentoring they could provide for less experienced colleagues and prospective candidates. At a time when most political parties are in a parlous state, this is careless at best.

EMPLOYERS MAY LOSE OUT

By failing to recognise and value the skills, judgement and other capabilities that former parliamentarians and council leaders can bring to the workplace, employers may lose out on using valuable skills. The extent of MPs' responsibilities may not be well understood, and those of council leaders even less so. Yet, they all perform a complex task as we have seen including strategic decision making, high-level budget management, conflict resolution and forging relationship with a myriad of different individuals, groups and institutions. It is delicate orchestration. Yet all too often, employers do not make effective use of politicians' knowledge, skills and experience, quite possibly to their detriment. Echoing Shaffir and Kleinknecht (2005) from Canada, Byrne and Theakston (2015) report on the nearly one quarter of their sample who felt hindered in their efforts to find a new job by having been an MP, almost as if they were *"soiled goods,"* although a larger percentage but still (just) a minority, 47 per cent, had felt that their background as an MP had been beneficial. There is a similar account from Australia where Coghill (2015, personal communication) suggests that the difficulty that some former backbenchers have had getting employment at anywhere near comparable remuneration arose in part because of a sense that they were, *"tainted by politics, irrespective of party."*

Quite aside from the directly transferable skills that former MPs and council leaders have, employers could make good use of the political nous that former politicians could bring. Many employers have little understanding of how political decisions are arrived at either at a national or a local level, a gap that former politicians can ably fill. On the other hand, there is unease in the UK about what is seen to be a revolving door between politicians and the private sector, particularly the corporate boardroom despite, as we have seen, clear evidence that this is not the case in the UK.

There is however understandable concern that former ministers should not be in a position to exert undue influence with advice on the propriety of employment in the two years following ministerial office provided in the UK by the Advisory Committee on Business Appointments (ACoBA). The power and resources of ACoBA and its lack of transparency have been questioned (for example by the Public Administration Select Committee in 2012). It may well be that there should be tougher regulation of employment after ministerial office but with more robust and transparent rules in place, surely there are benefits from former ministers sharing their expertise, both their political nous and their directly transferable skills, with other sectors?

Academia in some parts of the world recognises the value of former politicians. A number of former senior Australian politicians have moved into academic positions over recent years (Malcolm Fraser, Gareth Evans and Julia Gillard, for example), although this has not been without some contention (The Australian, 30 October 2013). In the USA, there is a well-worn path between politics and academia. The UK system however has traditionally been more resistant to politicians entering academia: both difficulty in funding positions and often an insistence on a background of formal academic writing have contributed to a less permeable interface between politics and academia (Kenny 2015, personal communication). It is however possible to make the journey into academia, and there is recent anecdotal evidence that more former MPs in the UK have followed that route, for example, Charles Clarke, David Blunkett, Vince Cable, David Willetts and Ed Balls.

CIVIC SOCIETY LOSES OUT

Civic society appears to waste the knowledge, skills and experience of former MPs and council leaders even more extravagantly than employers. In the UK, there has been little in the way of anything systematic to use the potentially rich resource that they offer, either in schools, universities and colleges or elsewhere. In contrast, the US Association of Former Members of Congress was set up in 1970, originally as an alumni association, similar to the Association of Former MPs in the UK. But in 1983, it became chartered by the US Congress and widened its ambitions: it is now dedicated to using this valuable resource to promote and educate about public service and strengthening representative democracy with extensive programmes in place to achieve these aims.

That former politicians are not systematically encouraged to share their knowledge, skills and experience is puzzling given the current disengagement from our political system. There is growing disillusionment with our system of democracy reflected in an extensive literature seeking to understand and analyse the reasons for this, well summarised by Hay (2007). While there are many complex factors that underlie current increasing distrust of and alienation from representative democracy, Stoker (2006) convincingly argues that an important part of the explanation is that there is little understanding about politics and especially of how it is in the nature

of politics inevitably to disappoint. Politics, by design, will involve compromise and messiness with both winners and, crucially, losers. He argues
(Stoker 2006 p. 83) that,

*"Understanding politics – its dynamics and its limitations – can limit
the disappointment that citizens appear to display in both mature and newer
democracies."*

In his modern day paean to the late Professor Bernard Crick, Flinders
(2012) takes up a similar theme; that if citizens understood politics better,
particularly with regard to its internal contradictions and tensions, they
might expect realistically, a little less of it.

Yet there is little attempt to enhance public understanding of what politics can—and, even more importantly, cannot—deliver or of the nature
of the political process. Instead, egged on by a raucous media, politicians
facing an election are more likely to succumb to the temptation to raise
expectations about what can be delivered, however improbable they may
be. And when those election promises predictably fail to materialise, public cynicism is stoked further and the gulf between politician and the citizen widened yet more. In the words of Coleman (2005), it is almost as
though each inhabited a different planet,

*"The academics, policy-makers and politicians are from Mars. The public
are from Venus."*

Stoker (2006, p. 205) urges a coming together of the two sides,

*"The sharp divide that has grown up between professional politicos and
ordinary citizens should become fuzzier, and needs to be bridged by a wider
range of channels of communication between the two sides through better representative politics and new forms and opportunities for citizen engagement."*

There are many potential ways to seek a rapprochement and enhance
understanding between politicians and citizens but why not include
making use of those who have been in political office but who are now
"ordinary citizens"? Who better to promote understanding of politics
than former politicians who have seen it from both sides of the fence?
Furthermore, they are less likely to be seen by the public as having any
sort of axe to grind.

The UK does have the Westminster Foundation for Democracy, established in 1992 following the end of the cold war, as an independent public
body sponsored by the Foreign and Commonwealth Office. While it provides expertise in developing parliaments, political party structures and civil
society organisations, its focus is on work overseas rather than within the
UK, and former politicians are not systematically asked to become involved.

Encouragingly, the Association of Former MPs has recently set up the Parliamentary Outreach Trust, registered as a charity with the Charity Commission in July 2015 and at arms' length from the AFMP (Austin 2015, personal communication). It aims to attract charitable funding for educational and good governance work in the UK and abroad so that former MPs from different parties can visit schools, colleges and universities to talk about political life and democracy. There appears to be no similar initiative involving former council leaders, although there have been moves through the Local Government Association to involve some former council leaders in mentoring newly elected leaders.

It is not just that former political office holders know the mechanics of how our system of representative democracy works, but, by virtue of no longer being in office, they can see the system from both sides: as an elected representative and back again as an ordinary citizen. This gives them unique insight into the perspective of both, and an unparalleled ability to speak the language of both. They have had to both make difficult compromises in office and understand how those compromises are felt and experienced as ordinary citizens. In former MPs and council leaders, there is a cadre of people who are in pole position to bridge the chasm between politics and the citizen. Instead, we allow them to scatter to the wind.

Former political office holders in the UK, with the exception of some recent former prime ministers, seem to disappear—banished to the Land of Oblivion as in ancient Greek democracies—as if they were instantly disposable. Keane (2011) observes that former heads of government usually do not go quietly but even former prime ministers can be hard to find: Jeremy Paxman recounts how difficult it was to contact former Prime Minister, Sir John Major (Paxman 2002, p. 272),

"One minute you're running the country. The next, no one even has your telephone number."

Paxman's difficulty in tracking down so prominent a political figure chimes with Marquand's (2014) notion of *"presentism."* Marquand's thesis has a much wider canvas than the fate of political office holders, but the idea of *"presentism"* may well be relevant to it. He laments the scorning of history and with it, the loss of memory, shared knowledge and identity in modern day Britain,

"An incurious 'presentism' – combining a lack of historical sense, a pervasive contempt for the wisdom of the past, a fascination with novelty simply because it is new and a propensity to over-react to every ephemeral focusgroup finding or tabloid whim – saturates public debate and shapes policymaking." (p. 66)

Perhaps in a similar vein, I was surprised to hear an incidental comment from one interviewee in this study that s/he had never had any ministerial handover during a re-shuffle except on one occasion when there had been a direct exchange of individuals between two ministerial positions. It is as though there is no relevant political history of a portfolio that can be usefully drawn upon coming into a ministerial post, even from a respected colleague in the same political party. This resonates with Byrne and Theakston's (2015) observation of how striking they found it that so many of their departing MPs had not met with those who succeeded them.

At a time when understanding of and engagement with our democratic system is so low, discarding what former politicians could offer to promote understanding of how our democracy works seems remarkably wasteful. But I go on to argue that we as a citizenry lose out further.

We All Lose Out

There have been debates on the nature of political leadership since classical times, but any healthy system of representative democracy in the modern day depends on a reasonable degree of fluidity between those who are elected to serve in political office and those whom they represent. The distinction between the two—holding office and not being in office—should be clear, but ordinary citizens should have a reasonable chance of gaining political office should they be able and motivated, and not be precluded from doing so by disproportionate risks that might be encountered. Put another way, the door into and out of political office should be well oiled. Or, as Baturo puts it, that political leaders who leave office and pursue their own careers reinforce, "*the rotation in office as norm*" and, in turn, strengthen democratic consolidation (Baturo 2016).

This thinking underlay one of the core principles for effective representation that was agreed in the work of the Councillors Commission (Department for Communities and Local Government 2007). The idea of a citizen legislator may always have been exaggerated (Riddell 1995) but nevertheless, as one of my interviewees in this study advocated,

"Everyone should do a bit of politics."

Or another who described her/his former MP partner as having seen the time in Parliament as a "*patch*" of her/his life, not the entirety, and to be moved on from.

I argue that in the absence of a reasonable degree of fluidity in our system, our democracy is diminished. Why? First, because it reinforces the separation of a political class from the rest of us; second, because it limits the range of people who are able or willing to come forward to serve in elected office; and third, with exit made more difficult than it needs to be, we all have fewer opportunities to share in the fullest experience of political citizenship—representing others.

These issues have become more charged in the early years of the twenty-first century with evidence of considerable disenchantment with representative democracy. Coleman (2005) writes elegantly,

"Democracy works best when voters and representatives connect: exchanging views, accounting for themselves to each other, and, ideally, sharing a common world."

In the absence of meaningful connection between voters and representatives, we all lose out: a relatively closed political class serves its citizens less well (Riddell 1996) whether at local or national level. A political class distant from its electorate risks being less effective in terms of the perceived authenticity of its conversation and communication, and in terms of its political judgements—a far cry from a common world.

A POLITICAL CLASS

The term "political class" has not always been used consistently but it was introduced in 1896 by the Italian lawyer and social theorist, Gaetano Mosca, and gathered pace in continental Europe from the 1970s (Oborne 2007). Mosca used the term to mean how politicians had moved away from representing voters and providing the essential link between citizens and state, and instead had begun to represent themselves.

Oborne (2007) has been among the most vociferous of commentators. He has no time for what he sees as the self-serving attitude and behaviour of the political class, and tellingly in the context of this book claims,

"The Political Class values only success. It rarely finds time for those who fail to measure up to these standards." (p. 16)

Other commentators (e.g. Riddell 1995; Mair 2013; Wright 2013; Kenny and Pearce 2014) have documented the growth of a political class in the UK and other western democracies in more measured tones, often as part of a much wider debate about democracy and the concept of "post-democracy." It is not possible to pursue this broader context here, but Mair (2013, p. 43) describes conventional politics as,

"Part of an external world which people view from outside."

Wright (2013), himself a former Westminster MP, writes in a similar vein of MPs being regarded as,

"Out of touch, living in a closed political world far removed from the concerns of those whom they represent."
If politicians could resist the tendency to become a separate political class, it would, Wright argues, be beneficial both for them and for us all. Wright suggests that the focus should be on the nature and composition of the contemporary political class itself as well as on political behaviour.

One of my interviewees, a former high ranking MP who had deliberately not taken up a pass for the House of Commons as s/he could have done, explained a conversation s/he had had with a journalist who was surprised to see her/him queuing to get into the Commons,

"I just had to go through the tourist entrance in the same way and he said, "Why is this?" and I said, "Well, actually, I've never ever. I've always believed that if the electorate say no, that's it, and I don't like the idea of a political class who are kind of perpetually there."

Her/his sentiments recall Keane's caution that an elision between holding top elected office and life after political leadership is not usually good for democracy (Keane 2011, p. 285).

But as Allen and Cairney (2015) write, the term "political class" is used to cover a multitude of alleged sins. They argue that there are three distinct concepts that can usefully be extracted from the "political class" narrative: a political elite, the professionalisation of politics and political careerism. The definition of a political elite may vary, but it is almost inevitable that there will be a political elite in any polity; the issue discussed in this chapter is its permeability and the ease of flow into and out of such an elite. With regard to this notion of fluidity, the concepts of the professionalisation of politics and political careerism are highly relevant.

We have seen in Chap. 3 how the balance of career versus non-career politicians in the UK has been changing in recent decades, and how the professionalisation of politics has gathered apace. The increase both in the proportion of career politicians (in Cowley's sense of having worked in the political sphere prior to gaining office) and in the professionalisation of politics has consequences on who gets into political office, who stays and who goes. In turn, who politicians are and who they are perceived to be will affect the degree to which voters and representatives connect: the degree to which each feels that they can connect with the other, account for themselves to each other and, crucially, share a common world.

Being an effective representative at local or national level is however a highly time consuming, energy demanding business. It is not for the faint hearted. Elected politicians need considerable resilience to withstand the significantly increased pressures. But on the other hand, people want to be represented by people who they feel understand the world as they see it.

It is not an easy balance to strike. As Coleman (2005) memorably writes,

"The challenge for democratic politicians is to be seen as ordinary enough to be representative, while extraordinary enough to be representatives."

This principle, I would argue, holds true at all levels of governance.

"Doing" politics does not necessarily mean standing for elected office, but attaining political office is a key and important means of doing so. In a representative democracy, it is elected politicians that ultimately and rightly make decisions. But if the difficulties of gaining political office, holding that office and leaving political office are too great, we narrow the group of people who will be able and motivated to stand to represent us. We therefore reduce the fluidity into and out of office. Within this context, I shall summarise the evidence presented in Chap. 3 on access to political office before considering the exit from office.

Entry into Political Office

Chapter 3 detailed the changing background of UK politicians over the last century or so. In essence, after centuries in which political office was effectively reserved for the most privileged, universal franchise along with the advance of the trade union movement and the Labour Party in the UK in the twentieth century started to open up access to political office. At both national and local levels, holding political office became more possible for those who came from less advantaged backgrounds. With the route into Parliament made somewhat more accessible, people from less privileged backgrounds began to be elected as MPs in the latter half of the twentieth century. With its tight apex, local council leadership was at least as slow, possibly slower, to open up. The case should not however be over-stated: MPs and councillors were still demographically starkly unrepresentative of the general population.

But now, political office seems to be becoming once again more restricted. There is evidence, for example from the Social Mobility and Child Poverty Commission, that in the twenty-first century, social mobility and access to all professions as well as politics have stagnated (Milburn 2014) and that there is a narrowing of access into political office.

In the 2015 UK General Election, as we have seen in Chap. 3, there was a further narrowing of the occupational background of candidates with an increasing proportion from politically relevant (for example, special advisers or journalism) backgrounds. And, despite a significant increase in the number of women and people from a black and minority ethnic background, the Westminster Parliament remains overwhelmingly white, male and privileged. The picture of councillors at local government is similar in these respects.

Furthermore, the chances of coming back into the Westminster Parliament after a defeat are likely to be fewer than they once were (Riddell 2013, personal communication). The stakes of getting into Parliament are raised.

The stakes are getting higher also for council leaders and directly elected mayors. While there may be advantages in taking on a demanding council leadership role full time, it will have implications that may not have been considered in the rush to follow a parliamentary model. Who might be precluded from standing in the first place if there is an insistence of the role being full time? Especially in more politically contested authorities, the pitfalls of giving up a career may be seen as too high to contemplate standing.

These concerns are not confined to the UK. From Australia again, Coghill observes how the knowledge of the difficulty in finding employment combined with a reduction in retirement benefits is,

"Expected to have a chilling effect on citizens offering themselves for candidature." (Coghill 2015, personal communication)

As we have seen, there have been profound changes in our elected representatives over a relatively short time; are they *"ordinary enough"* given the narrowing of the pool from which MPs are selected and elected? There is a larger cadre of professional politicians not only within the Westminster Parliament but also within the devolved governments of the UK, and now within local government—but little thought appears to have been given to its consequences.

Exit from Political Office

Once in office, we know that pressures on parliamentarians have increased (Weinberg 2012, 2015) such that perhaps only those with psychological defences that are most adaptive to these pressures may be able to withstand them. A minority may flee.

Those politicians who can stand, or even thrive in, the heat of office increasingly may not want to leave. As noted earlier, Keane (2011) similarly describes office holders as at risk of suffering from the malady of "*office dependency*," while one of my interviewees more prosaically described them as "*bed blockers.*" The stakes get raised still further.

This study suggests that we may encourage office dependency by making it more difficult than necessary for people to leave political office. There will always be some risk in any transition, but this research suggests that without some acknowledgement of the challenges of dealing with the sudden loss of political office, the risks for some may be simply too high.

There is anecdotal evidence of a significant number of MPs feeling trapped as the pressures on them have increased: not at ease in parliamentary office but feeling that the risks were too high to step down. Too late to return to earlier careers; too risky to leave and too soon to retire— "*Huis Clos,*" as one of my interviewees memorably likened it.

Observing the change in the nature of the House of Commons, King (1981) comments that career politicians will not want to go,

"*Career politicians will want to stay in politics. They will therefore want to stay in the House of Commons. Accordingly, they will defer their retirement from the House of Commons for as long as possible.*"

Echoing King, Riddell (1995) describes the determination of career politicians to stay in Parliament once they have been elected,

"*The new breed of full-time politicians is also determined to cling on to both office and seats in the Commons – though there was never a golden age of allegedly honourable politicians resigning on principle.*"

Paxman (2002, p. 281) is in no doubt either about the seductive, siren call to remain,

"*Once they are on the stage, the proportion willing to leave it voluntarily is tiny. Even Martin Bell, who entered the House of Commons at the May 1997 election as Mr Clean, swearing to stay there for only one parliament, found the place irresistible and scurried down from Cheshire to Essex in an (unsuccessful) search of a way of spending another five years as MP.*"

In a similar vein, Oborne paints a cogent and powerful picture of the higher stakes that MPs now face and the personal calamity that failure represents. He points out how politicians who had previously located their identities in areas other than politics were less likely to see electoral rejection or the loss of a ministerial job as a personal catastrophe. Furthermore, he suggests that they were more willing to contemplate resignation in the event of fault or dishonour (Oborne 2007, p. 326). Now, of the political class, he observes that,

"Its members care too much about politics. This single-minded fanaticism distinguishes the Political Class from earlier types of governing elites." This perspective chimes with my group of current MPs who, with the exception of someone who had already experienced the trauma of defeat, simply did not want to think about going. It was not a subject on which to dally.

Council leaders arguably have more of a personal and political imperative to think about leaving office given that their position within their party group may be keenly contested in some authorities, and a change of party control will inevitably lead to the end of their council leadership. Yet here too there was reluctance on the part of many to think too hard about how they might shape the ending of their time in office or to succession plan. While council leaders in office might have acknowledged that they should think about when and how they hoped to leave, any plans were often non-specific and put off to a later time.

Within local government, with increasingly full-time leaders, the risks of standing down increase. Like MPs, it may be difficult to return to the profession or job from whence they came. With the degree of uncertainty about future employment and no access now to the LGPS, standing down carries significant financial risks.

If we are to continue down the professional route in Parliament with local government leadership following helter-skelter in its wake, there is a compelling argument that the support on exit that is available to any professional losing their job should be available to elected representatives. As previously noted, advice in writing curriculum vitae and in effective interview techniques, for example, is standard now for most leaving professional jobs.

At present, however, most former MPs and council leaders have little of what is available in other occupational roles. Instead, they seem to disappear. It is virtually impossible even to track down who council leaders have been. In democratic terms, that is as it should be. But if the personal struggle is made so harsh and unforgiving, it is hardly surprising if this might be an unappealing prospect for those currently holding office. Might some therefore not be tempted to seek to remain in office for longer than they might otherwise? Might succession planning be too threatening? Why would one go given potential oblivion, possibly to face unemployment and financial insecurity? Might it be too risky for some even to embark on the possibility of standing in the first place given the risks involved? Might there be some groups for whom the risks would be seen to be especially high—those in jobs to which a return would be problematic, for example—thus influencing the nature and composition of those who get to be elected? Any what of their legacy when politicians outstay their time in office?

Powell's less well-known observation of Joseph Chamberlain—that an earlier resignation would have saved him from personal humiliation—could have been usefully borne in mind by a number of politicians since. Of Chamberlain, Powell (1977, p. 136) judged,

"The consequences of his failure to resign were never to be repaired."

The exit from political office—how it is viewed by those holding office, how it is experienced and managed by those making the transition and what happens subsequently—may be only a tiny part of a much wider, more complex landscape, but it may just have some bearing on the nature and composition of the political class. If political exit could be managed more gracefully as part of a broader appreciation of the importance of fluidity in political representation, our democracy might be enhanced.

The increasing professionalisation of politics at all levels and the predominance of career politicians in the Westminster Parliament as well as the increasing pressures of office diminish fluidity into and out of political office. It is becoming more difficult to access political office for many, it is becoming more uncomfortable to stay in office for some and it is becoming more risky to exit office. Recalling one of my interviewee's comment,

"It's becoming harder and harder and why would people take those kinds of risks with their lives?"

Diminishing the fluidity of access into, through and out of political office has costs for us all. By making it more possible for a wider range of people to step forward to serve in political office, we extend the opportunity of the fullest expression of political citizenship; and with a wider range of people having experienced political office, we increase understanding of and confidence in political representation.

Political office is becoming increasingly impermeable. While the UK political system is considerably more porous than some others—Keane (2011), for example, compares the UK favourably with Italy with its recycling of national leaders—I am suggesting that elements of sclerosis can be detected. The door into and out of politics needs oiling.

* * * * * * * * * * * * * * * *

This chapter has sought to illustrate how political exit has implications that extend far beyond the individuals immediately affected. In considering these implications, the distinction between the personal and the political needs to be held in mind—but this is not straightforward. In a well-functioning democracy, it is right that when a politician leaves office, s/he should lose all the trappings of that office: they are associated with the role and not with the person. It is a political necessity for us all that office holders relinquish all that goes with office. As Keane (2011) writes, *"enforcing the distinction between holding and leaving office is a key indicator of whether or not a form of government can be considered democratic."* But, as acknowledged earlier, a political life will almost inevitably mean that the personal and the political will be deeply entangled for the individual. All the more reason, therefore, that we should acknowledge and understand the personal challenges that accompany the exit from political office, even as we might celebrate a political changing of the guard.

REFERENCES

Allen, P. and Cairney, P. (2015). What Do We Mean When We Talk About the 'Political Class'. *Political Studies Review* doi: 10.1111/1478-9302.12092.

Austin, J. (2015). Personal communication.

Baturo, A. (2016). Democracy, Development, Career Trajectories of Former Political Leaders. *Comparative Political Studies* pp. 1–32.

Byrne, C. and Theakston, K. (2015). Leaving the House: The Experience of Former Members of Parliament Who Left the House of Commons in 2010. *Parliamentary Affairs* doi: 10.1093/pa/gsv053.

Coghill, K. (2015). Personal communication.

Coleman, S. (2005). *Direct Representation: Towards a Conversational Democracy.* London: IPPR.

Department of Communities and Local Government. (2007). *Representing the Future: Report of the Councillors Commission.* London: Communities and Local Government Publications.

Flinders, M. (2012). *Defending Politics: Why Democracy Matters in the Twenty-First Century.* Oxford: Oxford University Press.

Gonzàlez-Bailon, S., Jennings, W. and Lodge, M. (2013). Politics in the Boardroom: Corporate Pay, Networks and Recruitment of Former Parliamentarians, Ministers and Civil Servants in Britain. *Political Studies* 61(4) pp. 850–873.

Hay, C. (2007). *Why We Hate Politics.* Cambridge: Polity Press.

Keane, J. (2011). *Life after political death.* In J. Kane, H. Patapan, and P. `t Hart (Eds.), *Dispersed Democratic Leadership.* Oxford: Oxford University Press.

Kiefer, T. and Briner, R.B. (1998). Managing Retirement – Rethinking Links between Individual and Organization. *European Journal of Work and Organizational Psychology* 7 (3) pp. 373–390.

Kenny, M. (2015). Personal communication.

Kenny, M. and Pearce, N. (2014). New Statesman. 25 July-7 August 2014.

King, A. (1981). The Rise of the Career Politician in Britain – And Its Consequences. *British Journal of Political Science* 11 pp. 249–285.

Mair, P. (2013). *Ruling the Void: The Hollowing of Western Democracy.* London: Verso.

Marquand, D. (2014). *Mammon's Kingdom: An Essay on Britain, Now.* London: Allen Lane.

Milburn, A. (2014). *Elitist Britain?* Retrieved from www.dera.ioe.ac.uk. Accessed 23 November 2014.

Oborne, P. (2007). *The Triumph of the Political Class.* London: Simon & Schuster.

Paxman, J. (2002). *The Political Animal.* London: Penguin Books.

Powell, E. (1977). *Joseph Chamberlain.* London: Thames and Hudson.

Riddell, P. (1995). The Impact of the Rise of the Career Politician. *The Journal of Legislative Studies* 1 (2) pp. 186–191.

Riddell, P. (1996). *Honest Opportunism: How We Get the Politicians We Deserve.* London: Indigo.

Riddell, P. (2013). Personal communication.

Shaffir, W. and Kleinknecht, S. (2005). Death at the Polls. Experiencing and Coping with Political Defeat. *Journal of Contemporary Ethnography* 34 (6) pp. 707–738.

Stoker, G. (2006). *Why Politics Matters: Making Democracy Work.* Basingstoke: Palgrave Macmillan.

Weinberg, A. (2012). *Should the job of national politicians carry a government health warning? The impact of psychological strain on politicians.* In A. Weinberg (Ed.), *The Psychology of Politicians.* Cambridge University Press: Cambridge.

Weinberg, A. (2015). A Longitudinal Study on the Impact of Changes in the Job and the Expenses Scandal on UK National Politicians' Experiences of Work, Stress and the Home-Work Interface. *Parliamentary Affairs* 68 pp. 248–271.

Wright, T. (2013). What Is It About Politicians? *Political Quarterly* 84 (4) pp. 448–453.

CHAPTER 14

Reflections from 2015 and the UK General Election

Despite the evidence presented in preceding chapters that leaving political office is a major, yet unrecognised, transition for individuals, partners and families and that there may be wider implications for our system of democracy, there appears to be relatively little interest in this issue in the Westminster Parliament. Local government under the auspices of the Local Government Association has shown some stirrings of interest, but it is questionable how far this extends within the sector as a whole.

In 2015, three months before the UK General Election, I sent a summary report of the findings from my research that had just been published at the time (Roberts 2015), with a covering letter to the Whips Office in the House of Commons to the three (then) main political parties: Conservative, Labour and Liberal Democrat. Mindful that the Speaker of the House of Commons had held a reception before the General Election for all MPs who were standing down in 2015, I sent the report, again with a covering letter, to the Speaker's Office. I received only an acknowledgement from one political party and the Speaker's Office but no further inquiry. Of course, these are all very busy people with large postbags and they were soon to be in the maelstrom of an election but even so, might this lack of interest in engaging with the issue be related to the reluctance noted earlier of current office holders even to contemplate political exit? It is curious.

The context of the 2015 UK General Election was inevitably different from the election in 2010. As noted earlier, it was the first to be held under the Fixed Term Parliaments Act of 2011. For the first time, MPs

© The Author(s) 2017
J. Roberts, *Losing Political Office*,
DOI 10.1007/978-3-319-39702-3_14

in the 2010–2015 Parliament knew the date of the next election well in advance, its date no longer the prerogative of the British Prime Minister. MPs standing down in 2015 were therefore able to plan for the future with more certainty. It is possible that this affected the date at which they publicly announced that they would not contest the next election. Council leaders, on the other hand, have long known the date of their next electoral test (although under the Representation of the People Act 1983 the date can be changed by order of the Secretary of State to coincide with a European election in the same year).

Furthermore, the intensity of the debate on MPs' expenses had died down (Judge 2013)—at the 2015 General Election far fewer MPs (90) stood down in 2015 than in 2010 (149)—although suspicion of MPs' motives and the lingering perception of politicians feathering their own nests remained following public outrage after the 2009 expenses scandal (Byrne and Theakston 2015). The wider context of MPs' salary and other allowances needs however to be understood.

Payments to MPs

In recent Parliaments prior to 2001, MPs were reasonably well paid in terms of their basic salary, although not by comparison to some higher paid professions, but their expenses and allowances were modest and the rules governing them were unclear. MPs did not have money to employ more than one or two staff and those whom they did employ tended to be long-standing staff members who could be managed reasonably well without external advice. With the more generous expenses and allowances introduced through the Fees Office in 2001, MPs were able to employ more staff but, in turn, their responsibilities as employers significantly increased and thus their need for advice in these matters.

Relatively few (86) MPs stood down in 2005. In 2009, as the next General Election was approaching, many more MPs had announced that they were standing down. One insider at the House of Commons told me more about how the Fees Office had attempted to support MPs with the practicalities of standing down. The Fees Office had instigated contact with every MP who was standing down to offer a meeting to advise on employment matters concerning their staff and on their own financial matters pre- and post-election. For those MPs who were defeated in 2010, a similar meeting had been offered and an additional room had been made available for emotional support should it have appeared to be needed—

but this had not been widely known to MPs and it had rarely been used. It had been astutely observed at the time that MPs who had been defeated had had much shorter conversations with Fees Office staff than the more relaxed encounters with MPs who had stood down. They appeared to have had one eye on the door throughout, wanting to be told quickly what they had needed to know before they had got out, almost as if they had been embarrassed, or even ashamed.

By the time of the 2015 General Election, in the wake of the expenses scandal, the Independent Parliamentary Standards Authority (IPSA) had been established under the Parliamentary Standards Act 2009. IPSA was given the remit and powers to introduce independent regulation of MPs' business costs and expenses and, subsequently, pay and pensions. IPSA makes clear that its approach and rules,

"Are a clean break from the old system of self regulation by MPs and the House of Commons The new rules are fair to MPs and the public purse, workable and, crucially, transparent – anyone can go online and see what their MP has claimed for and what they are paid". (IPSA http:// Parliamentarystandards.org.uk/Pages/default.aspx accessed 8.11.15).

There is no doubt that the creation of IPSA was an attempt to restore public trust in what and how MPs were paid; it is however regarded by some MPs, fairly or not, with suspicion. On the other hand, it is one of the few institutions that have given substantial thought to the departure of MPs from Parliament.

It should be noted that MPs standing down from the 2015 election were for the first time eligible for less financial support than those who were defeated. MPs leaving in 2010 were the last to receive the Resettlement Grant and Winding Up Allowance, applicable to all.

In readiness for the 2015 General Election, IPSA took proactive steps better to support departing MPs with the practicalities of leaving office. Plans and their execution were thoughtful and thorough. It was instigated by a new emphasis within IPSA on the needs of the "user"—MPs—and an attempt to *"walk in their shoes."* Previously, no one had given any thought to the journey that departing MPs had taken. The consumer voice was now to be considered in this most ancient of institutions.

In preparation, in early 2014, IPSA set up a team dedicated to departing MPs as well as teams for new and returning MPs. No such team had ever been set up before.

For those MPs who had announced that they were standing down, IPSA contacted each in turn to offer an individual meeting with someone from the IPSA team and from the House of Commons Personnel Advice Service (PAS) (Simpson 2015, personal communication). At this meeting, each MP was given a pack of practical information that focused on the practicalities, including the winding-up budget and dealing with their staff. Each MP had a dedicated "election contact" to whom they could turn for advice throughout this period. A new website for MPs with all the relevant information was created in late 2014.

In early 2015, IPSA raised the possibility to all MPs in its bulletins that they could get in touch should they be concerned that they may not be successful in the coming election. "What if?" meetings were offered with individual MPs and a number took place.

Preparations by the time of the General Election were well laid so that, on 8 May, the day after the 2015 General Election, all 92 MPs who had been defeated were contacted. Training for the staff within IPSA was meticulous not only with regard to the practicalities of meeting with each MP but notably in readiness for a range of possible emotional reactions from MPs. In the initial contact, IPSA acknowledged the loss brought about by the MPs' defeat and offered slots to meet individually at times convenient to them, including at a weekend. Individual meetings were thoughtfully organised in a hub area at 7 Millbank rather than at Portcullis House where new MPs were joyfully assembling. These meetings were held with a member of the IPSA team who would go on to be their "election contact" and a member of the House of Commons PAS. By the end of September 2015, a number of former MPs remained in contact with the IPSA team, a longer time than IPSA had first anticipated but the nature of this involvement was with regard to the technical complexities of the winding up.

As helpful as this new process instigated by IPSA was, it should be noted that it was limited to the practicalities of the process of winding up MPs' offices, and it did not include anything such as signposting for help with future employment that might support the MPs themselves rather than just their staff.

Some Reflections from MPs Leaving in 2015

I had conversations with five former MPs—Liberal Democrat, Labour and Conservative—who had left Parliament at the 2015 General Election, either having stood down or after electoral defeat. I did not intend to compose a new research sample but instead to ask a small number of former MPs who had left political office very recently to reflect on the summary report of my research (Roberts 2015) in the light of their own experience and their observations of their colleagues. Four other former MPs and one former council leader did not get back to me following an initial approach.

These conversations took place from towards the end of 2015 to February 2016, only five to nine months after the General Election (compared with two years or so in the research study). It was therefore potentially a tough ask of these former MPs. Agree however they did, and with considerable grace.

RT. HON. LORD DAVID BLUNKETT

David Blunkett was Labour MP for Sheffield Brightside and Hillsborough from 1987 until 2015. He held prominent senior positions in the Blair Government from 1997: as Education and Employment Secretary, Work and Pensions Secretary and Home Secretary. He resigned from the Cabinet on two occasions: first in 2004 from the Home Office following allegations of fast-tracking a work permit amidst highly publicised difficulties in his personal life; and later in 2005 after allegations were made regarding a conflict of interest from which he was subsequently completely exonerated. He stood down in 2015. Before entering the House of Commons, Blunkett had been leader of Sheffield City Council from 1980 to 1987. He was elected as a councillor in 1970 at the age of 22, the youngest councillor at that time in Britain.

In May 2015, David Blunkett accepted a professorial Chair in Politics and Practice at the University of Sheffield: he had long written and spoken widely about representative democracy and citizenship, having many years earlier been a keen student of Professor Bernard Crick. The next month, in June, Blunkett agreed to chair both the College of Law and the David Ross Multi Academy Charitable Trust. He was awarded a peerage in the dissolution honours in August 2015.

Of my report, David Blunkett was supportive,

"It is an essential read because I think it starts to address some of the issues we've ignored in politics for far too long."

Blunkett had witnessed changes in Parliament over the last 20 years. In the 1990s, the flow in and out of politics, and especially the flow out, had been easier. There had been no register of interests and nothing like the same level of scrutiny as now. He was in no doubt of the reputational damage to politicians from the ill-advised actions on expenses of a few.

Blunkett knew all too well the high human cost to individual MPs both of holding office and of its leaving but he welcomed the inclusion of partners and families in my research given the very considerable impact on politicians' families. Politicians may have chosen to put themselves on the line in terms of being in the public eye but those close to them have not—there is no reason for them to be damaged. And yet they too are often caught in the crossfire.

Anyone losing a job, of course, will experience trauma, but the very public nature of the job of an MP compounds that trauma,

"It is a massive psychological and emotional and public hit all at the same time."

In Blunkett's view, this triple hit had been made worse by the decision of IPSA to limit very strictly what is available to an MP who loses their seat: what is, in effect, a severance payment is nothing like it was. For those who stand down, there is now little in the way of a financial cushion to allow former MPs time to adjust—the 2010 cohort was the last to receive such a payment. And, drawing on the evidence in my report, Blunkett thought that this was likely only to make the experience of leaving office more difficult.

Blunkett was clear that these issues were all tied up with the mistrust, disdain and *"almost now a dislike"* of politics and politicians. He was strongly of the view that public understanding of how politics works and what skills are both necessary for and gained in office is very limited. This is an issue close to Blunkett's heart: he is very engaged currently with work at the Crick Centre at Sheffield University on public perceptions and understanding of politics. He is clear that democracy cannot function without people being willing to put themselves forward on to the political front line to serve. If the experience of holding office or of its leaving is too risky, then only those who have the income, wealth, or personal connections will take on the task and *"that would be a disaster."*

Need it be so risky to hold high office? Why should politicians' personal lives or those of their family members that do not impinge on the politician's working life be the business of anyone else? Might the intensity of the media mill prevent people taking on senior positions that are in the spotlight in the first place? Do we really want to squander talent in such circumstances? After all, this would rarely happen in any other field.

Need leaving office be so risky? Politicians have, after all, a great deal to contribute to employers and to civic society once they leave office. Blunkett highlighted two examples internationally in the private sector where this had been the case: the BP spillage in the gulf off Louisiana in the USA, and the Volkswagen scandal concerning car emissions data. Neither BP nor Volkswagen seemed to have had any idea about how what had had happened might play out in the wider world with the public and with the media. Yet former politicians could have been helpful. Politicians are used to things going wrong—*"you get hammered and you learn about how to deal with that."* Their skills however are not mostly made use of.

Blunkett acknowledged that he had been fortunate to be able to move into academia, as a number of his former colleagues. In his case, he was helped by the relationships he had forged with the Politics Department at his local university (and alma mater) and the fact that he had been able to plan his departure from the Commons unlike former MPs who had been defeated. His transition from practical politics to academic politics had therefore been relatively smooth.

For most of his former colleagues, however, Blunkett felt their transition had not been so straightforward. And yet he was in no doubt that there was real talent ready and waiting to be made use of.

Not only were politicians' skills acquired in office but the skills that they may have had before entering the Commons were now more difficult to maintain. Blunkett acknowledged the strong (and often contrasting) views held on the issue of so-called "second jobs" but he saw the virtue of a backbench MP being able to keep their hands in to whatever profession or craft they may have been in previously in order to keep up their skills and their connections. As long as constituents were not adversely affected, this should not be a problem but it was nevertheless now much more of an issue than it had been (although curiously enough, not for journalists). There are real consequences for such constraints,

"The more there is a disconnect, the more the outside world says you add no value. The more people see it as a very narrow and confined experience and therefore the psychology is ... you've been in this very exclusive world, where is the added value, what can you bring to the table?"

And what of local government of which Blunkett had long experience as well as Parliament? He was clear that we were going in the wrong direction. Rather than acknowledge that being a council leader is valuable in its own right and for the knowledge and the experience that it brings, we instead expect them to take (for those undertaking the role full-time) an immediate reduction in income and a loss of pension rights. What might that mean for aspirant leaders' families? That Eric Pickles, former Secretary of State in the Department of Communities and Local Government, had taken away pension rights from councillors was,

"Wicked, a punishment for being in public service … We should be doing the exact opposite and say that we will make it possible for you to do this and we won't punish you, we should make it as easy as possible to go in and out of politics without detriment to you and your family."

Blunkett was clear that he was not suggesting special treatment, he was not advocating politicians receiving any more favourable treatment than anyone else but he felt strongly that they should not punished for public service.

Why not say, Blunkett suggested, that we would be willing to keep a job open to you during a period of council leadership so that you can go to it and come back as, for example, in France where you can move in and out of national and local government more easily?

In response to my notion of the importance of fluidity into and out of politics, Blunkett thought it made for better politics and better politicians, knowing that if you left political office, you knew that you could come back. If it were easier to go, people would be more willing to leave, get other experiences and come back. Even when Blunkett was first elected in 1987, he recalled there having been a bye-election about every three months (albeit partly because of conditions at work with *"ridiculous"* all night sittings and *"people were dying"* more often).

Blunkett reflected on his own experience of losing a Cabinet position and of standing down.

Of his first Cabinet resignation, Blunkett remembered,

"Its dramatic effect. It had an enormous impact on me. I was on the edge of a nervous breakdown partly because it was associated with my private life falling apart, the two were completely interlinked."

But he knew that he still had a job—his job as an MP—and he had strong support from many family members and friends. Without this hinterland the experience would have been dramatically worse. Maintaining a hinterland,

"Is crucial and we should encourage politicians to do that."

For Blunkett, *"the big hit"* was because his motivation as a minister had been to change the world, and having had the ability to take big decisions that make a difference taken away had been so very difficult. No longer able to influence on the same scale, no longer able to take decisions that make a difference.

Perhaps surprisingly in the light of Blunkett's previous experiences, his later experience of standing down in 2015 was also described as traumatic,

"The big trauma for me was actually making the decision and telling the constituency party. At the constituency, we were all in tears. They were − I was − traumatised at the meeting. It was a dramatic feeling to actually say that I have made my mind up and this is what I am going to do ... It had a dramatic impact on me."

Blunkett was thoughtful in his reflections of that time: he had been surprised by the impact of his announcement of standing down. Both he and his constituency party members went back a long way, both in his 28 years as an MP but also as a councillor for many years before that. Even so, he described himself as shaken, touched and humbled by what was said and the tears of that constituency meeting,

"That was the moment that really shook me. I went home that night to Margaret and said 'Pour me a glass of wine as I've got to sit down as I'm still shaking.'"

Blunkett had however made his mind up for a number of reasons: his concern that for another five years (now that fixed term Parliaments were in place) he would not be able to provide the energy and level of service that he felt would be necessary to his constituents; that he was unlikely to get back into the Cabinet even if Labour did win, and if it did not, the prospect of yet more years in opposition was not to be contemplated; and that he was so much more interested in academia. But it was not an easy decision.

Blunkett had grown up in the local area and loved the people in his community. If he were not the local MP, he would no longer have a voice in constituency matters, he would no longer be able to be in a position where he could sort matters on behalf of people he cared about. He had agonised, deciding privately to go in January 2104 but continually testing the decision out over the next few months. He knew that he had to go at some point, to bite the bullet, and surely it would be better to do so at the age of 68 when he was more likely to make a better transition to a different life rather than when he was in his 70s,

"It was a rational decision but it did not mean that I wasn't fearful."

Having come to a final decision, Blunkett organised the announcement of his standing down with thoroughness. He announced his decision to his constituency in June 2014 in order to allow them nearly a year to select a new candidate. Once he had announced his decision, Blunkett described his sense of relief that the decision was final and there was no going back. He had carefully organised news of his standing down with national and local media so that it came out at one time rather than *"dribbling out"* and so that he was not able to change his mind. He recorded one national radio interview in advance on the strict undertaking that the news was not to get out before. It did not.

At this time, Blunkett did not know if he would be appointed to the House of Lords or if he would secure a position at the University of Sheffield. The Lords had not been a factor in his decision to go. Indeed, he only knew of his appointment with any certainty six weeks before the election. He agreed that the Lords offers a soft landing to departing MPs, both the anticipation of it and, for him certainly, the knowledge that it offered a sense of purpose. As a peer, Blunkett was aware that he still had a platform in the public arena from which his voice could be heard and that this would not otherwise necessarily be the case.

That year following the public announcement of his standing down in June 2014 was both a liberating period for Blunkett and a time of anxiety because of the uncertainty. He recalled a conversation with Tony Blair who had said to him that he was right to go at that time. But, Blunkett responded to the former Prime Minister in vivid language,

"You were flying the plane, Tony. The rest of us jump out and have to see if the parachute opens".

Blunkett was very aware that many former MPs do not get a soft landing and that it was difficult to let go of political office. But he was in no doubt that politicians should resist the temptation to stay in office, uncertain of whether the parachute might open or not, only for their own personal interests. The decision should be based on wider interests, not just *"to stay in their comfort zone."* Personal fear was not a good enough reason to stay in political office.

Of the 2015 election, Blunkett considered the loss of many Labour seats as a bigger shock than in 2010. Labour losses in 2010 had been anticipated to some extent but not in England and Wales in 2015. He suggested that in addition to the personal trauma experienced by individual candidates from both Labour and Liberal Democrat parties, there had been a collective trauma; such was the scale of the losses in parts of the UK and especially in Scotland. It had, after all, only been realised some months previously that the Scottish National Party (SNP) would make such sweeping gains, wiping out almost every sitting Scottish MP. It had been rough going for all the Labour candidates in Scotland, Blunkett was sure, but especially for any new candidate who had been selected in a seat with a previous large Labour majority. They might well have given up a good job and moved home—changed their lives utterly—in order to fight the seat in the reasonable expectation that they would successfully contest the seat and enter the Commons. For some, he thought, the denial was such that it simply could not be talked about either before or even after the election; the scale of the defeat was simply too overwhelming.

That there may have been a collective trauma was in one sense protective because many had shared in the shock of unexpected defeat but, on the other hand, the scale of the losses sustained was likely to have had an additional impact, both personal and political.

RT. HON. PAUL BURSTOW

Paul Burstow was the Liberal Democrat MP for Sutton and Cheam for 18 years, from 1997 to 2015. He had previously unsuccessfully contested the seat in 1992. In May 2010, he was appointed Minister of State in the Department of Health until he was sacked in 2012. Before entering Parliament, Burstow was a councillor, initially for the Social Democratic Party, from 1986 until 2002. He was Campaigns Officer and then Chief Executive for the Association of Liberal Democrat Councillors from 1986 until his election as an MP. He was defeated in Sutton and Cheam by his Conservative opponent in May 2015 by a margin of nearly 4000 votes. Burstow's majority in 2010 was 1608.

Since Burstow's defeat, he has been appointed as Chair of the Tavistock and Portman NHS Foundation Trust and a professor at City University specialising in the impact of public policy and government on health and social care.

Of the findings of my report, Burstow felt that some chimed strongly for him personally while other elements resonated less. The anger and especially the hurt that was highlighted following defeat in the research struck a chord for Burstow, his wife and, he thought, his former colleagues. The anger, especially on the part of partners of former colleagues, arose more from the thoughtlessness of the political parties in terms of how they dealt with those who had lost office,

"That there is no organised attempt to make use of the assets that you have in terms of experience is quite striking."

Also striking a chord for Burstow was the reluctance of current MPs to think about leaving office. Very few would, he thought, unless possibly they had won previously by a very small margin and used their vulnerability as a way to galvanise themselves to avoid losing next time. He recalled that he had been routinely asked questions about what he would do after his time in office but he would always respond, "*It's not something I think about*". If you start thinking about what you might do in those circumstances, he said,

"*You are already on that psychological path to getting an outcome you do not want.*"

In contrast to the former MPs in my research, Burstow had neither fled from office nor had he found the journey of transition following an unexpected defeat an enormous struggle. He put this down to having "*crossed a psychological threshold.*" Together with his wife, he had decided in the summer 2014 that were he to be re-elected, he would not stand again in 2020. He had felt that by then, aged 58, he would still have had one or two big jobs left in him before he would contemplate slowing down. Burstow was therefore already thinking about how he would manage the transition from a public life to a more portfolio life style, with a range of activities in which he was interested. The fact that he had already started thinking in this way had, he thought, had a beneficial impact after he had failed to be re-elected.

Despite Burstow's small majority in 2010, he had been encouraged by independent polling to believe he could hold on in 2015. So he only realised that he might well lose during the course of the day of the election. Echoing my interviewees, he explained that,

"*It was striking that there were a number of people I was calling on, who had been canvassed as supporters, who wouldn't make eye contact, there was a shiftiness, an uncomfortableness … an embarrassment – why are you on my doorstep?*"

When he got home later after the polls closed at 10 o'clock, he told his wife that the result was not looking good. The exit poll that came out almost immediately after the polls closed chimed with Burstow's experience on the doorsteps. His fears were confirmed a couple of hours or so later by a member of his campaign team phoning to say the voting papers being emptied from the ballot boxes in areas where they were expecting to do well were not looking good.

At that point, Burstow recalls feeling,

"*Very frozen… I didn't want to get too emotional about it – in the sense that it would not have been good for anyone in the family, and I am not probably someone by inclination who does that. No sense of tears or anything like that*".

That Burstow's party, the Liberal Democrats, sustained such a massive electoral loss, had a protective effect, he thought,

"In a funny way, it helped … because I did not take it personally as what happened was not about me and my performance as a constituency MP … it was about a very, very well executed targeted campaign by the Conservatives in my constituency and a national narrative that posed the electorate the question who should run the country. In circumstances where the question being answered was not who would make the best MP, my incumbency couldn't overcome the tide. No personal sense of rejection of me. I felt sad for the party but it felt beyond my control".

Although Burstow felt sad at the collective political loss, his priority in the immediate post-election period and in the aftermath was to get on with his life and sort out what he was to do,

"Getting on with maintaining the rhythms of daily life and pursuing whatever opportunities I could create for myself. So I didn't have a lot of time to mull over, worry about that".

He did however feel very sorry for the losses sustained by his party and former colleagues and for those few who still remained, given the onerous task that they now faced, soldiering on in the Commons. Burstow felt that,

"The party has not been particularly brilliant nationally at supporting those colleagues lost their seat".

Burstow had received many sympathetic and encouraging e-mails, messages on Facebook, tweets, phone calls from his erstwhile constituents and party members and people in the voluntary sector with whom he had worked closely. He did receive a phone call early on from Don Foster, the Liberal Democrat Chief Whip in the last Parliament, who had called many other MPs in the party. He had not directly heard from the party leader—but acknowledged that the party leader was in shock himself. He did however receive a letter from the party President. It was however the follow through that was poor in terms of support. He acknowledged that the party organisation had little capability to put in much support for its defeated MPs. Such capability that it did have was expended on its staff, those who had worked for the Liberal Democrat party, often for many years, and who had suffered losses too and now faced a very uncertain future. Both the party and its MPs felt keenly a sense of responsibility for them.

Was there a party to thank Burstow and to acknowledge his 18 years as MP? There was, the weekend after the election but shared with his constituency neighbour, Tom Brake, MP, who had been successfully re-elected—possibly a bittersweet experience.

There was a gathering of former Liberal Democrat MPs at party head-
quarters the next month,

*"It was more of a debrief, the meal out afterwards was probably more
useful."*

Burstow and his former colleagues would have welcomed more support with the practicalities of getting on with life at this time: advice about
writing CVs; help with interview technique; how to do a good LinkedIn
page and be social media savvy in the search for employment; and, in the
modern era, the importance of checking and being aware of your social
media footprint in case of things previously written that might be unhelpful without context. Burstow and his fellow former colleagues were after
all going back into a very different labour market from whence they had
come many years before. They had not had to compete in this sort of market often for over two decades; electoral competition is very different. He
was not sure if the political parties should not undertake this role; perhaps
it fell to IPSA?

Of IPSA, Burstow felt it could do more. While he was contacted very
soon after the election by IPSA, he was clear that their support was unhelp-
fully limited to managing the process of winding up the office and fulfilling IPSA's business needs. It was not an exit interview; it was not about
the welfare or wellbeing of MPs who were suddenly out of a job. There
was no reason why IPSA could not have done both tasks albeit perhaps at
separate times. Burstow felt that IPSA had two classes of departing MPs: if
you chose to stand down, IPSA would provide more in the way of support
than if you were defeated. He acknowledged that a defeated MP received a
better financial package—depending on length of service—than one who
stood down but that the money was not a substitute for practical aid and
assistance for a working life after Parliament.

Burstow had been very proactive from the start in seeking alternative
work,

*"I was incredibly busy between May and end of July, winding up the office
and getting out there and … I have a very good address book, a lot of people
I have worked with – they took my calls and e-mails. I was very proactive. I
worked as if I was still working. I just carried on with a very clear purpose
in my mind in making contacts … in this world head hunters are constantly
making calls and if you are not out there and putting yourself around …
once you do, I found, that created opportunities. Not all of them have come
off, another role that I went for I didn't get but it was a good experience to
go through the process."*

He acknowledged his good fortune in having a friend who worked in a business school. He went through what Burstow might have to offer, what his needs were and he facilitated a few introductions for him. Burstow highlighted one example: having not been interviewed for many years, he had found going through a mock interview particularly valuable. Once some opportunities seemed to be opening up, Burstow and his family went away for four weeks over the summer, a little longer than normal—perhaps a useful marker between stages in his transition journey.

Burstow had long been interested in health and social care issues, and this had been his ministerial portfolio. He had come to realise that MPs who had specialised in a specific set of issues and become identified with them during their time in Parliament were better placed later than those who had remained generalists. Specialised knowledge and experience could transfer more readily into the private or charitable sector while generalists struggle more, finding it harder to convince recruiters of their value.

Entry into the academic world had come about by Burstow having first noticed that other former MPs had ventured into academia and then him pitching what he might be able to offer to a couple of academics he knew in health and social care. Initially as a Visiting Professor, Burstow had been attractive to City University for his ability to bring the experience of policy formation and execution to evidence and research, so maximising research impact.

Of his former colleagues, Burstow thought that quite a few were "*still in the search phase.*" His impression was that a number had put on hold pursuing options until after the summer of 2015, a time perhaps "*to lick their wounds.*"

Interestingly, he commented on how instructive it can be to look at the LinkedIn pages of former MPs. From these pages, it can be evident who has moved on and who has not. Many of his former colleagues focus heavily still on their role as a former MP,

"*Many are stuck in "That's what I was and that's what I am". Others have moved on, they have re-written their pages and they are re-presenting themselves to the world*".

This observation resonates with the importance in the transition journey, discussed in Chap. 11, of developing a new narrative of who you are now and what you do. Who was Burstow now and what did he do? He had a ready response,

"*I am a social policy thought leader and entrepreneur, manifested in my role chairing and my role as a professor of health and social care and the consultancy work that I am doing*".

That, I thought, was a neat, immensely useful narrative—and, unquestionably, forward looking. Burstow said that he often did not even talk about having being an MP at all. I was surprised at this, so relatively soon after the election. How had he been so resilient? We discussed this more later.

What about Burstow's sacking in 2012: did the findings of my research have any resonances with this event? There were some. He had not expected to be sacked, he did not see it coming and on the day, he had been told of his sacking, *"politely but fairly perfunctorily."* He rationalised that having himself been a Chief Whip, he could not have argued with the reason given—to make space for other MPs to have a chance to serve—but he acknowledged that it had been *"Devastating, really hurtful."* He had spent two years dealing with the challenges of very controversial health legislation while also undertaking detailed work drawing up social care reform. Now suddenly he was not to have the opportunity to take the social care reforms through Parliament. It had been immensely frustrating.

Burstow acknowledged that his ministerial sacking had at the time been more painful than the loss of his seat as it had felt much more personal. What had he done wrong? It appeared nothing. It was a very hurtful process. But he understood that tough decisions had to be made. Although smarting in the immediate aftermath, Burstow was determined not to waste time and to put his experience to good use. He went off then to find other opportunities. He subsequently chaired three independent commissions in the fields of health and social care but he was not loftily appointed to them: Burstow had proactively pitched his ideas to others and had to obtain the necessary (and considerable) funding. These commissions were described as fulfilling and interesting and they gave him a sense of purpose and a cause.

Does Burstow have a sense of purpose now? Emphatically yes—derived from his involvement still in health and social care and, in particular, mental health. He missed little from his time as an MP, other than the relationships with constituents. He memorably described his political exit,

"On being released, I took a very big gulp of air and found that there was fresher air outside".

Burstow felt that he was in a very different chapter of his life,

"I find myself on buses passing the House of Commons and it feels as though it was a different person's life. Almost as though it were another person. It is very strange".

How had Burstow been so resourceful and resilient? He reflected. He had been fortunate in having supportive family members and friends; the decision that he and his wife had made previously to step down in 2020 had been protective to an extent; and in retrospect, he had done some planning, albeit unaware of this at the time. He had got a better mortgage deal the year before in order to release some cash and this had meant that the family was less pressurised, having a financial cushion following his electoral defeat—although Burstow did not think that he could have artic-ulated this motivation to himself at the time. Furthermore, he had had a specialism as an MP that was more readily recognised as being transferable to the world outside Parliament, and he had had contacts and relationships that had helped. Having never much relished the "clubby" aspect of the Commons—he had commuted from home to and from Westminster each day—had probably contributed to him not much missing those aspects of Parliamentary life. He thought he had joined the Association of Former MPs but he had not gone to any its meetings. And lastly, Burstow had a hinterland in addition to family and friends—other interests and enthusi-asms that had stood him in good stead.

RT. HON. SIR VINCE CABLE

Vince Cable was Liberal Democrat MP for Twickenham from 1997 until he was defeated by 2017 votes in the May 2015 election by his Conservative opponent. His majority previously had been 12,140. He was Secretary of State for Business, Innovation and Skills from 2010 to 2015 and previously both Deputy Leader (from 2006 until 2010) and Acting Leader (in 2007) of the Liberal Democrat Party. Prior to being elected as an MP, Cable had been a university economics lecturer and later Chief Economist at Shell. In the 1970s, he had been a Labour Party councillor in Glasgow.

Since May 2015, Cable has published a book, *After the Storm*, on the state of the global financial markets and the British economy since 2008. He has been appointed as Professor in Practice in Economics at the London School of Economics and as Visiting Professor at St Mary's University in south-west London and at Nottingham University.

Despite Cable's large majority in 2010, his defeat that was a shock to many in 2015,

"Didn't feel a massive blow."

Cable was clear that his defeat was part of *"the general tsunami"* that swept away the majority of his former Liberal Democrat colleagues, regardless of their personal performance. That his personal defeat was a part of this wider picture alleviated any sense of guilt. He was in no doubt that it was the ruthlessness of the Tory election machine that had set out to destroy the Liberal Democrats, targeting vulnerable seats with a persuasive narrative,

"From Number 10, there was a national campaign that sought to convince constituents in Twickenham that they must not risk chaos; that the key decision was who was to be elected as Prime Minister, not who was to be elected as the local MP."

Cable and his party nationally had known a year before the election that the Liberal Democrats were some way behind; the polling figures on the party leaders were making it very obvious. Views in the party had varied between the optimists who thought they might lose half their seats and the pessimists who thought that they might be wiped out. Nevertheless, even on election day, Cable thought that in his seat, there was a 50:50 chance of winning. Local canvassing had shown that the Liberal Democrat vote was holding up and that Cable was ahead of the Tory candidate. In the event, the large group of *"soft Tories"*—that is, those who said that they might well vote for Cable personally—on the day did not,

"En masse they turned their back on us in the last 48 hours".

The national exit poll on election night made clear how badly the night was going to go but it was not until the middle of the night that he knew that he had lost his seat.

Cable went as far as to say that the experience had been,

"Quite hard ... it was obviously upsetting."

The widely circulated footage of Cable walking with dignity but silently at dawn from his count, declining to speak to reporters scurrying after him, spoke volumes. Even as Cable was sped away, television cameras pressed up close towards his face against the car window.

Despite the brutal effectiveness of the Conservative campaign nationally, Cable was at pains to say how charming his opponent in Twickenham had been and her generosity in her tribute to the work that he had done in the constituency at the count. Cable is a fair and courteous man. But what was the impact on him personally?

He denied any anger with the Tories—winning election is after all the name of the game—but he had been angry *"to some extent"* with the leadership of the Liberal Democrats for not more effectively positioning the party. It had apparently been widely recognised that if the Liberal Democrats had kept around 30 MPs then Cable might well have taken over the leadership but, with their number of MPs down to eight, and Cable himself ejected, the picture was very different.

How long had Cable thought about staying in Parliament? He had toyed with the idea of standing down in 2015 but had thought that he would stay for just one more term. He recalled some slight ambivalence towards him from a few younger former Parliamentary colleagues—a sense that, at his age, he should perhaps make way, despite the high regard in which he was held.

After Cable had been reselected, he shut his mind to any notion of standing down—it would have seemed as though he were turning his back on the constituency—but he acknowledged that he was running *"not with enormous enthusiasm."* He described himself a bit disengaged, and not quite in line with the leadership in terms of the party's intellectual framework.

Cable missed his old department, the Department of Business, Skills and Innovation (BIS) and his constituency but not Parliament. Cable had come to a point, it seemed, when there were other things that he wanted to do with his life, and the attraction for him of the House of Commons itself was waning. Having had the experience of being a Cabinet minister,

"Made me realise that Parliament was not that important. Attending a select committee might make you raise your game a bit. Otherwise it is a very minor factor ... the power lies with the executive."

Cable remembered with affection the event organised not long before the election by the Permanent Secretary at BIS for all staff in the Methodist Hall. Cable was to paint the vision for the future and in so doing to maintain morale among staff. Was it a valedictory moment?

"Well yes, I suppose it was."

Cable fondly remembered the moving ovation that staff had given him that he deeply appreciated,

"The staff were lovely."

In retrospect, this event had been both a valediction from Cable's government department and from Parliament, an important marker of his transition from office.

Cable had made sure to secure agreements with the Tories about what was to be protected at BIS under a new coalition but with a Tory majority, all bets were off.

With journalists camped outside his house, Cable left London with his wife for her farm in the country the day after the election. He described himself as phlegmatic about the loss of his seat given that he had distanced somewhat from the Commons and going back to the backbenches had little appeal. His wife was apparently relieved: 18-hour days had been Cable's norm as a Cabinet minister. But now there was no going back.

And then? Cable had to get on with all the practicalities of sorting things out: of thanking staff; making sure that his office was properly wound up (not a short process); and, of course, Cable did not have a job to go to. He had however come to realise that he had skills that could be made good use of. Among these were a strength in communicating a complicated idea simply and directly—a rare skill.

Was there any acknowledgement of his work as an MP? Plenty. He had received a deluge of letters and had been met by so many people in the street in his constituency who said that they had voted for Cable that he wryly wondered how he could possibly have lost. Others, often Labour voters, told him they would have voted for him had they realised that he was in danger of losing (an echo of tales told to Byrne and Theakston 2015). Everyone suddenly seemed to be extremely nice. Cable's reaction was more one of amusement than exasperation or anger, as some of my interviewees.

There were other acknowledgements: a big thank you party for those who had helped Cable's campaign (organised and paid for by Cable) at which the local party expressed their appreciation to him and a similar event for his financial donors; a number of other thank you events for Cable organised by various organisations; and *"a few nice letters"* from the Liberal Democrat party, including the party President.

Cable turned down the offer of a peerage. He explained that he had done 18 years in Parliament and it was time for other things. He had a very full life and a large extended family from two happy marriages that was very important to him. Cable had always been very critical of the House of Lords and its system of appointments. The Upper House had got *"gross"* in size. Many peers were appointed for reasons that had little to do with merit—and he did not want any of that. But some of Cable's friends were quite angry with him for his decision, almost, he thought, as though it were an uncomfortable reflection on them.

Instead, Cable returned to academia with his appointment to two professorships in economics; he has published a book, a sequel to his book on the financial crisis of 2008; he has participated in many book events across the country; and he is on the board of a couple of smaller companies involved with grassroots projects. He was very clear that he did not wish to be on boards in the corporate world—with Cable's pedigree, he would have been highly sought after for such non-executive positions but this was not for him. He was not quite as busy as he was but he was much more in control of his time,

"No longer the constant scrutiny, I can choose to do the media I like, I can say what I want to do."

Perhaps in contrast to Cable's time as a minister and an MP, people uniformly seemed to be very friendly and very respectful. He had some contact with former colleagues but he was not a member of the Association of Former MPs (but he did have a House of Commons pass).

Cable seemed very comfortable in his own skin and despite his recent and largely unexpected defeat, to have adjusted relatively smoothly to this new chapter in his life. He readily described his identity now that seemed to integrate politics (a social democrat), family (of enormous importance), academia and communications, and ballroom dancing (that took up a great deal of his post-Parliamentary life).

Of relevance, perhaps, in understanding Cable's resilience is that he was 54 years old when he was first elected as an MP, unusually old now to enter Parliament for the first time. He had admittedly stood as a Parliamentary candidate in his 20s for Labour but then he had other priorities—family and later caring for his wife—that had diverted him from political office for some time. Cable had therefore developed a career and an identity as an economist as well as having a great deal invested in his family and other interests—an extensive hinterland in comparison with many other MPs that has stood him in good stead subsequently.

RT HON SIR JIM PAICE

Jim Paice was the Conservative MP for South East Cambridgeshire from 1987 to 2015, holding the seat with comfortable majorities (17,502 in 2010). He served in junior roles in government in the Ministry of Agriculture, Fisheries and Food and the Department of Employment in the early 1990s. Paice was appointed as Minister of State for Agriculture and Food in the Department for Environment, Food and Rural Affairs (DEFRA) in the coalition government from 2010 until he was removed in a reshuffle in September 2012. He was honoured with a knighthood in 2012. Prior to his election as an MP, Paice had an extensive background in agriculture, as a hands-on farmer and an agricultural training manager. From 1976 to 1987, Paice was a member of Suffolk Coastal District Council, becoming its youngest ever chairman in 1983.

Paice did not contest the 2015 General Election, having decided before 2010 that he would stand for the last time in the General Election of that year. He made the public announcement of his decision to leave in March 2013. Until November 2015, he was Chairman of First Milk, a famers' co-operative. He continues on his small farm of Highland cattle and he is on their Breed Council. In addition, Paice is a director of Camgrain, a local grain business; a trustee of the Game and Wildlife Conservation Trust; a trustee of NIAB, a not-for-profit plant research and information centre; and a governor of a nearby school.

Paice had little disagreement with my report and our subsequent conversation had many resonances with its findings.

I asked about Paice's removal from government in 2012. The phone call from David Cameron making clear that he was to make way for a Liberal Democrat minister at DEFRA had come *"completely out of the blue"*: many were astonished at his sacking as Paice had been very well regarded in the agricultural portfolio. He had known that he would not have been further promoted but being Minister for Agriculture had been the only job in politics that Paice had ever really wanted and, given his background, for which he had seemed ideally suited. He had been *"a bit dumbstruck"* at hearing the news (while fulfilling ministerial duties at a national livestock exhibition) and came to admit that he had been *"pretty bloody angry, seething"* but he had to take it on the chin. He returned to London but never went back to his DEFRA office—*"you're out when you're out"*—and he left Westminster for the week. Paice held a goodbye drinks party at his flat for those civil servants with whom he had worked most closely at the Department two or three weeks later—in effect, an important transition ritual.

Paice recalls a bruising time, still to some extent to this day: he had been deeply disappointed not to have been able to finish what he had set in motion as minister where he had genuinely wanted to make a number of policy changes. On the other hand, he had been overwhelmed with letters and messages of support from the farming community and, only a few weeks later, he had been delighted that his work had been unexpectedly recognised by way of a number of awards, including the prestigious Farmers' Weekly award of Farmers' Champion of the Year. Some months later, Paice recalls with just a touch of vindication, how the Prime Minister, responding to a question on the Common Agricultural Policy, had complimented Paice's agricultural expertise prompting Labour benches to retort, *"Then why did you sack him?"*

Paice reflected on his departure from Parliament: he had been an MP since the age of 38 and he had seen colleagues become *"quite sad"* as they sat in the Commons well into their 70s, years after they had held front-bench positions or, in some cases, never having done so. This was not a future to be emulated. That the dates of the 2010–2015 Parliament had been fixed had meant that it had been easier to plan and had influenced the timing of Paice's public announcement but not the decision to go itself. Some of his colleagues had been surprised that he was leaving relatively early (in his mid-60s) but Paice felt that it was just the right time. He had always had other interests, he had accomplished much of what he had set out to do, and he had got the ministerial job that he had always wanted. He was aware of how the role of an MP had changed significantly during his time in the Commons, in part owing to the rise of social media. As an MP even in a seat with a large majority, the pressure to be campaigning throughout a Parliament was now ever present, an uncongenial prospect. This in turn had changed the type of people that the political parties were seeking as candidates. He sadly recalled one applicant for parliamentary candidature who had been turned down—despite having had excellent credentials from business and local government—on account of not having been enough of a campaigner. That had influenced Paice's decision to go. He ruefully reflected that,

"We are choosing not on the basis of how good an MP someone will be but on whether they will become an MP and that's not what Parliament is about."

He thought it was all part of the devaluation of politics: public demands and expectations of MPs had risen enormously but politics and politicians had been increasingly demeaned by the public and the media, well before the expenses scandal.

It was not easy to leave the Commons, he thought, and he had always believed that there should be a generous resettlement package for MPs, most of whom now were entirely dependent on their parliamentary salary for income. While recognising the need for party discipline, Paice was nevertheless concerned that MPs may become *"overly subservient"* to their party for fear of losing both their seat and income, at a time when they should be exerting their independence.

Following his public announcement that he was going, Paice felt *"a bit of relief that it was out of the way, everybody else knew what I had known for a long time."* In the subsequent two years, he took pains to support the Conservative candidate who had been selected to contest the seat, readily willing to step back from any constituency limelight, unlike perhaps some of his colleagues. Paice's moment of leaving Parliament, he recalls, was very low key: he had a drink with a few colleagues, said goodbye, shook hands with a doorkeeper and walked out—no fuss, no ceremony—and remarkably different from the excitement of 28 years previously when he had first arrived. Of note, Paice and his wife went abroad for most of the 2015 election campaign including Election Day itself—*"it was the break – the longest time we'd been away for a very long while"*—and, of course, a clear marker of the transition from long public service in office.

How did no longer being an MP feel? It was *"quite odd … initially like a holiday,"* but the break was permanent and not temporary. Paice had always lived a very busy life but it became apparent that now there was no longer any deadline, a most unusual—and odd—sensation that lasted for about six months at least. He had solid family support having invested a great deal in his relationship with his sons over the years despite the pressures of parliamentary life and frequent absences. He had received a lot of acknowledgements from constituents and from those with whom he had worked closely but notably, he had had no contact from anyone within the Conservative Party since he had left Parliament nearly ten months previously. Paice's expertise had remained untapped by the party. He attributed this partly to having not pushed himself forward, for example declining to seek elected office as a Police and Crime Commissioner, but he was mindful that former MPs' insights into policy development, in his case on agriculture, could potentially be useful.

Paice observed that,

"People management in Parliament is terrible … absolutely awful."

The Conservative Party had at one time appointed a "pastoral whip" but there had been little practical support for this role.

What had Paice missed? On the occasion of the public announcement of his standing down in 2013, he had told his local paper, *The Ely Standard,* that he would miss,

"The camaraderie, the hot house of gossip, being in the thick of it, I will miss that."

Three years on, he agreed that this was precisely what he missed in contrast to *"the drudgery and the routine."* Paice was unsure how his former colleagues had dealt with political exit, not having seen any of his former colleagues. Yet he had been a very sociable MP, had he not, and lived not too far from London? With some wistfulness, he acknowledged that seeing his former colleagues would be a reminder of the past, just a little painful despite him having been clear that he had had enough of elected office and had no regrets about his decision to leave. Paice admitted that retirement took some getting used to despite his evident enjoyment of life currently. Standing down had been, I think, to his surprise,

"A bit raw ... a bigger wrench than I thought it would be, giving up all that camaraderie, realising that you're never going to do that again ... a lot that you've stopped, given up."

He could recognise that by his decision to go, he had, in Tony Wright's words, done it to himself and that it had inevitably involved a measure of loss.

How would Paice describe himself now? *"A farmer"* was his immediate reaction—and then, *"and a former Minister of Agriculture"*—but he demurred a little at the word, "former." He was keen to stress that,

"When you retire, it's not all over ... and 'former' means that was behind but what is the future? I __am__ a farmer ... and recognising that there is life ahead."

Indeed so.

JO SWINSON

Jo Swinson was the Liberal Democrat MP for East Dunbartonshire, where she was brought up, from 2005 to 2015. After graduating from the London School of Economics in Management, she worked as a marketing manager in the private sector and contested a Parliamentary seat in 2001 and a Scottish Parliament seat in 2003. On entering the Commons in 2005, she was its youngest MP. She was a minister from 2012 to 2015 in the coalition government in the Department of Business, Innovation and Skills, with additional responsibility for Women and Equalities.

East Dunbartonshire had been a marginal seat but Swinson lost her seat—as did most other Scottish Labour and Liberal Democrat MPs—in 2015 to the SNP by 2167 votes. Her husband, also formerly a Liberal Democrat MP, lost his seat at the same time. She has since taken on a number of positions: as a non-executive director of tech company Clear Returns; Chair of the charity Maternity Action, and advisory roles with comparethemarket.com and the Advertising Standards Authority.

Having read my summary report, Swinson was glad that the subject of MPs losing office was being studied given the magnitude of the transition and she agreed with many of the recommendations. She affirmed the importance of context and, particularly in 2010, the expenses issue that had embroiled all MPs catching even those who had done nothing wrong, in the cross fire,

"Reading your report took me back to 2009 and that atmosphere."

The context of 2015—*"a massacre of Liberal Democrats"*—was very different. Although Swinson had observed former colleagues dealing with their loss of office differently, that so many Liberal Democrats had lost their seats had meant that there had been *"a safety in numbers."*

While defeat had not perhaps been inevitable, winning her seat had been an enormous challenge and, hence, she said that she had not taken the loss of her seat personally even though East Dunbartonshire was Swinson's home. She had known the seat was marginal in 2005 and her majority was smaller in 2010—she honestly acknowledged an element of hurt at the time, having been highly regarded as a constituency MP,

"One of the first lessons that I learnt was that it was not necessarily related to how good a job you've done."

Swinson had known the likely consequences of going into a coalition with the Tories, traditionally hated in the west coast of Scotland, and that her seat would be imperilled. On the other hand, after the Scottish referendum, she had seen a way in which she might be able to win with the tactical votes of both Tories and Labour supporters coming in behind her against the SNP. It was close, but in the event, the nationalist tide was too strong.

So, safety in numbers was the key factor (as for both Paul Burstow and Vince Cable) in not attributing defeat personally. Conversely, that so many MPs in Scotland lost their seats at the same time had meant that there was potentially a crowded field for jobs where political experience was valued. Swinson graphically likened the situation to a factory closure.

Swinson only knew for sure that she had lost her seat a few minutes before the announcement. She described knowing what she had to do on the platform at the count: lose with dignity (she related to the experiences of others in my report); not cry; do her media interviews and, most importantly, to thank all of those who had supported her. The most difficult aspect had been to get the balance right between not crying but still being able to access and convey the genuine emotion of having loved serving as MP for the constituency. No mean task but she had pulled it off—helped by being able to meet up with her mother only later,

"She'd have put a hand on my arm and it would have set me off."

The tears came the next day, listening to her party leader, Nick Clegg's speech.

Having barely slept, Swinson flew to London to meet up with her husband and son who had travelled from Chippenham. Being reunited with her son after three weeks was the priority. A toddler, of course, makes no allowance for parental exhaustion but he,

"Was the best tonic ... he didn't let us wallow in any way."

While Swinson agreed that it would be sensible to prepare for the eventuality of defeat, she stressed how difficult in practice that was. The focused mindset necessary to fight an effective campaign makes it all but impossible. The one thing that Swinson did do however, a year before the election and still a minister, was to join LinkedIn. Now she realised how difficult it can be to get in contact with those she had known as a minister as it was the Department that would organise all meetings.

In the immediate aftermath of the election, Swinson did stay off Twitter for a few days, *"it had become so vile ... cybernats on Twitter are a different breed apart and I didn't want to read lots of gloating."*

However, she had later been pleasantly surprised to read many more positive comments from people of all political persuasions and none about her, *"almost as though it were an obituary."* Tellingly, she commented how much less abuse she now gets on Twitter—as a woman in the public eye, abuse had been *"pretty much run of the mill."*

Swinson experienced a double whammy from having been both a Liberal Democrat and a Scottish MP but also from the fact that both she and her husband lost their seats simultaneously. The loss of his seat (in Chippenham) was always possible. Despite the short-term insecurity, Swinson thought that it had been better, certainly in retrospect, that both had lost rather than just one or the other. Had one partner still been an MP, she reflected, it would have been *"pretty miserable"* for one to watch the other go into the Commons each day. Furthermore, as a family, they would not have been able to take advantage of not being an MP—being able to socialise and go away more freely.

Instead, both Swinson and her husband had been able to deal with leaving Parliament together, each understanding what the other was going through and being able to provide mutual support. Positive acknowledgements of her time in office there were aplenty. Interestingly, however, Swinson had forgotten penning in a political blog, Liberal Democrat Voice, at the end of May 2015,

"I had to read them in small batches over the next few days: it's often the words of kindness that bring the raw emotions to the surface the most ... On one level, the pain I felt was deeply personal."

She was aware that she was now—nearly nine months on from the General Election—in a different frame of mind. But she admitted it was hard to return to the constituency (where her family still live) and be asked what she is now doing now. At the beginning especially,

"It was horrible when you don't have any semblance of an idea what you are going to do ... haven't had time to prepare ... do you say I'm the former MP... I used to be ... you crave being able to say that you are doing something current."

Wisely, Swinson wished not to be defined by the past.

Swinson ventured as far as to say that the period after the election had not been a happy time in terms of the result but she is convinced now that,

"In the end up I'll look back and think it was a good thing ... I loved being an MP and I can't see how I'd ever have chosen voluntarily to leave. But I now have lots of opportunities to do other things that I care about and change world in different ways."

Knowing that she did everything she could have done had been a great help; at the end of the day, the electorate took things out of her hands. She was not plagued by "what if's?" and losing had freed her from the personal responsibility of making a decision to move on from Parliament.

Furthermore, even if Swinson had just hung on to her seat, she would have returned to a shrunken Liberal Democrat team of just nine: back to opposition in Westminster to see the Tories press ahead with policies that in coalition the Liberal Democrats had stopped; in a tiny minority in Scotland where the hostile political environment *"is different from the normal political divide and that in itself can be unpleasant."*

Swinson would have made it work as effectively as she could, but for her, the prospect was less appealing than driving change as a government minister. She was not therefore troubled by the loss of her immediate political future. She was aware that, in this way, she differed markedly from former Tory MPs who lost: the future for them might well have been very different—ministerial promotion, and possibly for some, to the Cabinet.

The months since the election for Swinson had been both scary and exciting. It had been,

"A huge learning curve, unlike anything since I became a minister ... all quite exhilarating ... trying things on for size."

She had talked to many people, including a former minister and a peer; she had read a book[1] that had helpfully stressed the importance of "test and learn"—try different identities—rather than "plan and execute."

There was however little support, coaching or signposting for such an endeavour.

Insightfully, Swinson was aware of how since 2002, she had been on *"rigid train tracks"* utterly focused on being an MP. In contrast now she was in *"a wild flower meadow"* where she could meander as she pleased, learn a great deal and take time to enjoy things under less pressure. She was pleased to be out of her comfort zone—uncomfortable but necessary—although she acknowledged that it should not go on for too long. Swinson now had more shape to what she was doing and she had an immediate narrative,

"I am building an interesting portfolio, I have a couple of advisory roles, non-executive positions and I am writing a book (on equal power between men and women)."

She was determined to be flexible and versatile, manifested in her new business card (produced within three weeks)—*"it made me feel professional"*—that was very simple but had slightly different photos suited for different identities.

But what about the delicate issue of income?

Swinson was earning and she was optimistic that both she and her husband would come to earn more than when they were MPs. She was aware that doors were more open for her as a former minister than for her colleagues who had remained on the backbenches whose skills, she felt, were not understood.

Of her former colleagues, she had observed how varied the response had been. What had made the difference? Swinson thought a lack of a support network was an issue for a number, having other elements in life other than being an MP as hard as that might be given the pressures, and transferability of skills from preceding careers, and underlying resilience. Her young son had been the most powerful reminder of what was really important in life. That said, it is hard to reconcile the demands of parenthood and Parliamentary life. Swinson had seen the challenges that faced former Scottish Labour MPs who had lost their seats in 2015: some had been in place for many years in seemingly impregnable seats and now had a far harder task to redefine themselves. They had not signed up for the level of uncertainty in their seats that Swinson had in East Dunbartonshire.

While Swinson would not rule out standing as an MP sometime in the future, interestingly, she would not describe herself as a politician now. Politics had been *"a hobby"* before she became an MP and so it was again now. That she identified herself so clearly in other ways—despite the fact that she became an MP at such a young age—has surely stood her in good stead.

REFLECTIONS ON THE CONVERSATIONS FROM 2015

The conversations with the five MPs above who left political office in 2015 were not chosen on any rigorous methodological basis other than that they included both former MPs who had stood down or had been defeated, MPs who had been in different parties, both men and women, and I suspect the toughest criterion, that they would be willing to talk to me on an attributable basis. The five who readily agreed to talk with me will therefore be a selective group, relatively resilient and probably not typical of all of those who left Parliament in 2015, itself a different cohort than the group of MPs who left in 2010, as discussed earlier.

David Blunkett's story powerfully illustrates how poignant and emotionally charged standing down from political office can be. He had chosen to go, entirely within his control and for readily understandable reasons but still it was a difficult and an emotionally draining time. Standing down from a constituency where relationships have been forged over years and a role that has become such a significant part of a person's identity is not a straightforward issue. With a berth both in the Lords and at Sheffield University, David Blunkett has had a parachute but still, he wisely reflects on the anxieties of bailing out. And he looks more widely at the possible broader implications.

Jim Paice's experiences had some similarities to those of David Blunkett, even though his public announcement of standing down had been much less emotionally charged. He came to recognise that leaving Parliament was a transition of more significance than perhaps he had bargained for.

What of defeated MPs? That it was only defeated former MPs from the Liberal Democrat party who agreed to talk with me on the record may reflect the point they all made: that they had been protected to some extent by the fact that so many of their MPs were felled—there had indeed been a "*safety in numbers*"—recalling the potentially protective effect of group rather than individual exit (Ebaugh 1988) referred to in Chap. 3. Liberal Democrat MPs had been punished by the electorate for having entered into a coalition with the Conservative Party in 2010, and they felt that they had been targeted in 2015 by their erstwhile coalition partners. However hard they may have campaigned, the odds were stacked against them, thus absolving them from a sense of personal responsibility.

Furthermore, if it is the case that part of the grief of losing a Parliamentary seat arises from the loss of a future and what might have been, this again shielded the Liberal Democrats. They had sacrificed a great deal politically in their pact with the Conservatives. Had they retained their seats, they would have been part of a much diminished band, condemned to opposition, and they felt that they would have had to stand by and watch their former coalition partners ride roughshod over what they had previously protected.

While the broader context painted is of crucial importance, there are in addition individual factors that have contributed to resilience of these five former MPs through resignation from senior office, standing down and electoral defeat. All five had strong family and social support; with other sources of identity, they were not solely wedded to their identity as an MP or politician; they had all been government ministers which is likely to have been helpful in acquiring new roles that had been important for moving on; they had been positively acknowledged for their contribution as an MP and/or minister; two had received knighthoods, one a peerage; and they were open to different avenues albeit drawing on their specialist areas of expertise; and, with limited evidence available to me, seemingly resilient in terms of personality. Swinson's recognition that the electorate had made the decision for her that she had been unlikely ever to make for herself provides food for thought.

NOTE

1. *Working Identity* by Herminia Ibarra.

REFERENCES

Byrne, C. and Theakston, K. (2015). Leaving the House: The Experience of Former Members of Parliament Who Left the House of Commons in 2010. *Parliamentary Affairs* doi: 10.1093/pa/gsv053.

Ebaugh, H.R.F. (1988). *Becoming an Ex*. Chicago: The University of Chicago Press.

Judge, D. (2013). Recall of MPs in the UK: 'If I Were You, I Wouldn't Start from Here. *Parliamentary Affairs* 66 pp. 732–751.

Roberts, J. (2015). *Losing Political Office*. Milton Keynes: The Open University Business School.

Simpson, A. (2015). Personal communication.

CHAPTER 15

End Thoughts

The stories here are powerful. But most of them have not been voiced in a public domain, still less heard. For a number, they have not been voiced even privately. Even eight years on from a previous defeat, a politician who had by then regained a seat could say,

"I haven't really been able to have that sort of conversation properly with anyone."

Yet these are people who have both had the great privilege to be an elected representative but who have in turn given an enormous amount—many years of immensely hard work and commitment, and often at considerable personal cost—to our democratic system in which we all have a stake.

Political mortality is not a comfortable subject to discuss. We shy away from lingering long over exits of any kind. The nature of political office and its intoxicating allure for many makes contemplating its end deeply painful. That politics is all about the promise of the future; that political parties exist to fight elections, to win and to stay in power make it all the more difficult for any space to be made for thinking about politicians going in the other direction. That there was a barely any response to a summary report of this study from the Speaker or from the Whips Office of the three main political parties at the time in early 2015 underlines how little interest the parties have in addressing political exit.

In this study, a minority of MPs quietly fled from a role that no longer held any appeal. Others, whether they had stood down or had been defeated, mourned to varying degrees. How they fared in a new chapter

© The Author(s) 2017
J. Roberts, *Losing Political Office*,
DOI 10.1007/978-3-319-39702-3_15

of their lives depended on many different factors. Many of these will be up to the individuals concerned and their families. But we all have some wider responsibility too.

Recalling Runciman (2013) quoted at the beginning of this book, my contention is that we are complicit in shielding politicians from intimations of their own mortality. Just as former political office holders may avoid painful reminders of what once was, it appears that we avoid them. I make no apology for using this powerful quote again:

"Ex-MPs are like rotting fish. Failed politicians are the worst of the worst. That's what I feel and there's an unspoken feeling that the failure is contagious."

Whether they were champing at the bit to go or whether they were torn unwillingly from office, politicians who have lost office have something powerful to contribute, both about their individual experience of holding office and its loss, about the impact of it on those close to them and about how our democratic system works (or not). Those thoughtful, highly capable former MPs who may have chosen to go after one or two terms have something important to tell us—but there are no exit interviews for them, as there are in other occupations or in Canada, where exit interviews with MPs have recently been conducted.[1] The waters close over immediately. Former council leaders are, if it is possible, dropped even more invisibly.

Our democracy depends on politicians failing to win. But the silence about what happens then—broken only occasionally by a harsh, salacious, almost punitive edge in the immediate aftermath of a defeat—is deafening. Why? The electorate may wish for their pound of flesh, for political triumph or revenge. But is it really the case that *"failed"* politicians are like *"rotting fish"* or *"lepers"* from whom to keep well away? Is an integral part of our democratic system really so unbearable to think about? We might push away such uncomfortable thoughts, but we do so at some risk to us all in terms of the implications for our system of representative democracy. Can't we be braver?

NOTE

1. http://www.samaracanada.com

REFERENCES

Runciman, D. (2013). *The Confidence Trap*. New Jersey: Princeton University Press.

APPENDIX

RESEARCH QUESTIONS

My research aimed to make a contribution to the identified gaps in the literature. I therefore asked the following research questions:

- What is the experience of losing elected political office for the office holder?
- What are the consequences of the loss of political office on individuals and their families?
- What, if anything, could be done to mitigate the consequences?
- What can current politicians tell us about the period prior to exit and how the matter is (or is not) approached while in office?
- Are there any wider implications from the information gathered for our democratic system?

STUDY DESIGN

This was a flexibly designed, qualitative study that allowed for some modification of the design of the study as it progressed. It was envisaged, for example, that there might be some change to specific questions and prompts both within any one interview in response to what was being brought up at the time by the interviewee. It was possible also that additional themes might emerge from interviews that had been insufficiently considered.

© The Author(s) 2017   257
J. Roberts, *Losing Political Office*,
DOI 10.1007/978-3-319-39702-3

Furthermore, in order to address the fourth research question, the original design specified that the views of long-serving politicians about how long they intended to stay in office would be ascertained. As the study progressed however it became clear that the views of politicians currently in office, both long-serving politicians and those who had been in office for shorter times, would be more useful in order to get a broader picture. This research question was therefore modified to its current wording and omitting the original word, "long-serving."

METHODOLOGY

(i) Sampling

I sought to recruit 10 former political office holders, a mixture of former MPs and former council leaders, to each group: Group 1, former office holders who had decided to stand down; and Group 2, former office holders who had been electorally defeated. In both these groups of former office holders, I intended to interview the partners that they had at the time of the loss of office where possible. Group 3 were current office holders, both MPs and council leaders or directly elected mayors: I did not seek to interview their partners.

While the first two groups were clearly defined for ease of later analysis, in reality the individuals in these two categories are better considered as lying on a dimension. Politicians choose to stand down more or less voluntarily: politicians may, for example, choose not to contest an election because they fear that local factors and/or the national electoral cycle will lead to defeat at the ballot box; or there may have been pressure to stand down from others for personal reasons. In this study, there was one individual who was included in the "defeated" group given that s/he was de-selected in acrimonious circumstances although s/he had later formally stood down. It was nevertheless hypothesised that there would remain differences between the two experiences—of not contesting an election and of defeat—that justified the separation of the two groups in the design of this study.

I intended to adopt a stratified sampling approach whereby a sample of former and current office holders was to be compiled reflecting a range of different backgrounds and experience—or strata—of the politicians in order to gain as much insight, depth and breadth as possible within a small study.

Within each group, therefore, I sought to recruit as diverse a mix of former office holders as possible, in terms of political party, geography, gender, age and, for MPs, seniority within the Commons.

I intended to recruit former MPs from those who had left political office at the 2010 General Election. There is readily available information about such MPs: a list of MPs in the 2005 to 2010 Parliament; a list of those MPs who had announced that they were to stand down in 2010; and a list of the General Election results from all constituencies. In addition, there was considerable publicity about a number of individual MPs who had decided to stand down prior to the election and about a number who later were electorally defeated in May 2010.

There is no similar available information about former council leaders. I had therefore to find out details of former leaders in a piecemeal fashion, by seeking advice from a variety of different individuals within the local government sector, and by checking out council websites where there had been a change of control. I was looking to recruit former council leaders of unitary authorities or counties—councils with a broad range of responsibilities—who had not only lost their leadership role but also at the same time their seat. In addition, local authority elections in different areas take place in different years (some "all out" and some staggered, "in thirds," that is with a third of council members facing election in three years over a four-year cycle) and the extent of political change at a local election may well depend to different degrees on the national electoral cycle.

I focused initially on leaders who lost their position in 2010 but given how few did so because of the factors above, I soon broadened my search to leaders who had lost their seat and position in the couple of years before and after 2010. It was considerably more difficult to identify potential participants and find out their contact details than I had anticipated.

I contacted every council leader whom I could identify that fitted the criteria for the study. Although there was relatively less possibility of stratifying the sample, in the event the sample contained a reasonably good mix of leaders in terms of age, political party, gender and geography.

As there was a larger pool of MPs from which to select possible participants, I was guided by the need to stratify the groups as above. I contacted specific former MPs who would provide the necessary stratification using personal contacts and recommendations or via websites.

(ii) Contacting potential participants

I first wrote a letter, sent either electronically or by post, to potential participants, outlining the research project and seeking permission to contact them again. My initial letter made clear the aim of the study, an outline of the methodology and gave strict undertakings with regard to confidentiality. It was envisaged that the interview would last no longer than one and a half hours. Letters to the former politicians (Group 1 and 2) explicitly mentioned that I would like to interview their partners if possible. Of those whom I contacted, 22 in all, one did not reply. I have no reason to believe that my letter, sent twice through different routes, did not reach this one potential participant who did not respond. Of the 21 who did reply, all but one was willing to participate.

Both the potential participants who did not take part had been electorally defeated. I attempted to understand a little more from the one potential participant who responded but declined to be interviewed, about the reasons for not participating, but s/he did not wish to be drawn.

I used the same means to contact current MPs and council leaders/mayors. It was considerably easier to identify them and to find their contact details. I wrote to 13 current politicians of whom 11 replied, and all but one of those who did respond agreed to be interviewed. Two MPs did not respond.

A second contact, usually by e-mail, was sent to those who responded positively in order to take forward the practical arrangements for the interviews. This included mention of the possibility of audiotape recording the interview. A number contacted me by telephone, in which case arrangements were agreed on the phone and confirmed by e-mail.

(iii) The sample of former political office holders (Group 1 and 2)

By design, the former MPs had all left office in 2010. There were, however, very few leaders who left office in 2010 and as a result, those whom I interviewed left office in years ranging from 2008 to 2012, with half having left in 2011.

All the participants in Groups 1 and 2 were interviewed in 2012 and 2013. The length of time that had elapsed since interviewees had left political office varied, far more so for council leaders than MPs because the year in which leaders had moved on from office also varied considerably for reasons explained above.

All the former MPs were interviewed about two years after they left office following the May 2010 General Election (range 23 to 27 months). The time that elapsed for leaders ranged from 12 months to just under four years (47 months), with most interviewed between 12 and 18 months after they had left office.

Participants came from all three main political parties and from different regions of England. None of the participants came from Wales or Scotland but this was not by design; the potential costs of travel to Northern Ireland did however exclude their former office holders from the study as well as a different and more complex party political structure. Participants ranged in age from those who were in their thirties to one in their seventies, and they included four (25%) women, a reasonable number given the percentage of female MPs and (even lower) percentage of female council leaders. The aim was not however to achieve representativeness per se but more to bring into the sample participants from a wide range of different backgrounds.

Participants had been in office, either as a council leader or as an MP for widely varying lengths of time: from under one year to 27 years. Those who had stood down, Group 1, had been in office from four years to 23 years; those who had been defeated, Group 2, had been in office from under one year to 27 years. Across the two groups, the council leaders had been in office from under one year to 20 years while the MPs had been in Parliament from five to 27 years.

In one case, it turned out that the former leader had determined to step down from both her/ his leadership position and as a councillor but planned it in a staggered manner a year before the local election. S/he had organised to spend the last year in a high-profile, more ceremonial role instead.

In Group 1 (the 10 who had stood down), I interviewed four partners out of the eight who had partners at the time of leaving office and were still with them. In Group 2 (the 10 who had been electorally defeated), I interviewed seven of the nine who had partners although in one case this included an adult child (suggested to me at the interview by the interviewee, as there was no current partner). I had suggested that these interviews would last no longer than one hour.

(iv) The sample of current politicians (Group 3)

I interviewed 10 current politicians, a mixture of MPs (four) and council leaders (four) and directly elected mayors (two). They had been elected to their current position for widely varying times—from two to over 30 years—and ranged in age from their forties (just) to their sixties. I interviewed participants in Group 3 from the end of 2013 to May 2014.

Seven were men and three women; they came from all three (then) main political parties and from widely different regions of England.

The design of the study did not include seeking to interview partners of current politicians, in Group 3.

(v) Interviews

(a) Setting

Interviews took place in a number of different settings, very much at the preference of and convenience to the interviewees. My only stipulation was that it needed to be somewhere private that could be experienced as a safe, contained space and where confidentiality could be assured.

In many cases in Groups 1 and 2, interviews took place in participants' homes in different parts of the country; others at Local Government House in central London; and a few in or outside of relatively empty cafes. I conducted two interviews with partners by Skype for logistical reasons.

In most cases, I interviewed partners immediately after the interview with the former MP/ leader but usually separately. In one case, the couple remained together throughout both interviews. In some cases, I interviewed the partner on a different (later) date.

The setting was more straightforward for Group 3: either at the Westminster Parliament or at Local Government House, the county hall or borough town hall.

(b) Interview protocol

The protocol for the semi-structured interview was compiled from a core of question headings designed to elicit the information needed to address the research questions: the facts of what happened before, during and after the loss of political office, as well as feelings, beliefs and attitudes about the transition from office.

Question headings were informed by the literature that I had read prior to the design of the interviews and from theoretical ideas from, for example, Attachment Theory and Family Systems Thinking, as well as the author's own reflections as both a health professional and a former council leader. There was considerable caution exercised with regard to the latter in recognition of the risk of personal bias. Care was taken to guard against undue bias by discussion with the supervisor and an academic peer group based first at Warwick University and later at The Open University. In addition, two former MPs and one former leader (two of whom had been defeated, one had stood down, but none was interviewed subsequently) were consulted for their comments and any views they might have about the relevance, salience, language and any possible omissions in the interview protocol. Their comments led to some additions to possible probes in the interview protocol.

The introduction to the interview went over the background to and the purpose of the research before making very clear the boundaries that had been set around the study. The strict safeguards in place to maintain confidentiality were explained and it was emphasised that no individual would be identifiable from any output from the research.

Consent was sought (and granted in all cases) to audiotape the interviews on the understanding that the recordings would all be deleted once the project had been completed.

GROUPS 1 AND 2

The interview began deliberately with a very open-ended question—what first comes to mind when you think about the loss of your political office?—in order to encourage wide-ranging thoughts and reflections on the issue that were relatively untainted by any other questions on my part. In those cases where there had been a loss of both ministerial office and a parliamentary seat, possibly at different times, I deliberately left open at this stage which loss was the focus of my enquiry. The interviewees were able then to tell me which had been the more significant loss and their reflections about both.

The main body of the interview probed first the experience of holding office in order better to understand the experience of its loss, before asking in detail about the subsequent loss. I was interested to know the facts of what happened, the attitudes and feelings of interviewees, what they had done (their behaviours), and how they made sense of it all. I was keen to understand both the direct experience of the office holder as well as their views about the impact on a partner and children and any wider family.

The partner interview was very similarly constructed and designed to elicit partners' views about the impact of the loss of office both on the former office holder but also on them and any other members of the family.

Specific key questions were asked, as in the interview protocol, of all interviewees. I had given thought to likely probes arising from each question (also indicated on the protocol), but the probe depended very much on the response of each participant. The interviewees were encouraged to talk in depth about their reflections on the issues being raised; their responses were not curtailed.

As the interviews came to end, participants were asked for any additional comments that they might have had in order not to lose any material that they thought might be relevant.

The interviews were conducted in such a way that interviewees were encouraged to reflect, to muse, and to bring whatever they thought might be important to them into the conversation. All questions in the protocol were covered but not necessarily in the order in which they were written. The researcher listened with care: my stance was one of interest and curiosity. Although the subject matter was very different, the style of interviewing bore some similarities to that used in my clinical role, conducting sensitive interviews as a child and adolescent psychiatrist and as a systemic family therapist.

Notes of key points from the interviewee were jotted down during the course of the interview, in part as a fall back in case of a technical problem with the voice recorder. Although I had not initially written any additional notes after an interview, I came to write brief reflections on anything I had found notable as soon as possible after interviews had been conducted.

The duration of interviews with former office holders ranged from a whisker under an hour to three and a half hours, but most were around two hours long. Partner interviews were shorter, from about half an hour to just over one hour.

Group 3

The interviews with current politicians in Group 3 were similarly structured as those in Groups 1 and 2 except of course they did not include any section on the experience of loss of office, apart from the one case where a current politician had lost office previously before regaining a seat. The interviews included questioning on how long the politician was thinking of seeking to remain in office, the factors that influenced their thinking, and what they may have learnt from seeing colleagues move on from elected office.

Interviews with current politicians were shorter, from half an hour to a little over one hour or so. This was because the interview protocol was shorter, that current politicians were usually more pressed for time and, I came to realise, many had less emotionally invested in the subject matter. My impression was that this was particularly so for the MPs in the sample, except notably for the one who had previously experienced a defeat. Council leaders seemed more curious by the research study perhaps because the issue of how long to seek to remain in office felt more salient.

For all three groups, the interviews were transcribed but again with great care taken to safeguard confidentiality with a code known only to the author and supervisor used for each rather than the name of the participant.

METHOD OF ANALYSIS

My intention from the outset had been to explore in depth the range of experiences of a group of former politicians and to draw out relevant themes rather than to aggregate the data numerically. When however certain experiences featured repeatedly, I have given some broad indication of numbers.

Some themes flowed naturally from the design of the interview protocol (e.g. the decision to stand down, the facts of what happened at the time of the election and immediate reactions to electoral defeat) but others emerged from close attention to the data.

I approached the analysis of the data from the interviewees in the following way:

(a) I initially thoroughly read all the transcripts of interviews several times until I became very acquainted with their detail. Certain themes emerged from the data, for example, the way in which those who planned to stand down had marked their transition from office (or not).

(b) Having developed a group of themes from both the interview protocol and the transcripts, I went back over all the interviews and scrutinised them in detail to identify and document everything that pertained to these themes. At all times I took care to ensure that none of the participants could be identified from what I had quoted.

(c) I reviewed the transcripts again, attempting to stand back somewhat and identify anything in the interviews that I had missed or where I might have given undue weight—too much or too little—to any particular passages, or where I might have introduced any misinterpretations or distortions from the data. I recognised that it can be easy to give too little bearing to data that is relatively moderate and neutral.

Permission to quote on an unattributable basis was sought in all cases.

Index[1]

[1] Note: Page numbers followed by "n" denote notes.

© The Author(s) 2017   267
J. Roberts, *Losing Political Office*,
DOI 10.1007/978-3-319-39702-3

The manufacturer's authorised representative in the EU is Springer
Nature Customer Service Centre GmbH, Europaplatz 3, 69115 Heidelberg,
Germany. If you have any concerns regarding our products, please
contact ProductSafety@springernature.com

Printed and bound by CPI Group (UK) Ltd, Croydon, CR0 4YY
23/04/2026
02095633-0001